"In this outstanding volume, Stephen Chester brin
the Protestant Reformers to bear on the vexed qu
tween Paul's understandings of justification and ur
model of gracious exposition both of the Reformers
This is a must read for students of Paul's letters at all levels."

—BEVERLY ROBERTS GAVENTA
Princeton Theological Seminary

"For anyone interested in the history of Pauline theology on a host of crucial
issues—justification, sin and original sin, the law, grace, faith and works, union
with Christ—Chester provides an education in one volume, exemplary in its clear,
concise exposition. He focuses on the connections and disconnections between
the Reformers both with earlier theologians and with contemporary Pauline
scholarship (particularly the New Perspective on Paul). Few can be the readers
who will not learn much from his careful study."

—STEPHEN WESTERHOLM
McMaster University

"In this eminently readable book, Chester navigates the Reformers' readings of
Paul with nuance and clarity. In addition, he puts them in conversation with more
recent trends in Pauline scholarship, disentangling similarities and differences.
His approach is refreshingly irenic, fair, and charitable as he disentangles the
complexities of differing points of view. The result is a brilliant reclamation of the
Reformers' liberating insights into the all-encompassing grace of God in Christ.
This book is a treasure that belongs on the shelf of every scholar and pastor who
cares about Paul's gospel."

—SUSAN EASTMAN
Duke Divinity School

"Stephen Chester has a welcome habit of exposing the uninformed judgments
that mar Pauline scholarship, especially in relation to the Reformation. Here he
both shortens and supplements his earlier work, developing his key points with
sparkling clarity. Students and teachers who are grappling with the central themes
of Paul's theology will be enormously grateful for Chester's deep understanding
of the Reformers and his critical dialogue with them."

—JOHN M. G. BARCLAY
Durham University

"*Paul through the Eyes of the Reformers* is a grand tour. The stops and sites focus on the sixteenth-century Reformers, but the tour includes the history of reading Paul's letters from Augustine to the medieval era, and from the period after the Second World War to the present. Placing the Reformers in conversation with their interpretative ancestors and (often critical) heirs, Stephen Chester facilitates a patient, not uncritical, but finally appreciative understanding of Reformation interpretations of Paul. Through Paul's letters, the Reformers encountered the surprising grace of God; by reading Paul with the Reformers, this book also announces the surprising grace Paul calls the gospel."

—JONATHAN A. LINEBAUGH
Beeson Divinity School

PAUL THROUGH THE EYES OF THE REFORMERS

Living under Grace

STEPHEN J. CHESTER

WILLIAM B. EERDMANS PUBLISHING COMPANY

GRAND RAPIDS, MICHIGAN

Wm. B. Eerdmans Publishing Co.
2006 44th Street SE, Grand Rapids, MI 49508
www.eerdmans.com

Book design by Lydia Hall

Printed in the United States of America

30 30 29 28 27 26 25   1 2 3 4 5 6 7

ISBN 978-0-8028-7848-9

Library of Congress Cataloging-in-Publication Data

A catalog record for this book is available from the Library of Congress.

For Gordon Palmer, David Easton, and David Kersten
with gratitude for their leadership, guidance, and friendship

Contents

*Part 3 Justification by Faith and Union with Christ
          in the Reformers' Exegesis*

Part 4   Reading Paul with the Reformers Today

CONTENTS

Preface

The main purpose of this book is simply to provide a sharper and more succinct statement of the argument of my much longer volume *Reading Paul with the Reformers* (Grand Rapids: Eerdmans, 2017). As in the earlier volume, I seek to show that the dismissal of the Reformers as misinterpreters of Paul characteristic of scholarship within the New Perspective on Paul (hereafter NPP) was itself misguided. Following the inauguration of a new era in Pauline studies with the publication in 1977 by E. P. Sanders of *Paul and Palestinian Judaism*, the legitimate impulse to move beyond misrepresentations of Judaism as a crude religion of works-righteousness was accompanied by an ill-judged wholesale rejection of the Reformers' Pauline exegesis.

Without having significantly engaged the Reformers' exegesis, Pauline scholars assumed not only that the Reformers' analogy between Paul's opponents and their own had helped to distort later scholarly accounts of Judaism but that they were also the source of other major errors. The Reformers were ultimately responsible for portrayals of the apostle Paul in his former life as a Pharisee struggling with inability to obey the law and a guilty conscience. They were also ultimately responsible for narrowly forensic accounts of Paul's teaching on justification that reduce it to a cold contractual legal fiction. In fact, neither of these other errors are characteristic of the Reformers' Pauline exegesis. Further, without usually recognizing it, NPP scholarship itself typically relies at some significant points upon exegetical conclusions first developed by the Reformers. Finally, again without recognition, NPP scholarship also sometimes rejects important aspects of the Reformers' Pauline exegesis only to affirm other aspects of their exegesis in intensified form.

Given the complex combination in NPP scholarship of legitimate criticism, straightforward misunderstanding, and unrecognized appropriation of the Reformers' Pauline exegesis, simply to understand that exegesis accurately is an urgent task. This task of descriptive analysis is undertaken in part 2 of this book. Here the attempt is made to lay out clearly what the Reformers heard Paul say about both the human plight apart from Christ and about salvation in Christ (chapters 6 and 7). This comes after material that places the dramatic shift in Pauline interpretation brought about by the Reformers in the context of the very different perspectives on Paul offered by their medieval predecessors, perspectives themselves developed in the pervasive shadow of Augustine (chapters 3–5). All of this provides a platform from which to offer a reevaluation of the relationship between the NPP and the exegetical legacy of the Reformers (chapters 8 and 9). Although the NPP represents a significant advance in understanding Paul in his Jewish context, the Reformers' exegesis nevertheless offers a different vantage point from which critically to evaluate contemporary interpretation and identify continuing weaknesses.

Part 1 (chapters 1 and 2) attempts to prepare the ground for this argument using new material that did not appear in *Reading Paul with the Reformers*. A fuller account is provided of the evolution of NPP scholarship, especially of attitudes within it toward trajectories of interpretation perceived to stem from the Reformers. This account shows that any assumption of a general opposition between the NPP and the exegetical legacy of the Reformers is not borne out by the history of scholarship. Across recent decades, trends in the interpretation of Paul and those in the interpretation of Luther track each other closely. As scholars in each discipline responded to the intellectual currents and needs of their own contexts, the interpretations offered of Paul and of Luther did not grow further apart but in fact resembled each other in significant ways. Only by ignoring the parallels between recent perspectives on Paul and on Luther can the complex nature of the relationship between the NPP and Reformation be obscured.

Part 3 of the book takes a different turn. Although the Reformers developed extensive shared commitments in their interpretation of the Pauline texts, there were differences among them. This was particularly so in how the christological dimensions of justification by faith were expressed. All agreed that justifying faith looks away from the self and to Christ, receiving an alien righteousness that comes from outside themselves to those who believe. Yet there were a variety of perspectives among the Reformers about how alien righteousness is received through Christ, and how justification relates to Paul's statements about being united with Christ and to the renewal experienced by believers. These differences are clarified by exploring their treatment in the work of the three most influential Pauline exegetes among the Reformers: Luther, Melanchthon, and Calvin (chapters 10–14). Here it emerges that Luther and Calvin in different ways both make union with Christ central to justification. Melanchthon does not do so, emphasizing instead that justification is "on account of" Christ, whose saving death pleads the case of believers before the heavenly throne.

Part 4 of the book probes the implications of these differences concerning justification, arguing that it is Luther's and Calvin's integration of union with Christ and justification that has particularly significant resources to offer for the task of interpreting Paul today. The benefits that this procedure can offer in understanding Paul are explained, and an example offered of their impact on understanding a particularly important text in Reformation and contemporary debates about Paul (chapter 16). This concluding chapter is prepared for by new material that places the Reformers' Pauline exegesis in dialogue with developments in Pauline interpretation that have in recent years clearly moved beyond the framework established by the NPP itself (chapter 15). Inevitably, even a new perspective eventually becomes an older one. The task of recontextualizing Paul for changing contexts goes on, and, as it does so, we have much to gain by attending to the voices of those who, like the Reformers, have undertaken the task before us.

The writing of this book has taken place in the years following a move in 2019 to my current position at Wycliffe College at the University of Toronto. I am grateful for the research leave that has allowed me to produce this volume. I have also deeply appreciated the help and friendship of my colleagues at Wycliffe College, both faculty and staff, as I settled into a new context during the tumultuous years of a global pandemic. My wife Betsy and I have been blessed by the friendship and fellowship of all at the Living Room Church in Midtown, Toronto. Without any of this support, I would not have been able to complete the task.

As I look further into the past, there are many who have shaped my journey and shown me what it means faithfully to follow Christ. I owe particular debts of gratitude to Gordon R. Palmer (who supervised my work as a volunteer at Ruchazie Parish Church, 1988–1989), to David Easton (who supervised my work as probationer minister at Burnside Blairbeth Church, 1994–1995), and to David W. Kersten (under whose leadership as dean of the seminary I worked at North Park Theological Seminary, Chicago, 2012–2019). This book is dedicated to them with affection and respect.

Abbreviations

Unless otherwise stated, all other abbreviations follow *The SBL Handbook of Style: For Biblical Studies and Related Disciplines*, 2nd ed. (Atlanta: SBL Press, 2014).

AB	Anchor Bible
ASD	*Opera omnia Desiderii Erasmi Roterodami recognita et adnotatione critica instructa notisque illustrata*. Desiderius Erasmus. Amsterdam: North Holland, 1969–
BibInt	*Biblical Interpretation*
CNTC	*Calvin's New Testament Commentaries*. John Calvin. Edited by D. W. Torrance and T. F. Torrance. 12 vols. Grand Rapids: Eerdmans, 1959–1972
Comm. 1 Cor.	*Commentary on 1 Corinthians*. John Calvin
Comm. 2 Cor.	*Commentary on 2 Corinthians*. John Calvin
Comm. Eph.	*Commentary on Ephesians*. John Calvin
Comm. Gal.	*Commentary on Galatians*. John Calvin
Comm. Gen.	*Commentary on Genesis*. John Calvin
Comm. Phil.	*Commentary on Philippians*. John Calvin
Comm. Rom.	*Commentary on Romans*. John Calvin
CR	*Philippi Melanthonis opera quae supersunt omnia*. Philip Melanchthon. Edited by Karl Bretschneider and Heinrich Bindseil. 28 vols. Vols. 1–28 of the *Corpus Reformatorum*. Halle: Schwetschke & Sons, 1834–1860
CTS	*Calvin Translation Society Edition of Calvin's Commentaries*. John Calvin. 46 vols. Edinburgh: Calvin Translation Society, 1843–1855
CWE	*Collected Works of Erasmus*. Desiderius Erasmus. Toronto: University of Toronto Press, 1974–
EC	*Early Christianity*
ExAud	*Ex Auditu*

IJST	*International Journal of Systematic Theology*
Institutes	*Institutes of the Christian Religion*. John Calvin. 1559 ed. Translated by F. L. Battles. Edited by J. T. McNeill. 2 vols. Philadelphia: Westminster, 1960
JSNT	*Journal for the Study of the New Testament*
JTI	*Journal of Theological Interpretation*
KJV	King James Version
LCL	Loeb Classical Library
LQ	*Lutheran Quarterly*
LW	*Luther's Works*. Martin Luther. American ed. 55 vols. Original ed. 17 vols. New Series. Saint Louis: Concordia; Philadelphia: Fortress, 1955–1986, 2010–
MBWT	*Melanchthon's Briefwechsel: Kritische und kommentierte Gesamtausgabe*. Philip Melanchthon. Edited by Heinz Scheible. Stuttgart-Bad Cannstatt: Frommann-Holzboog, 1977– (*T* = *Texte* volumes)
MSA	*Melanchthons Werke in Auswahl* [*Studienausgabe*]. Philip Melanchthon. Edited by Robert Stupperich. 7 vols. Gütersloh: Mohn, 1951–1975
NRSV	New Revised Standard Version
PrTMS	Princeton Theological Monograph Series
RCSNT	Reformation Commentary on Scripture: New Testament. Edited by Timothy F. George. Downers Grove, IL: InterVarsity Press, 2011–
RSR	*Recherches de science religieuse*
SJT	*Scottish Journal of Theology*
ST	*Studia Theologica*
ThQ	*Theological Quarterly*
TynBul	*Tyndale Bulletin*
WA Br	*D. Martin Luthers Werke: Kritische Gesamtausgabe; Briefwechsel* (*Weimarer Ausgabe*). Martin Luther. 18 vols. Weimar: Böhlau, 1930–1985
WA DB	*D. Martin Luthers Werke: Kritische Gesamtausgabe; Die deutsche Bibel* (*Weimarer Ausgabe*). Martin Luther. 15 vols. Weimar: Böhlau, 1906–1961
WUNT	Wissenschaftliche Untersuchungen zum Neuen Testament

PART ONE

---

*The New Perspective
on Paul and the Reformation*

CHAPTER ONE

The New Perspective on Paul: Context

I n April 1978 the TV miniseries *Holocaust* was broadcast in the United States. While profoundly painful for survivors, the series was viewed by approximately 120 million people at a time when the population of the country was approximately 222 million. When the series was shown in West Germany in the following year, it was viewed by approximately twenty million people, which was around one-third of the population. Although the Holocaust had happened more than thirty years previously, the almost unimaginable scale and barbarity of the murder of six million Jews by Nazi Germany had led in Western societies to a delayed reckoning with these events. As the United States Holocaust Memorial Museum comments, "The initial horror at the revelation of what had happened gave way to a kind of numbed silence, out of which there only gradually emerged the realization that these were realities with which one must come to terms."[1] At the level of popular culture, a TV drama like *Holocaust* was part of this difficult coming to terms.

The same process was taking place for Christian churches. *Nostra Aetate*, the 1965 declaration of the Second Vatican Council on relations with non-Christian religions, included a condemnation of anti-Semitism. There followed in succeeding decades over one hundred statements made by various denominations concerning Christian-Jewish relations. In the United States, discussions between the Evangelical Lutheran Church of America and Jewish representatives began at a series of meetings in the 1970s and culminated in a 1994 declaration by the church to the Jewish community. For the Lutheran World Federation, its 1984 assembly

---

1. https://www.ushmm.org/research/about-the-mandel-center/initiatives/ethics-religion -holocaust/articles-and-resources/jews-and-christians-the-unfolding-interfaith-relationship (accessed November 2, 2020). As of June 2024, this article is no longer directly available on the USHMM website but can be accessed via an internet search using the article title.

marked a new start in global dialogue between Jews and Lutherans. In all such conversations, a significant part of the context was discussion of the causes of the Holocaust. Even if certainly not a sufficient cause, and even if exercising its influence in conjunction with other powerful and complex factors, what part had Christian attitudes toward Judaism played in making anti-Semitism acceptable in European culture?

1.1. Pauline Interpretation and Reckoning with the Holocaust

In a different form, the same reckoning was also beginning to take place in the academic world, including the discipline of biblical studies. In 1977, the Texan scholar E. P. Sanders (1937–2022) published *Paul and Palestinian Judaism*.[2] Sanders's book challenged existing scholarly descriptions of Second Temple Judaism,[3] arguing that they reflected a biased and negative portrayal of Judaism untrue to the primary sources. It was the right book at the right time, and it made an enormous impact on Pauline studies. For up until then, dominant portrayals of Paul's theology had positioned it in contrast to Second Temple Judaism as it had been previously defined, but if such standard portrayals of Judaism were erroneous and prejudiced, then a new account of Paul's theology was also needed. Over the next few years, just such a new account of Paul's theology emerged, and it became a scholarly movement, widely referred to using the label the "New Perspective on Paul" (NPP). In truth, this movement was never as monolithic as the label suggests, with many differences of opinion among its advocates. Yet there were some shared characteristics that did make it at least a coherent *constellation* of readings of Paul. One of those shared characteristics was the unanimity with which advocates of the NPP rejected previously dominant patterns in Pauline interpretation.

The previously dominant patterns they rejected were often collectively identified as the "Lutheran" interpretation of Paul,[4] a designation that pointed to the roots of these discredited ideas in trajectories of interpretation stemming from the Protestant Reformation of the sixteenth century. To read Paul in this Lutheran

2. E. P. Sanders, *Paul and Palestinian Judaism* (London: SCM, 1977).

3. The designation "Second Temple Judaism" covers the period from the rebuilding of the Jerusalem temple after the return from exile in Babylon in the late sixth century BCE down to its destruction by the legions in 70 CE at the climax of the Jewish Revolt against Roman rule (66–70 CE).

4. On the problematic nature of the terminology, see James B. Prothro, "An Unhelpful Label: Reading the 'Lutheran' Reading of Paul," *JSNT* 39 (2016): 119–40.

way was anachronistically to misunderstand Paul. It was major Reformation interpreters of Paul, such as Martin Luther (1483–1546) and John Calvin (1509–1564), who were primarily responsible for the biggest ever wrong-turning in Pauline interpretation.

This questioning of the heritage of the Reformation in one way made perfect sense, for there are some of his later writings in which Luther expresses vile and utterly indefensible anti-Jewish sentiments.[5] Yet NPP scholarship did not in fact pay attention to these details or even display any evidence that the work of the Reformers was being read. Instead, the Reformers simply appeared from time to time as the discredited dark backdrop against which the insights of the NPP might be advantageously positioned. The question of whether what the Reformers said about the interpretation of Pauline texts was being accurately understood and portrayed was not explored.[6]

Nor did NPP scholarship very often present itself as part of the wider reckoning with the Holocaust taking place in Western societies. Instead, it largely presented itself within the existing conventions of historical-critical scholarship. Detailed attention was paid only to other recent interpreters, and studies were usually focused solely on the first-century horizon. Neither the late twentieth-century context of NPP scholarship nor the work of the many previous generations of Pauline interpreters was much discussed. The scholarly task was to present an accurate description of ancient realities. Yet interpretation is a self-involving task, and the self is shaped by historical forces. To seek accurately to portray the past without attending to the context of the interpreter is itself insufficiently historical because interpretations can be offered only from within the flow of history. The past is always viewed from a specific location: "Truth is to be found as we live in this flux, not by leaping out of our historical skins."[7] It was unhelpful for NPP scholarship to fail clearly to acknowledge that much of its energy came from the pressing contemporary need for a less prejudicial account of Judaism. Unhelpful also were suggestions from some of its detractors that precisely because a contemporary need could be traced, the NPP was necessarily historically suspect.

---

5. Luther's tract of 1543, *On the Jews and Their Lies* (*LW* 47:121–306), is especially problematic.

6. The term "Reformers" can be used with historical validity in a variety of ways. It could be used to refer to all advocates of reform who could be labeled "Protestant," or even more broadly to include also advocates of reform who remained within the Roman church. I use it more narrowly to refer to the early Lutheran and early Reformed exegetes (e.g., Luther, Melanchthon, Calvin) who established the trajectories of interpretation that are still of significance in debates concerning the NPP.

7. John K. Riches, "Reception History as a Challenge to Biblical Theology," *JTI* 7 (2013): 185.

1.2. Pauline Interpretation and Reception History

The tendency of NPP interpreters to reject the Reformers as interpreters of Paul without engaging their work was therefore itself also problematic. Precisely because the NPP rejected trajectories of interpretation stemming from the exegesis of the Reformers, that exegesis formed a crucial aspect of the context of NPP interpreters. To understand it would have helped to clarify important aspects of their own historical location as interpreters. Yet even though the relationship between past interpretations and contemporary ones was so clearly an issue at stake, the origins of the past interpretations being rejected were little discussed. There was a failure to attend to the reality that in biblical scholarship, one of the most significant factors shaping interpreters and their present contexts is the work of previous interpreters. Whether the influence exercised takes the form of attraction or aversion, it is impossible to escape. If we critically engage with it, we may better understand ourselves as interpreters and so be better equipped for our own interpretative work. If we ignore it and claim to evade it, then it will be unrecognized but no less powerful.

In recent decades, this concern has been met by the rise of reception history as a field of scholarly activity within biblical studies. Reception history seeks to understand "both how works influenced their readers; and how successive generations of readers influenced the understanding of texts and works."[8] Continuity and innovation occurs within unfolding traditions of interpretation. In the process, there may be paradigm shifts within disciplines when existing interpretations no longer answer the questions contemporary readers are asking. New paradigms arise within which these questions can be answered. Given the coincidence in time between the rise of the NPP and the reckoning with the Holocaust taking place within Western culture, the NPP provides a classic example of such a paradigm shift. The new questions being asked about attitudes toward Judaism provoked new interpretations of the Pauline letters that answered them.

To make these observations is certainly *not* to argue that interpretations are merely culturally relative. New Testament scholars base their judgments on the grammar of the texts and our knowledge of various dimensions of the contexts of the author and first readers. Some interpretations fit this available evidence a

---

8. Anthony C. Thiselton, "Reception Theory, H. R. Jauss and the Formative Power of Scripture," *SJT* 65 (2012): 290–91. The key influences upon the development of reception history are the German philosopher H. G. Gadamer (1900–2002) and the German literary theorist H. R. Jauss (1921–1997). See Robert Evans, *Reception History, Tradition and Biblical Interpretation: Gadamer and Jauss in Current Practice* (London: T&T Clark, 2014).

lot better than others. They are historically plausible in a way that others are not. Reception history simply highlights for us that these judgments are always made by scholars influenced in one way or another by traditions of interpretation. Given the significance of the Reformers within the reception history that forms the context of the NPP, to engage in contemporary Pauline interpretation in a critically aware manner requires attention to their interpretation of the Pauline Letters.

The purpose of this book is to pay such attention. One of its major aims is to help to equip readers as Pauline interpreters by offering an accurate portrayal of the Reformers' exegesis. My purpose in doing so is to dispel misunderstanding of their Pauline interpretation, for the assumptions made about their exegesis within NPP scholarship are not entirely correct. The Reformers have sometimes been rejected on the grounds that they held positions that they did not in fact hold. Contemporary interpretation also sometimes owes debts to them, that is, scholars within the NPP adopt exegetical positions first advocated by the Reformers without recognizing their origin.

Further, engaging with the Reformers' Pauline exegesis takes advantage of one of the most important opportunities provided by reception history. By studying interpreters from previous eras, we are enabled to see exegetical issues from a different perspective. Our assumptions are challenged, which alters and refines our sense of viable interpretative possibilities. The Reformers are far from the only past Pauline interpreters from whose study we might benefit in this way, but they are prominent among them. They have insights into the interpretation of the Pauline Letters that can be a significant resource for our own attempts to interpret those letters in and for contemporary contexts. Sometimes they will help us to identify arguments that challenge widely help contemporary positions and to identify features of Paul's theology to which our own interpretation should attend.

Nevertheless, the purposes of this book do *not* include turning the clock back by discrediting the NPP and restoring the Lutheran interpretation of Paul as it was understood before Sanders. The NPP did represent a significant and salutary step forward in the portrayal of Judaism. The Reformers can aid us in our own interpretative task only if we construct a dialogue with them about key interpretative issues. This requires us critically to sift their exegetical conclusions before bringing them into conversation with our own questions and concerns. Some positions held by the Reformers accurately understood and those held by most contemporary interpreters are indeed in straightforward conflict. Sometimes it must be concluded that the Reformers made errors in interpretation. They are not right on every issue, and it would be unhelpful in our own interpretation simply to repeat what they said. We are interpreting for different times and simple nostalgia for the interpretation of a previous era would merely evade contemporary challenges.

We should also avoid patronizing the Reformers, or other interpreters of the past, by engaging with their work only to allocate praise or blame for the degree to which their conclusions either anticipate our own or fail to do so. The expectation that interpretations of the past ought simply to mirror those of the present is itself anachronistic. Instead, our goal should be to enter a critical conversation with their work, reading their exegesis in a discriminating manner, both reaching different conclusions from them where necessary and taking inspiration from them when appropriate. We cannot and should not return to the past, but in our own efforts to interpret the Pauline texts accurately we can and must make use of the resources provided by important interpreters of previous eras like the Reformers.

CHAPTER TWO

Parallel Disciplines:
Pauline Theology and Luther Studies

A s we have already seen, it was problematic for New Perspective on Paul (NPP) scholarship to neglect the history of reception in general and the place of the Reformers in particular. More attention was needed to the NPP's own historical location within a wider context in which Western culture was coming to terms with the horrors of the Holocaust. Precisely because the NPP was rejecting trajectories of interpretation perceived to stem from the Reformers, more attention also ought to have been paid to the accuracy of perceptions of the Reformers' Pauline interpretation current among New Testament scholars. It is not possible helpfully to correct the Reformers' misinterpretations of Paul while perpetuating misinterpretations of the Reformers themselves. Reliance upon such misinterpretations also denies us access to the insights and resources they have to offer us for the task of interpreting Paul in and for contemporary contexts.

2.1. Recognizing Shared Trajectories of Interpretation

However, there was a further connected reason why NPP scholarship should not have neglected the Reformers in general and Martin Luther in particular. This was not only because Luther was one of Paul's most influential ever interpreters, for whom Pauline interpretation was central to his theology. It was also because important new developments in the interpretation of Luther across recent decades mirror in significant ways new developments in the interpretation of Paul. This is perhaps unsurprising given that, at least in part, contemporary Luther scholars are engaged in interpreting Luther interpreting Paul. Yet it is little recognized that in the decades around the rise of the NPP, the interpretation of Luther's theology was subject to change and development in ways that parallel the history of Pauline scholarship in the same period. If we are to escape from simplistic binary contrasts between the NPP and the exegesis of the Reformers, then before we explore the work of the Reformers themselves, it is necessary to place these parallel developments in Pauline interpretation and Luther interpretation alongside each other. As we shall see, the recent history of the two disciplines suggests a relationship between them much more complex than the straightforward overcoming of error inherited from Luther that is celebrated within NPP scholarship.

2.2. The Rise of the NPP

Although E. P. Sanders included some discussion of Paul's theology in *Paul and Palestinian Judaism*, his argument instead focused largely on the nature of Second Temple Judaism. Sanders documented at length a history of interpretative bias, especially in nineteenth- and twentieth-century German scholarship, in the presentation of Jewish sources. He sharply questioned portrayals of Judaism as a legalistic religion that was preoccupied with petty regulations and taught salvation by works. Despite the aspirations of scholars to objectivity, their vision of Judaism implicitly positioned it as a religion gone wrong: it stood in negative contrast to Protestant Christianity's emphasis on divine grace.

Sanders instead sought to provide a more genuinely neutral evaluation by considering the pattern of religion presented by Second Temple Judaism. He found in Second Temple sources a religion that, while centrally concerned with obedience to God's law, was also fully aware that its covenant relationship with God was based upon prior divine grace. The obedience that was so important was not a crude attempt to earn God's favor but rather a grateful response to grace already given. In terms of Israel's relationship with God, *getting in* depended upon grace. The importance of obedience related instead to *staying in* a relationship already established by God.

The significance of these conclusions for interpreting Paul is that in both Romans and Galatians he insists several times that justification is by faith and not by "works of the law" (Rom 3:20, 27, 28; Gal 2:16 [×3]; 3:2, 5, 10). It was the phrase "works of the law" (*erga nomou*) that Protestant interpreters traditionally took as the negative component of a contrast between the grace entered into through faith in Christ and the attempts to earn God's favor characteristic of Judaism. Paul was an opponent of works-righteousness. Yet if Sanders was correct about the pattern of religion current within Second Temple Judaism, it did not teach works-righteousness. Whatever Paul was opposing, it was therefore unlikely to be works-righteousness. A new account of what Paul meant by "works of the law" and of their significance within Judaism was clearly needed.

In 1977 Sanders said little specifically about the phrase "works of the law," but he did describe what he regarded as the overall pattern of religion found in Paul. In rejecting the law, the covenant, and the election of Israel as means of salvation, Paul is working out the implications of his central conviction that God sent Jesus as Savior. It is not that Paul identifies a particular problem with Judaism such as works-righteousness. Rather, he recognizes that if Judaism as it existed could have brought salvation, then the sending of Christ would have been pointless. It is what Paul now believes about Christ that determines his attitude toward Judaism, not dissatisfaction with Judaism that leads him toward Christ: "*This is what Paul finds wrong in Judaism: it is not Christianity.*"[1]

Similarly, Paul's "thought did not run from plight to solution but from solution to plight." He believed that the world needed a Savior, and that sin was the plight from which all needed to be delivered, as a reflex of his conviction that God had indeed sent such a Savior. If one had been sent, a Savior must have been necessary. Paul's insistence on justification by faith is therefore largely simply "a negative argument against keeping the law as sufficient or necessary for salvation." Much more significant for Paul's theology than justification by faith is his use of the concept of being "in Christ" and multiple associated images (such as being joined to Christ or conformed to Christ) to speak of a union between Christ and believers. Those who believe participate in Christ, and it is in the participatory categories of his thought that "the real bite" of Paul's theology is found.[2]

Sanders's argument provided a reason for Paul's general conviction that the law was unable to provide a path to salvation, but he did not offer a specific interpretation of the phrase "works of the law." Paul therefore appeared somewhat arbitrary in the application of his convictions about Christ and the law to Judaism. This gap in Sanders's argument was soon filled by the British scholar James D. G. Dunn (1939–2020), who provided an interpretation of the "works of the law" that did not involve Jewish works-righteousness.[3] Dunn argued that in a context like Paul's gentile mission where the relationship of Israel to other nations was at stake, some issues were more sensitive than others. At a formal level, Paul's phrase refers to all

---

1. E. P. Sanders, *Paul and Palestinian Judaism* (London: SCM, 1977), 552.

2. Sanders, *Paul and Palestinian Judaism*, 443, 492, 502. I do not distinguish between the phrase "union with Christ" and the phrase "participation in Christ" but use the two to refer to the same broad category of vocabulary in the Pauline texts, especially his frequent descriptions of believers as existing "in Christ" and related phrases.

3. See especially Dunn's 1983 essay "The New Perspective on Paul" republished in the volume *The New Perspective on Paul*, rev. ed. (Grand Rapids: Eerdmans, 2008), 99–120.

that the law requires, but there were several key Jewish practices that demonstrated the separation of Jews from other nations and their loyalty to the covenant.

Circumcision, food laws, and Sabbath observance were boundary markers delineating Jewish identity, and it is to these practices that the phrase "works of the law" makes special reference. Its target is those Jewish believers in Christ who regarded as illegitimate Paul's preaching of a gospel that did not require gentiles to become law observant. For Paul, the affirmation by these opponents of the necessity for "works of the law" is "tantamount to saying 'God is God of the Jews only.'"[4] Judaism had gone astray not through works-righteousness but through an ethnocentric identification of righteousness with Jewish identity. For Paul, the attempt to impose such works on gentiles was based upon a misunderstanding of the requirements of God's covenant with Israel and missed the divine intention to bless also the nations (Gen 12:3). Paul's insistence that justification is by faith and not by "works of the law" is therefore his polemical response to objections to his mission to gentiles. It is his answer to the question, "How is it that Gentiles can be equally acceptable to God as Jews?"[5]

Dunn's achievement was to offer an account of Paul's theology that was consistent with Sanders's revisionist portrayal of Second Temple Judaism, but which also granted Paul his own distinctive critique of his opponents' perspective on the law. Although there remained some differences between them, in a subsequent work published in 1983, Sanders coordinated his own position with that advocated by Dunn. He, too, accepted that Paul was questioning the identification of righteousness with Jewish identity.[6] Key exegetical components of a new interpretative paradigm were being formulated, and it was in the early 1980s that the term "New Perspective" itself emerged.

The importance of these developments was recognized by another British scholar, N. T. Wright (b. 1948), who in the same years had independently developed ideas similar to those of Dunn.[7] Wright is a synthetic thinker, concerned both with exegetical detail and much larger theological patterns and frameworks. He seeks to integrate all the motifs of Paul's theology into a single synthesis and to relate this to the wider biblical narrative. Wright rapidly pushed beyond simply challenging traditional portrayals of Judaism, and beyond simply offering a

---

4. James D. G. Dunn, *The Theology of Paul the Apostle* (Edinburgh: T&T Clark, 1998), 363.

5. Dunn, *Theology of Paul*, 340.

6. E. P. Sanders, *Paul, the Law, and the Jewish People* (Philadelphia: Fortress, 1983), 47: "What is wrong with the law, and thus with Judaism, is that it does not provide for God's ultimate purpose, that of saving the entire world through faith in Christ, and without the privilege accorded to Jews through the promises, the covenants, and the law."

7. See N. T. Wright, "The Paul of History and the Apostle of Faith," *TynBul* 29 (1978): 61–88.

revised understanding of the phrase "works of the law." He also formulated a new position on the nature of justification itself.

Traditional Protestant accounts took Paul's justification language to be forensic—that is, an image drawn from the world of the law courts. God as judge declares righteous those who believe on the basis of Christ's atoning death, so forgiving their sins. Justification deals with the fundamental human problem, which is sin and the separation from God that results from it. While Wright also recognizes that justification is a forensic image in the sense that it anticipates the last judgment, he argues that God's declaration has a somewhat different nature: "'Justification, as in the verbs of Galatians 2:16–17 . . . denotes the verdict of God himself as to who really is a member of his people."[8] Justification concerns membership of God's covenant family, and faith is the badge or identity-defining characteristic of that family. God's verdict that someone is a member of the covenant family is made possible by Christ's sacrificial death, and the members of that family will receive forgiveness, but the vocabulary of justification is primarily covenantal. Membership of the covenant family provides the context in which forgiveness of sins takes place.

In this way, Wright offers an account of justification that provides a matching counterpart to the NPP's interpretation of the "works of the law." In Wright's view, Paul argues that justification does not come through Jewish identity as it was demarcated by practices such as circumcision, the food laws, and Sabbath observance. Instead, it comes through faith in God's Messiah whose saving death accomplishes a worldwide family composed of both Jews and gentiles. For Paul, both what justification is and what it is not concern covenantal membership and identity.

2.3. Before the NPP

In fact, the ideas advocated by the NPP were not entirely new. Scholars of Judaism such as George Foot Moore (1851–1931) had earlier disputed the accuracy of its portrayal as a religion of works-righteousness.[9] Within Pauline scholarship itself, as long ago as 1904, William Wrede (1859–1906) had argued that Paul's teaching about justification served two polemical purposes: "(1) the mission must be free from the burden of Jewish national custom; (2) the superiority of the Christian

---

8. N. T. Wright, *Justification* (Downers Grove, IL: InterVarsity Press, 2009), 121.

9. See George F. Moore, *Judaism in the First Centuries of the Christian Era: The Age of the Tannaim*, 3 vols. (Cambridge: Harvard University Press, 1927–1930).

faith in redemption over Judaism must be assured."[10] Otherwise justification is not of great importance to Paul, for whom participation in the death of Christ and the indwelling of the Spirit are of central significance in salvation. For Paul, faith is simply the means by which the individual appropriates what Christ has accomplished for humanity as a whole: "the history of salvation is the content of his faith."[11]

In the same era, Albert Schweitzer (1875–1965) held a similar position but did not regard Paul as simply polemical. Instead, Paul advocated justification by faith as a result of thinking through systematically the implications of Christ's death. Now that a new age has dawned, the law is redundant because those who die with Christ also die to the law. Nevertheless, it is telling that justification by faith appears in Paul's letters only when he is arguing with those who believe in justification through the law. The heart of Paul's theology lies elsewhere: "The doctrine of righteousness by faith is therefore a subsidiary crater, which has formed within the rim of the main crater—the mystical doctrine of redemption through the being-in-Christ."[12]

Closer in time to the rise of the NPP, Krister Stendahl (1921–2008) focused on the issue of Paul's conscience. In the 1960s, Stendahl pointed out that there is little evidence to support the then widely held view that before his Damascus Road experience, Paul had struggled with an inability to obey the law. Far from being psychologically prepared by such an introspective struggle for his transformation from persecutor to apostle, "Paul was equipped with what in our eyes must be called a rather 'robust' conscience. In Phil 3 Paul speaks most fully about his life before his Christian calling, and there is no indication that he had any difficulty in fulfilling the law."[13] Stendahl thus provided the basis upon which Sanders was able to argue that Paul worked from solution to plight, for Paul himself had experienced Christ as solution before he ever recognized a plight from which he needed to be saved. Paul's insistence on justification by faith should not be understood as a consequence of his Damascus Road experience but as an apologetic teaching, "hammered out by Paul for the very specific and limited purpose of defending

---

10. William Wrede, *Paul* (London: Green, 1907; German original 1904), 127.

11. Wrede, *Paul*, 115.

12. Albert Schweitzer, *The Mysticism of Paul the Apostle* (London: Black, 1931; German original 1930), 225. Schweitzer had developed similar ideas in his earlier volume *Paul and His Interpreters* (London: Black, 1912; German original 1911).

13. Krister Stendahl, *Paul among Jews and Gentiles* (Philadelphia: Fortress, 1976), 80. Stendahl originally published his enormously influential essay "Paul and the Introspective Conscience of the West" in 1963.

the rights of Gentile converts to be full and genuine heirs to the promises of God to Israel."[14]

The crucial difference made by the work of Sanders was therefore not so much that he adopted highly original positions. It was instead the cogency and detail with which he documented his conclusions about the nature of Second Temple Judaism. The result was that scholarly positions became mainstream that had previously been held only by a minority and vice versa. While the NPP was never monolithic, and there were significant differences among the scholars who identified with it, there was a rapid and definite paradigm shift in Pauline studies. The dramatically altered understanding of the "works of the law" meant that Paul's gospel was no longer positioned primarily in opposition to works-righteousness but instead in opposition to ethnocentrism. In Western contexts, being reshaped by globalization and large-scale immigration, on the one hand, and by secularization, on the other, and where large numbers of Christians now belonged to ethnic minorities, this emphasis suited contemporary needs.

Further, the redefinition of the nature of justification wrought by the NPP altered the significance within Paul's theology of individuals and their faith. In traditional Protestant accounts, not only did justification lie at the heart of Paul's theology, but it was also rooted in his personal experience on the Damascus Road.[15] The definition of justification in legal terms as the gift of right standing before God through the forgiveness of sins also helped to focus attention on the faith of individuals as the means through which the gift is received. Yet once the NPP gained hold, Paul's Damascus Road experience was often perceived as of less significance in shaping his theology than the practical issue of Jewish and gentile believers living together as a single people of God. Also, justification defined in forensic terms was no longer perceived to lie at the heart of Paul's theology.

For some, its significance was diminished in favor of alternative categories in Paul's thought such as participation in Christ or salvation history (the calling of the gentiles into the people of God). For others, as we saw with Wright and his emphasis on covenant, it was redefined in different terms that integrated it with the participatory and salvation-historical aspects of Paul's theology. And some of Paul's most succinct and compelling statements of the importance of faith came to be understood not as a reference to the faith of believers in Christ but instead to the faithful-

---

14. Stendahl, *Paul among Jews and Gentiles*, 2.

15. For a defense of the significance of Paul's experience for his theology, see Seyoon Kim, *The Origin of Paul's Gospel*, 2nd ed., WUNT 2/4 (Tübingen: Mohr Siebeck, 1984). This study is based upon Kim's PhD thesis, itself completed in 1977.

ness displayed by Christ himself on their behalf.[16] As a result, the salvation of the individual became a less dominant concern, with more attention given both to the communal level (i.e., the significance of Israel and the church) and the cosmic level (i.e., God's reclaiming and renewing of creation through Christ) of Paul's thought.

These major transitions in the interpretation of Paul happened quickly, and the NPP rapidly came to represent majority opinion among English-speaking Pauline scholars. This is not to say that its rise was undisputed. For example, many of its characteristic positions were contested in a nuanced manner by Stephen Westerholm (b. 1949), who accepted important aspects of Sanders's reevaluation of Judaism while rejecting its application to Paul. Westerholm argued that Paul had despaired of the human capacity to obey God's law in a manner untypical of Judaism. Paul therefore "attributes salvation to divine grace to the exclusion of any role by human works in a way which is not typical of Judaism. And the tenet that justification by faith alone is both necessary to Paul and pointless from the perspective of Judaism."[17] Yet although Westerholm succeeded in establishing himself as the most compelling critic of the NPP, he was not able to secure acceptance of his alternative proposals by a majority.

2.4. Perspectives on the Reformers within the NPP

That the NPP succeeded so quickly in altering majority opinion within its discipline raised questions for its proponents about the interpretations of Paul they rejected. If the NPP was correct, why had views so inconsistent with it previously dominated the discipline of Pauline studies? What accounts for the errors of the still recent past? A very clear explanation had already been offered by Krister Stendahl: "We all, in the West, and especially in the tradition of the Reformation, cannot help reading Paul through the experience of persons like Luther and Calvin. And this is the chief reason for most of our misunderstandings of Paul."[18] When the NPP rejected the Lutheran interpretation of Paul, it was therefore not using the label to identify Lutheranism as a specific Christian tradition. Instead,

---

16. See Richard B. Hays, *The Faith of Jesus Christ: The Narrative Substructure of Galatians 3:1–4:11*, 2nd ed. (Grand Rapids: Eerdmans, 2002). Hays's study was first published in 1983. This shift in the understanding of Paul's statements about faith will be discussed further below (see 8.2). It was not supported by all within the NPP and was disputed by James Dunn but secured very wide acceptance within North American Pauline scholarship.

17. Stephen Westerholm, *Israel's Law and the Church's Faith: Paul and His Recent Interpreters* (Grand Rapids: Eerdmans, 1988), 142. See also Stephen Westerholm, *Perspectives Old and New on Paul: The "Lutheran" Paul and His Critics* (Grand Rapids: Eerdmans, 2004).

18. Stendahl, *Paul among Jews and Gentiles*, 12.

the label served more broadly to identify Protestant interpretations of Paul's letters dominated by exegetical trajectories stemming from the Reformation.[19] It was from Reformation roots that came all the most serious perceived errors that the NPP sought to correct: the identification of Judaism with works-righteousness, the introspective struggle with the law that prepared the ground for Paul's Damascus Road transformation, and the centrality of justification by faith defined as a legal declaration of the forgiveness of an individual's sins.

The consequence of this identification of error in Pauline interpretation with the legacy of the Reformation was that, for several decades, the Reformers received little attention or only negative attention in NPP scholarship. E. P. Sanders wrote that Luther's interpretation of Paul "has been influential because it corresponds to the sense of sinfulness that many people feel, and which is part and parcel of western concepts of personhood, with their emphasis on individualism and introspection. Luther sought and found relief from guilt. But Luther's problems were not Paul's, and we misunderstand him if we see him through Luther's eyes."[20]

More recently, in N. T. Wright's monumental study *Paul and the Faithfulness of God*, neither the Reformers nor Reformation interpretation forms a major theme, but, in various scattered references, what Wright takes to be their significance is set in erroneous contrast to his own conclusions.[21] Such contrasts served a rhetorical purpose, identifying NPP scholarship with responsible historical interpretation of Paul and of Second Temple Judaism and identifying those who question its conclusions with the regressive and discredited interpretations of the Reformers.[22] Yet this negative characterization of major Reformation interpreters is not based on any substantial engagement with their work. It is largely a general judgment based upon popular perceptions of the interpretative positions they represented.

2.5. The Luther Renaissance and Bultmann's Interpretation of Paul

This sense that the traditions against which the NPP reacted are simply a known quantity that can confidently be characterized in negative terms was unfortunate.

19. Somewhat confusingly for those new to Pauline studies, this positions Stendahl, a Lutheran bishop, as one of the principal opponents of a Lutheran reading of Paul.

20. E. P. Sanders, *Paul* (Oxford: Oxford University Press, 1991), 49.

21. N. T. Wright, *Paul and the Faithfulness of God* (Minneapolis: Fortress, 2013), 1:24, 42, 67, 115, 141, 385, 461, 514. Note, however, the somewhat more positive evaluation of Calvin, positioned in contrast to Luther, in *Paul and His Recent Interpreters* (Minneapolis: Fortress, 2015), 27–32.

22. It is only fair also to note that those NPP scholars who themselves actively identified with Protestant ecclesial traditions often received ill-informed and sometimes extreme criticism from nonscholarly sources who misunderstood their proposals as a betrayal of the Christian gospel.

For in fact, the interpretation of the theology of the Reformers, especially that of Luther as the founder of Protestantism, was itself undergoing significant change. The Luther rejected by the NPP turned out to belong to a particular phase in the history of the reception of his thought. The phase in question was that of the Luther Renaissance, a movement in German and Scandinavian scholarship spanning the period from roughly 1900 to 1960.[23] Confronted by the many cataclysmic crises of modernity characteristic of those decades, with individual liberties threatened by totalitarian systems, Luther scholars emphasized the experience of justification as foundational to a positive religious contribution to a free society. While the Luther Renaissance was itself a complex scholarly phenomenon with different strands and internal tensions, the picture of Luther that dominated was that of an advocate of personal conviction and conscience. It is the inner religious life of the individual that is of ultimate importance.

The words "Here I stand," attributed to Luther at the Diet of Worms (1521), where he refused to bow to the institutional authority of the Roman church, sum up his status as a hero of the freedom of the individual conscience. While Luther's mature theology certainly remained a focus of interpretative activity, immense scholarly energy was expended on the young Luther's spiritual and intellectual development that led to his acts of defiance. It became something of a scholarly holy grail to pinpoint the date and content of Luther's moment of "Reformation breakthrough," when, after many struggles with spiritual despair (his *Anfechtungen*), he reached a new understanding of the righteousness of God in Romans,[24] and hence also a new assurance of salvation, incompatible with the teaching of the church.

This kind of interpretation of Luther's theology as focused upon individuals and their religious experience could be accepted within various Christian traditions. At one end of the theological spectrum, the main emphases of its account of Luther fitted with the concerns of liberal Protestantism: "His [Luther's] inward conviction, not his concrete doctrines and time-dependent expressions, was the object of liberal admiration. . . . [R]eligious expressions are secondary acts of the

---

23. See the essays in *Lutherrenaissance: Past and Present*, ed. Christine Helmer and Bo Kristian Holm (Göttingen: Vandenhoeck & Ruprecht, 2015).

24. Readers new to Pauline interpretation should note that in Greek, the verb "justify" (*dikaioō*) and the noun "righteousness" (*dikaiosynē*) are cognate terms. Old English had a verb cognate to the noun, but it was displaced by the Norman French "justify." This means that the phrases "righteousness by faith" and "justification by faith" are alternative English designations for the same aspect of Paul's theology. There is also a long-standing and lively debate about how Paul's phrase "the righteousness of God" relates to his teaching about justification. For Luther's own account of his breakthrough, written many years later, see *LW* 34:336–37.

human mind; they must change in the course of history. Each era has the task to seek productive dialogue with its own tradition and with contemporary attitudes towards living articulations of inward religious experience."[25]

Yet it was also capable of being adapted to the needs of those belonging to more conservative church traditions. While those in evangelical or pietist contexts were not about to adopt liberal Protestantism's flexible approach to many traditional Christian doctrines, their own brands of Christianity emphasized the significance of a personal experience of conversion. Portrayals of Luther centered around his personal spiritual journey and his moment of "Reformation breakthrough" to a new grasp of justification by faith could be congenial in these contexts too. Whatever their theological persuasion, thoughtful Protestants could appropriate Luther as the one who through his own experience truly understood Paul and his Damascus Road experience.

The Luther Renaissance thus offered a portrayal of Luther that responded to and reflected particular twentieth-century contexts. As times shifted, this portrayal of Luther was itself to be challenged through a fresh reading of his texts. Just as Pauline studies underwent paradigms shifts, so too did Luther interpretation. Yet on both sides of these paradigm shifts, trends in the two disciplines reflect each other. In the era before the rise of the NPP, we can see these similarities by comparing some aspects of the Luther Renaissance with the work of Rudolf Bultmann (1884–1976), who dominated the interpretation of Paul in the mid-twentieth century.[26]

At one level, Bultmann was quite distant from the kind of emphasis on personal religious experience characteristic of Luther studies in the same era. For Bultmann offered an interpretation of the New Testament structured by the categories of existential philosophy. He felt that if the Christian gospel was to be heard and accepted by modern people, supernatural elements incompatible with a scientific worldview needed to be explained in other terms. He demythologized the New Testament so that the question of the historical status of its claims of direct divine intervention in the life of the world became secondary. Thus, for example, to discuss whether the resurrected Christ truly appeared to Paul on the road to Damascus would be to ask the wrong question. The mythological content of Paul's experience is not its essential aspect.

---

25. Jörg Lauster, "Luther—Apostle of Freedom? Liberal Protestant Interpretations of Luther," in Helmer and Holm, *Lutherrenaissance*, 147.

26. For evaluation of Bultmann as an interpreter of the New Testament, see *Beyond Bultmann: Reckoning a New Testament Theology*, ed. Bruce W. Longenecker and Mikeal C. Parsons (Waco, TX: Baylor University Press, 2014).

Bultmann's existential approach appealed instead to the idea that, while science and belief in supernatural intervention are incompatible with each other, human subjectivity nevertheless cannot be explained entirely in scientific terms. Our experience of what it is to be human exceeds, and cannot be adequately captured by, scientific description. It is in relation to this existential realm that the Christian gospel ought to be proclaimed, and, for Bultmann, the essential content of that proclamation is that human beings find authentic existence when they become radically dependent on God as the true ground of their being. The cross remains at the center of the gospel for Bultmann, but not as a historical event. Instead, it is an existential event in which a person's acceptance of the effectiveness of Christ's death for their sins is the gateway to dependence upon God and to authentic existence.

Therefore, while supremely uninterested in various ways in the contents of religious experience, Bultmann nevertheless attached enormous significance to faith as an act of decision. It is only when human beings come to faith in Christ through such existential acts of decision that they leave behind all boasting and all reliance on themselves and their own resources. This emphasis on faith and on dependence upon God enabled Bultmann to offer an interpretation of Paul that is existential. Justification by faith is reinterpreted in terms of existential decision, but it remains at the heart of Paul's theology, and it relates primarily to the individual dimension of his thought. Their decision for the gospel brings individuals to a radically revised self-understanding. Further, the dependence on God proclaimed by Paul stands in contrast to his opponents' devotion to the works of the law and their attempts at works-righteousness. For Bultmann, Judaism is characterized by "the self-reliant attitude of the man who puts his trust in his own strength and that which is controllable by him."[27]

Thus, despite Bultmann's radically existential approach to Pauline interpretation, his perspective on Paul remains recognizably "Lutheran." Justification by faith is still the essential Pauline teaching, Judaism is still a religion of works, and, while the struggles of the introspective conscience as such are not a focus for Bultmann, its place is occupied by his emphasis on individual decision. And, in fact, in German Luther scholarship in the same period, there had been a significant existential strand. While all recognized that Luther was a thinker of his own time, his theology was often regarded as of enduring significance because his enormous emphasis on trust in God's promises was held to point the way toward a distinctively modern way of thinking about human existence. If faith in divine words of promise makes all the difference to who we are, as Luther argues in his teaching

27. Rudolf Bultmann, *Theology of the New Testament* (London: SCM, 1952), 1:240.

on justification, then this points toward an account of reality as constituted by language and by the relationships created through linguistic acts such as promises. On such accounts, the promises to which faith responds clearly represent God, but, since to a significant degree reality is constituted by language, it is not clear whether God has a reality independent of the human language within which the promises are expressed and received.[28]

It was within the same scholarly context that Luther was also widely perceived as a hero of the individual conscience, and, with significant scholarly voices presenting his thought in broadly existential terms, there seemed little need for New Testament specialists to question Luther's significance for Pauline interpretation. NPP scholars could simply ascribe the origin of erroneous trajectories in Pauline theology to the Reformers, especially Luther, while at the same time rejecting Bultmann's interpretation of Paul as merely their most modern manifestation. Yet the differences between Luther's perspective on Paul and that of Bultmann are substantial, and, whatever its merits, to interpret a sixteenth-century thinker in existential terms is clearly not the only possibility. In retrospect, it is unsurprising that existential interpretations of Luther came to be challenged by new paradigms in interpretation. And just as there were family resemblances between Bultmann's Paul and the existential Luther, so too there would be family resemblances between the NPP and new interpretations of Luther.

2.6. The NPP, the Apocalyptic Luther, and the Finnish Luther

In 1982 the Dutch historian Heiko A. Oberman (1930–2001) published in German a biography of Luther with the subtitle *Man between God and the Devil*.[29] It rapidly became the most influential treatment of Luther of its time and was published in English translation in 1992. The subtitle was indicative of the book's contents, for Oberman sought to interpret Luther more fully as a figure of the sixteenth century. To this end, he emphasized the apocalyptic nature of Luther's thought. Luther regarded the world as a cosmic battleground between God and Satan and understood his conflicts with the Roman church as part of that struggle and therefore as an eschatological act of God: "In the apocalyptic spotlight, both Luther's

---

28. A fine exposition of this approach to interpreting Luther is provided by Oswald Bayer, *Martin Luther's Theology: A Contemporary Interpretation* (Grand Rapids: Eerdmans, 2008).

29. Heiko A. Oberman, *Luther: Man between God and the Devil* (New York: Image, 1992). The contrast with the title of the best-selling biography of Luther in the previous generation by Roland Bainton (1894–1984), *Here I Stand: A Life of Martin Luther* (New York: Abingdon-Cokesbury, 1950), is suggestive.

hearty affirmation of human life in the face of evil and his harsh polemics against the agents of the devil made sense. As Luther saw it, the true church was under siege, the end was near, and there was no hope that human power alone would save the world."[30]

At a similar time, apocalyptic was becoming of major significance in the interpretation of Paul. The German New Testament scholar, Ernst Käsemann (1906–1998), himself a student of Bultmann, reacted strongly against his teacher's existential approach to Paul. In contrast to revised self-understanding as a result of individual decision, Käsemann asserted the importance of the cosmic level of Paul's thought. For the apostle, human beings are not autonomous, and the fundamental issue facing them is under whose lordship they stand. The heavenly and the earthly are two dualistically opposed spheres of power, and human beings are integrated into one or the other. The cross initiates God's breaking of the hold of evil over humanity and the world, and early followers of Jesus lived in imminent expectation of the manifestation of God's complete victory. In offering this picture of Paul, Käsemann drew on previous work by historical-critical scholars on the apocalyptic literature of Second Temple Judaism in which "the world is frequently portrayed as under the sway of demonic powers which can be broken only by divine intervention, often culminating in some final cosmic battle, preceded by a time of great suffering."[31]

Käsemann had developed his apocalyptic interpretation of Paul in essays produced throughout the 1960s and 1970s. However, his maximum impact on English-speaking scholarship came following the publication in 1980 of the translation of his great Romans commentary.[32] In the same year, the Dutch scholar Jan Christiaan Beker (1924–1999) offered an interpretation of Paul framed in apocalyptic terms. This was followed in subsequent decades by important studies from Martinus de Boer (b. 1947), his teacher J. Louis Martyn (1925–2015), and Douglas Campbell (b. 1961).[33] Although Käsemann himself remained committed to a Reformation doctrine of justification, this mediation into English-speaking Pauline scholarship of his apocalyptic view of Paul took place in ways largely consistent

30. Scott H. Hendrix, "The Work of Heiko A. Oberman (1930–2001)," *RSR* 28 (2002): 123–30.

31. John K. Riches, *Galatians through the Centuries* (Oxford: Blackwell, 2008), 81.

32. Ernst Käsemann, *Commentary on Romans* (Grand Rapids: Eerdmans, 1980). The German original had been published in 1973.

33. Martinus C. de Boer, *The Defeat of Death: Apocalyptic Eschatology in 1 Corinthians 15 and Romans 5* (Sheffield: JSOT Press, 1988); J. Louis Martyn, *Galatians*, AB 33A (New York: Doubleday, 1997); J. Louis Martyn, *Theological Issues in the Letters of Paul* (Edinburgh: T&T Clark, 1997); and Douglas A. Campbell, *The Deliverance of God: An Apocalyptic Rereading of Justification in Paul* (Grand Rapids: Eerdmans, 2009).

with the NPP. His attention to the cosmic level of Paul's theology meant that the salvation of the individual could be seen only in the context of God's reclamation and renewal of creation. And while Käsemann could still position Judaism in relation to Paul's gospel as emblematic of corrupt human religiosity, he could also himself be sharply critical of church traditions and had been sufficiently politically engaged so as to be imprisoned by the Nazi regime in the 1930s.

Käsemann perceived the Nazi movement itself as representing a secularized form of salvation history. He was therefore uneasy with interpretations of Paul that emphasized the category of covenant. He did not eliminate all salvation-historical elements in Paul but did insist that the "divine 'salvation-plan' (*Heilsplan*) operates through disjuncture and disaster (*Unheil*), and thus only by miracles of grace."[34] However, in the hands of J. Louis Martyn and others, this aversion to salvation-history was considerably intensified. This intensification was to such an extent that Martyn could insist that in Galatians, God's covenantal promises to Abraham, fulfilled in Christ, are not to be identified also with the intervening history of Israel: "there are no through-trains from the scriptural, patriarchal traditions . . . to the gospel of God's Son."[35] This position inevitably led to conflict with the kind of strongly covenantal reading of Paul offered by N. T. Wright. However, Wright did not dispute that Paul's theology was apocalyptic. He instead argued that its apocalyptic dimensions properly belong within a covenantal context. Few disputed that Paul could legitimately be termed an apocalyptic thinker.[36] The apocalyptic Paul fought and conquered in the same decades as the apocalyptic Luther.

Alongside his emphasis on its apocalyptic nature, Käsemann also regarded participation in Christ as crucial to Paul's theology. This was another aspect of Käsemann's Pauline interpretation that could be received with appreciation in NPP contexts, and, in the first decades of the twenty-first century, there has been a groundswell of interest in participation among Pauline scholars.[37] Käsemann's handling of participation in Christ took a particular form. He argued that Paul al-

---

34. John M. G. Barclay, *Paul and the Gift* (Grand Rapids: Eerdmans, 2015), 143.

35. Martyn, *Theological Issues*, 221.

36. An exception is provided by the work of Stanley Stowers and his students. See Stanley Stowers, *A Rereading of Romans: Justice, Jews, and Gentiles* (New Haven: Yale University Press, 1994), and Emma Wasserman, *The Death of the Soul in Romans 7: Sin, Death, and the Law in Light of Hellenistic Moral Psychology*, WUNT 2/256 (Tübingen: Mohr Siebeck, 2008).

37. See Constantine R. Campbell, *Paul and Union with Christ: An Exegetical and Theological Study* (Grand Rapids: Zondervan, 2012); Michael J. Gorman, *Participating in Christ: Explorations in Paul's Theology and Spirituality* (Grand Rapids: Baker, 2019); Grant Macaskill, *Union with Christ in the New Testament* (Oxford: Oxford University Press, 2013); and Michael J. Thate, Kevin J. Vanhoozer, and Constantine R. Campbell, eds., *In Christ in Paul: Explorations in Paul's Theology of Union and Participation*, WUNT 2/384 (Tübingen: Mohr Siebeck, 2014).

lows the forensic and participatory tracks in his theology to interpret each other.[38] This meant that for Käsemann, the significance of participation did not diminish that of justification. What mattered was less which of these two tracks was the most important in Paul's theology and more how they related to each other.

This is itself important, for once again there was a significant parallel development in Luther studies. Beginning in the 1970s, there arose a new Finnish school of Luther interpretation, led by Tuomo Mannermaa (1937–2015), who argued that Luther taught that justification itself involves union with Christ. As Luther says about Gal 2:15–16, "Faith justifies because it takes hold of and possesses this treasure, the present Christ... the Christ who is grasped by faith and lives in the heart is the true Christian righteousness" (*LW* 26:130). On this view, God justifies on the basis of faith, but faith is itself a divine gift in which Christ is present. It is this presence of Christ in the faith of the believer that creates the possibility of living the life of Christ (Gal 2:19–20).

The Finns' ideas were for some time not readily accessible in English. However, in the 1990s and early twenty-first century, this changed dramatically.[39] The Finnish perspective was widely debated, and it proved controversial. This was partly because the Finns' emphasis on union with Christ challenged existential accounts of Luther. If the significance of faith for Luther was not exclusively its receipt of divine words of promise and the divine declaration of righteousness that resulted, but also the gift of Christ present within it, then Luther may not so clearly point forward to a modern way of thinking about reality as constituted by language and the relationships created through linguistic acts. He may belong as much to the medieval world where discussions of the nature of reality employed the category of substance.

Perhaps even more contentiously, the Finns' views challenged the boundary between justification and renewal. In most traditional Protestant appropriations of Luther's teaching, including Lutheranism's own confessional statement, the Formula of Concord (1577), the transformation of believers through union with Christ is a consequence of justification and not a component of justification itself. Keeping justification and renewal distinct was thought to guard against the danger of slipping back into a form of works-righteousness, but, on the Finnish view, in the person of Christ present in faith, God's grace as the forgiveness of sins exists in inseparable unity with the gift of renewal. For the Finns, this certainly does not imply salvation by works (since although justification involves renewal, such

---

38. See especially Ernst Käsemann, *Perspectives on Paul* (Philadelphia: Fortress, 1971), 171–72.

39. See Carl E. Braaten and Robert W. Jenson, eds., *Union with Christ: The New Finnish Interpretation of Luther* (Grand Rapids: Eerdmans, 1998); Tuomo Mannermaa, *Christ Present in Faith: Luther's View of Justification* (Minneapolis: Fortress, 2005); and Olli-Pekka Vainio, ed., *Engaging Luther: A (New) Theological Perspective* (Eugene, OR: Wipf & Stock, 2010).

renewal is not its basis or cause), but others have not always been convinced. Yet whatever one's perspective on these complex debates, the Finns have undoubtedly succeeded in putting union with Christ at the heart of the discussion of Luther in the same decades that it was returning to the heart of the discussion of Paul.

There is thus a strikingly similar pattern in the recent history of the two disciplines. Existential accounts of Pauline theology characteristic of the post–World War II era were displaced by apocalyptic ones, but these, too, were then followed by a period of deep interest in participation in Christ that persists to the present. Within similar time frames, existential accounts of Luther's theology were challenged by apocalyptic ones and then by ones emphasizing union with Christ. The significance of this is not that scholars in the two disciplines were directly influenced by each other. Nor should it be regarded as simply coincidental. It is rather that the same intellectual currents impacted both disciplines at similar times. This is scarcely surprising given the centrality of Paul for Luther and the Reformation, but it does have an important consequence.

It would be preposterous when evaluating the current status of Luther's Pauline interpretation (i.e., how helpful Luther's work is for contemporary interpreters of Paul) to ignore the NPP and base the assessment only on Pauline scholarship prior to Sanders. It is similarly unfortunate to identify Luther and the other Reformers as Paul's misinterpreters in chief based only upon interpretations of Luther formulated prior to Oberman and to the Finnish school. The parallel developments in the two disciplines suggest that the relationship between the interpretation of the apostle and that of the Reformer is more complex than the belated correction by the NPP of an erroneous interpretation of Paul offered by Luther.[40] Before reaching conclusions about the Pauline interpretation of the Reformers, it is necessary to gain an accurate understanding of their Pauline interpretation, and to identify where their work and that of recent Pauline scholarship both cohere and stand in conflict. It is then necessary also to evaluate where such conflict means that positions held by the Reformers must be rejected and where they offer helpful resources for contemporary interpreters. When all this is done, Luther and the other Reformers will prove to have far more to offer contemporary Pauline interpretation that the rhetoric of NPP scholarship often suggests.

---

40. See Risto Saarinen, "The Pauline Luther and the Law: Lutheran Theology Re-engages the Study of Paul," in *Luther and the Gift* (Tübingen: Mohr Siebeck, 2017), 225: "Luther's theology is closer to the insights of the new perspective than has been previously assumed."

PART TWO

---

*Reformation Interpretation and
the New Perspective on Paul
as Paradigm Shifts*

CHAPTER THREE

Perspectives on Paul before the Reformers: Augustine

The argument of this book from this point forward falls into two further distinct parts. Part 3 (chapters 10–14) concerns the nature of justification and its place in Pauline theology. Here the contention that the Reformers' Pauline exegesis still has worthwhile resources to offer to contemporary interpreters will be pursued through an examination of individual Reformers. We will explore what Luther, Melanchthon, and Calvin each have to say about justification, and we will pay attention to how they differ from each other as well as to their agreements.

3.1. Comparing the Reformers and the NPP

Before then, however, part 2 (chapters 3–9) will pay attention to the fact that just as the New Perspective on Paul (NPP) represents a paradigm shift in the interpretation of Paul, so too did the Reformers' Pauline exegesis. They also broke in very significant ways with previously dominant trajectories of interpretation, and they together established a new tradition of reading Paul that transformed the legacy of Pauline interpretation inherited from the patristic and medieval eras. Notwithstanding some significant disagreements among themselves, there is a wide range of vital exegetical issues about which early Lutheran and early Reformed interpreters agree with each other over and against their Roman opponents.

Once the contours of this new Reformation tradition of interpreting Paul have been established, then the following key claims will be advanced about the relationship between it and the NPP (chapters 8–9):

1. The relationship between the Reformers' interpretation of Paul and the NPP cannot accurately be portrayed in straightforwardly antithetical terms. There

are exegetical positions widespread within NPP scholarship that in fact depend upon arguments made by the Reformers, especially in relation to Paul's anthropology (e.g., the meaning of terms such as "sin," "flesh," etc.).

2. There are other ways in which NPP interpreters intensify one aspect of the Reformers' Pauline interpretation at the expense of others. For example, the Reformers' own considerable emphasis on divine initiative in salvation is so heightened in some recent apocalyptic interpretations of Paul that little space is left to discuss the significance of human faith. Similarly, N. T. Wright so intensifies the theme of covenant, a theme integral to Reformed theology, that justification must be rethought in entirely covenantal terms in a manner incompatible with Reformation accounts.

3. NPP interpreters sometimes simply misunderstand the Reformers' interpretation of Paul, something most strikingly apparent in Stendahl's false assumption that their interpretation of Paul depended upon the apostle possessing an introspective conscience.

4. NPP interpreters nevertheless rightly perceive that Reformation accounts of what Paul means by the "works of the law" stand in genuine disagreement with their own. Here it must be acknowledged that the Reformers err in taking Paul's phrase to indicate Jewish commitment to works-righteousness. The issue for interpreters today is not this but whether the NPP's own exclusive emphasis on boundary markers in the interpretation of Paul's use of the phrase is itself exegetically sustainable.

These four claims together will constitute an assertion of the Reformers' continued relevance for contemporary Pauline interpretation. Yet since each of them depends upon establishing a historically credible account of the Reformers' Pauline exegesis so that it can be compared with that offered by NPP scholarship, they cannot be argued immediately. A thorough exploration of the Reformers' Pauline exegesis and the paradigm shift they achieved within their own historical context is necessary first (chapters 5–7). This in turn means that we cannot simply explore the Reformers' own Pauline exegesis. We must begin by understanding the traditions of Pauline interpretation against which they reacted (chapters 3–4).

3.2. Comparing the Reformers' and Medieval Pauline Interpretation

A helpful way to picture the paradigm shift in Pauline interpretation wrought by the Reformers is through the analogy of language and grammar. The Reformers' language of Pauline theology is a new language, radically different from the language of Pauline theology spoken by their medieval predecessors. It was sometimes unfathomable to those for whom that earlier language was native. The Reformers can speak this new language because in their shared exegetical conclusions, they have developed what can aptly be termed a new "exegetical grammar" of Pauline theology. In any language, its grammatical rules and principles structure and enable its use, ensuring its intelligibility within that language community. Similarly, the Reformers' shared exegetical conclusions about fundamental aspects of Paul's meaning provide a structure for, and so enable, their new interpretations of Pauline texts.[1] Interpretative disagreements between them take place within this new exegetical grammar that is radically different from that within which their predecessors interpreted Paul.

Yet the Reformers' new exegetical grammar was not intended to produce mere novelty. They "strove for a *reformation* in the sense of the restoration of the original form of the true congregation of Jesus Christ—and in this respect a renewal of the contemporary Church: *renovatio* [renewal] not *innovatio* [innovation]!"[2] They regarded themselves as the true Catholics, prophetically offering the opportunity for repentance and restoration to a stiff-necked people who would not listen. They therefore engaged in significant ways with the identity and history of the church. Luther wrote a tract *On the Councils and the Church* (1539) in which he displayed considerable knowledge of the work of the first four ecumenical councils—Nicaea (325), Constantinople (381), Ephesus (431), and Chalcedon (451)—and their relevance for the ecclesiological issues of his own day (*LW* 41). Calvin asserted that even in the worst times, God had maintained a living church through the preservation of baptism and other vestiges of true catholicity. Scripture alone was the Reformers' supreme authority, but that required rather than precluded engagement with its previous interpretation and application, especially by the church fathers.[3]

This sense of continuity should help us to avoid once common sweeping characterizations of the Reformation as the sudden springing into being of the modern world. Such characterizations stemmed from the debate between Karl Holl (1866–1926) and Ernst Troeltsch (1865–1923) about whether the Reformation

---

1. I am here adopting and adapting a concept of Luther's own. He speaks of "a new and theological grammar" (*LW* 26:267) that replaces a previous "moral grammar" (*LW* 26:268). He applies this new grammar to the task of interpreting texts that might seem to speak of righteousness by works. Rightly understood, these texts speak of deeds of love as the fruit of faith that grows from justification rather than as in any sense the basis on which justification is granted.

2. Berndt Hamm, "How Innovative Was the Reformation?," in *The Reformation of Faith in the Context of Late Medieval Theology and Piety: Essays by Berndt Hamm*, ed. Robert J. Bast (Leiden: Brill, 2004), 254.

3. See Diarmaid McCulloch, "Calvin: Fifth Latin Doctor of the Church?," in *Calvin and His Influence 1509–2009*, ed. Irena Backus and Philip Benedict (Oxford: Oxford University Press, 2011), 37–38.

represents the dawn of the modern world or a continuation of the Middle Ages. Recent scholarship has come down firmly on the side of continuity.[4] Luther was focused on correcting what he perceived as abuses in the life of the church, subjecting them to the test of Scripture, not launching a new era. Volker Leppin, the author of a recent major biography of Luther, sharply questions interpretations of Luther based upon "the idea of a radical disjunction between Luther's theology and the theology of the Middle Ages."[5]

Yet while recent judgments in favor of continuity are extremely helpful in placing Luther and others firmly in the context of their own time, this also should not blind us to the scale of change represented by the Reformers' conclusions about Pauline interpretation. For it is in the Reformers' Pauline exegesis that general arguments in favor of continuity find their greatest challenge. Although worked out in dialogue with patristic and medieval predecessors, the Reformers' new Pauline exegetical grammar differentiates them sharply from such predecessors. It overturned widespread assumptions stretching back centuries about the meaning of key terms and concepts. Their undeniably frequent dependence on predecessors for particular exegetical points should not be allowed to obscure the fact that these continuities exist within a radically altered framework.

In relation to key issues in Paul's description of the human plight apart from Christ (e.g., the nature of sin, the law, and the conscience), and in relation to his description of salvation in Christ (e.g., the works of the law, grace, and faith), the Reformers developed a powerful new consensus that contradicted the perspectives of their opponents.[6] In doing so, they established a new Pauline exegetical grammar that structured subsequent conversations about Pauline interpretation and helped to define what was plausible. They also in the process overturned a long-established, alternative way of thinking about the nature and process of salvation itself based upon the interpretation of the Pauline texts. This previous paradigm also possessed the characteristics of an exegetical grammar. For it, too, generated consensus about key issues in Paul's theology, and it, too, provided a framework within which remaining disagreements could be debated.

---

4. On this discussion, see Gerhard Müller, "Luther's Transformation of Medieval Thought: Discontinuity and Continuity," and Volker Leppin, "Luther's Transformation of Medieval Thought: Continuity and Discontinuity," in *The Oxford Handbook of Martin Luther's Theology*, ed. Robert Kolb, Irene Dingel, and Ľubomír Bakta (Oxford: Oxford University Press, 2014), 105–14 and 115–24.

5. Volker Leppin, "Martin Luther, Reconsidered for 2017," *LQ* 22 (2008): 375.

6. A partial exception to this consensus, and therefore a distinctive voice within early Protestant exegesis, is Martin Bucer. See Brian Lugioyo, *Martin Bucer's Doctrine of Justification: Reformation Theology and Early Modern Irenicism* (Oxford: Oxford University Press, 2011), 37–102.

3.3. Augustine's Pauline Exegetical Grammar

The medieval Pauline exegetical grammar that the Reformers rejected had a very clear source, for it was profoundly shaped by Augustine of Hippo (354–430). Ever since Augustine's dispute with Pelagius (c. 354–418) in the early fifth century, it had been widely recognized that Paul teaches that salvation begins with divine initiative. It cannot be otherwise, since the impact of sin means that fallen human beings can act justly only as a result of the gift of God's grace granted in initial justification. Sin itself Augustine conceives of as a preference for lesser goods, especially the self, over the highest good, which is God. Yet while this preference is entered into freely, it results in the bondage of the human will. Given over by God to its misdirected desires, the will is now "darkened in understanding and chilled in affection."[7]

There is a disorder in the self that leaves the rational human mind perpetually swamped by cupidity invested with the compulsive force of habit. The human will is left unable to choose the good, but not because of an external force restraining it. The good is instead unattainable because the will is no longer able truly to desire it, wanting rather those things that alienate the self from God. Commenting on what Paul says about misdirected desire/covetousness (*epithymia*) in Rom 7, Augustine notes that "it's our debility, it's our vice. It won't be detached from us and exist somewhere else, but it will be cured and not exist anywhere at all."[8] The human plight thus consists in a profound sickness of the will.

The Old Testament law can reveal to human beings languishing in this condition what God requires and can demonstrate their sinfulness, but it is unable to grant the power to obey. Augustine comments on Gal 3:21–22 that "the law was not given, therefore, to take away sin, but to imprison all under sin. For the law showed that what the Jews, blinded by custom, could regard as righteousness was sin, so that having been humbled in this way they might recognize that their salvation does not rest in their own hands but *in the hand of a mediator*."[9] As he says elsewhere, "Prior to the Law we do not struggle, because not only do we lust and sin, but we even assent to sin. Under the Law we struggle but we are overcome. We admit that we do evil, and by that admission, that we do not really want to

---

7. William S. Babcock, "Augustine on Sin and Moral Agency," in *The Ethics of St. Augustine*, ed. William S. Babcock (Atlanta: Scholars Press, 1991), 101.

8. Augustine, *Sermons 148–183*, trans. Edmund Hill, The Works of St. Augustine III/5 (New York: New City, 1992), 42 (151.3).

9. Augustine, *Augustine's Commentary on Galatians: Introduction, Text, Translation, and Notes*, trans. Eric A. Plumer (Oxford: Oxford University Press, 2003), 171 (25.9).

do it, but because we still lack grace we are overwhelmed."[10] The law tells human beings the truth, but it cannot enable them to obey the truth.

For these reasons, Augustine is convinced that no one can make themselves righteous. Righteousness is possible only through the gift of grace, which is available solely because of the person and work of Christ. Augustine says that the righteousness of God in Rom 1:17 is "not that by which God is righteous, but that with which he clothes a human being [*induit hominem*] when he justifies a sinner [*iustificat impium*]."[11] In this way, Paul's statement about God's righteousness is clearly connected with his later assertion that God justifies the ungodly (Rom 4:5). The priority of divine initiative in salvation is unambiguously asserted.

Yet once the initial gift of infused grace is received in baptism, Augustine considers it the Christian's responsibility to cooperate with this gift by performing meritorious good works in love of God and neighbor. The purpose of the justification of the ungodly is to *make* them righteous in substance and behavior: "What else, after all, does justified (Rom. 3:24) mean but: made righteous [*iusti facti*] by the one, of course, who justifies sinners (Rom. 4:5), so that from sinners they become righteous [*fiat iustus*]?"[12] Grace is something infused into those who believe, and there is not only initial justification but also justification as a lifetime process in which individuals make progress and gradually become more Christlike.

Paul's statements that justification is not by works of the law do not tell against this role for meritorious good works in justification since he is speaking only of initial justification and not about justification as a lifelong process.[13] Paul intends to say that good works do not contribute to initial justification, not to deny that works of charity play a crucial part in the ongoing process of justification. Indeed, far from faith and works functioning as opposites, faith is foundational to this ongoing process. For there is nobody who "can act justly [*operat iustitiam*] unless first

10. Paula Fredriksen Landes, *Augustine on Romans: Propositions from the Epistle to the Romans, Unfinished Commentary on the Epistle to the Romans* (Chico, CA: Scholars Press, 1982), 5–7 (proposition 18). This work is listed in the bibliography under Fredriksen Landes.

11. Augustine, "The Spirit and the Letter," in *Answer to the Pelagians*, trans. Roland J. Teske, The Works of St. Augustine I/23 (New York: New City, 1997), 158 (9.15). See David F. Wright, "Justification in Augustine," in *Justification in Perspective: Historical Developments and Contemporary Challenges*, ed. Bruce L. McCormack (Grand Rapids: Baker, 2006), 55–72.

12. Augustine, "Spirit and the Letter," 178–79 (26.45).

13. A minority of medieval commentators followed Ambrosiaster (an unidentified fourth-century commentator on Romans) in taking Paul's phrase "works of the law" to refer to Jewish ceremonies only and not to the moral law. This was not held to contradict the view that good works play no part in initial justification but merely to indicate that it was not Paul's purpose directly to comment on the issue.

justified [*iustificatus*]."[14] Faith is a gift of grace that then expresses itself in works. Augustine interprets Paul's quotation of Hab 2:4, "The one who is righteous will live by faith," with reference to the Christian life: "Having obtained this grace of faith, as a result of your faith you will be just, since *the just person lives from faith* (Rom. 1:17), and you will gain God by living from faith. When you have gained God by living from faith, you will receive immortality and eternal life as your reward."[15]

Here Augustine plainly means that faith is the source of good works: "Faith gives the proper foundation to our works; it gives them the proper orientation, and the good works which flow from faith are the steps by which we reach God."[16] In this understanding of Rom 1:17, human works can play no part in initial justification, but, once the gift of God's righteousness is received, works are vital if the Christian is to gain God and eternal life. The divine grace granted in initial justification enables the human obedience necessary for ongoing justification so that "when God crowns our merits [*merita nostra*], he only crowns his own gifts [*munera sua*]."[17] There can be no merit without grace given by God, so merit in no sense constitutes an independent claim upon God, but it is nevertheless real within the divinely initiated lifelong process of the justification of the believer. Augustine "characteristically does not attribute justification to good works or to faith and good works,"[18] but he equally never says that justification is by faith *alone*. For in justifying, God gives back to human beings the capacity to will the good: "grace should be understood as the gift of what is most deeply our own: our own true will."[19]

Within the ongoing process of justification, the sins of believers result in a loss of grace, but the merits of their good works, and their accessing of the grace made available through the sacraments of the church, result in its increase. The effects of grace "are inaugurated in the sacrament of baptism and consummated in the sacrament of the Eucharist."[20] There are mortal sins (e.g., murder) that might endanger the whole process but also a whole host of less serious venial sins

14. Ps 110:3. See Augustine, *Expositions of the Psalms 99–120*, trans. Maria Boulding, The Works of St. Augustine III/19 (New York: New City, 2003), 288.

15. Augustine, *Homilies on the Gospel of John 1–40*, trans. Edmund Hill, The Works of St. Augustine III/12 (New York: New City, 2009), 75 (3.9) in reference to John 1:16, "grace upon grace."

16. Stanislaus J. Grabowski, *The Church: An Introduction to the Theology of St. Augustine* (Saint Louis: Herder, 1957), 327.

17. Letter 194.5.19. See Augustine, *Letters 156–210*, trans. Roland Teske, The Works of St. Augustine II/3 (New York: New City, 2004), 296.

18. Wright, "Justification in Augustine," 65–66.

19. Lewis Ayres, "Augustine," in *The Blackwell Companion to Paul*, ed. Stephen Westerholm (Oxford: Wiley-Blackwell, 2011), 351.

20. Grabowski, *Church*, 415.

in relation to which works such as fasting, almsgiving, and prayer are efficacious. The Christian is still tempted to sin and faces struggles between the Spirit and the flesh (Gal 5:17). Such struggles "will not cease save at the resurrection of the body."[21] Nevertheless, there is a distinct difference between sin as it impacts the baptized and sin as it impacts those who are not Christians.

In a series of sermons on Rom 7 and 8 preached in Carthage, probably in 419,[22] Augustine distinguishes between suggestion, inclination or desire, and consent. Sin is suggested to people "either through the senses or through our own free association of ideas."[23] This then arouses inappropriate and misdirected desires, to which people give consent and then act. Such misdirected desires are expressions of human self-love and prominent among them are bodily desires. What distinguishes the person of the Christian is that baptism deals with original sin and with the guilt arising from such desires. Misdirected desires themselves remain, but, for the Christian, guilt no longer results so long as these desires are not consented to and acted upon. It is possible in a new way for the Christian to refuse to consent to such sinful desires or act upon them. Sin still threatens to disrupt healthy hierarchies between soul and body, and between reason/the will and the other faculties of the soul, so that the lower parts refuse to obey the higher. Yet sin can now be resisted.

This is the personal experience of Paul who summons Christians to the same fight. In this boxing bout between contrary desires, the conscience of the Christian is central: "Christ is watching you fighting. The ring is your conscience, where two contestants are matched, mind and flesh. . . . A hard struggle; but the one who is watching you fighting can help you when you are in danger of losing. . . . And what does winning now mean for you? Not consenting to evil desires. Because you can't help having those evil desires, can you? But winning means not consenting to them."[24]

When these battles in the conscience of the Christian are won, grace increases and merit follows: "We have been justified; but this justice can grow, as we make progress." When they are lost, then the goal of justice recedes: "Have we no justice at all? We certainly do have some. Let us be grateful for what we have, so that what

21. Fredriksen Landes, *Augustine on Romans*, 5–7 (proposition 18).

22. See Augustine, *Sermons 148–183*, 40–108 (sermons 151–56).

23. Eugene TeSelle, "Exploring the Inner Conflict: Augustine's Sermons on Romans 7 and 8," in *Engaging Augustine on Romans: Self, Context, and Theology in Interpretation*, ed. Daniel Patte and Eugene TeSelle (Harrisburg, PA: Trinity International, 2002), 118.

24. Augustine, *Sermons 148–183*, 80–81 (154A.3–4). Although on the same text and displaying consistent content and imagery, this sermon is not actually from the Carthage series.

we don't have may be added to it, and we don't lose what we do have."[25] As the battle in the conscience rages, grace and justice are added to or depleted, restored or eroded. The changes involved are changes in being, in the substance of what the person is, as the Christian progresses on a journey toward God. In the imagery of the later medieval age, the Christian is a pilgrim. Augustine understands Paul to be speaking of life "as a *via* [path] for our transformation."[26]

25. Augustine, *Sermons 148–183*, 116–17 (158.5).
26. Daphne Hampson, *Christian Contradictions: The Structures of Lutheran and Catholic Thought* (Cambridge: Cambridge University Press, 2001), 83.

CHAPTER FOUR

Perspectives on Paul before the Reformers:
The Medieval Era

Augustine's enormous prestige in the Western church ensured that his approach to interpreting Paul dominated throughout the medieval period. While the world of medieval Pauline interpretation is rich and varied, its variety exists within the exegetical grammar established by Augustine. His distinction between the initial act of justification and justification as a subsequent lifelong process is ubiquitous. The initial act of justification relies exclusively on divine grace, but baptized Christians cooperate with this gift and grow in grace through meritorious good deeds and through the grace that continues to be available in the Eucharist. As Christians grow in grace, they are transformed so that they become righteous people in substance and behavior. This growth is won through struggle in their conscience as they resist inappropriate desires—that is, refusing to consent to and act upon them. It is this series of key convictions, this exegetical grammar, based upon Augustine's interpretation of Pauline texts, that structures medieval Pauline interpretation.

*4.1. Augustine's Pauline Exegetical Grammar: New Developments
in the Medieval Era*

This Augustinian heritage was complemented by a new development in the life of the church that impacted all interpreters and constituted an additional shared element: the sacrament of penance. From the ninth century onward, the practice of private penance became widespread in Europe, and the Fourth Lateran Council (1215) required all Christians to make confession at least once a year. Penance came to play an important role in thinking about justification: the grace of baptism begins justification, but the merit of penance serves to counter the loss of grace and justice incurred by the sins of the baptized. The process of confession, an act of penance, and sacerdotal absolution restores justification.[1]

From the medieval perspective, penance thus sits comfortably within the soteriological framework established through Augustine's exegetical grammar. It does not compromise divine initiative in salvation since nobody begins to be justified through penance. It is not the basis of God's initial gift of grace but rather aids the Christian on the pathway of transformation by providing a mechanism through which setbacks are surmounted. Along with the clearer development of the doctrine of purgatory, where progress toward a state of righteousness could continue even after death, the sacrament of penance helped the Christian to merit heaven. This positioning of penance in relation to justification also makes it less surprising that Luther's initial breach with Rome could not be contained. A dispute focused on the sale of indulgences and so also on particular aspects of the doctrine of penance rapidly widened to encompass far broader soteriological issues.

In addition to the emergence of the sacrament of penance, there was also development in relation to Augustine's teaching about faith. He had insisted that faith never comes alone but is always expressed in the works of the Christian. However, medieval exegetes developed an explanation of how this occurs that resulted in a distinction between two kinds of faith. In Gal 5:6 Paul says that what counts is not circumcision or uncircumcision but "faith working through love." Following Peter Lombard (c. 1096–1160),[2] Thomas Aquinas (1225–1274) takes this phrase to refer specifically to "faith, not unformed, but the kind that worketh by charity: 'Faith without works is dead' (Jas. 2:26). For faith is a knowledge of the word of God 'That Christ may dwell by faith in your hearts' (Eph. 3:17)—which word is not perfectly possessed or perfectly known unless the love which it hopes for is possessed."[3]

On this view, the gift of faith granted in initial justification is a kind of knowledge or quality of mind and is unable by itself to justify. It is a cognitive acceptance of the facts of the gospel and as such is unformed. Only when such faith is shaped or formed by love can it become active and capable of the meritorious deeds necessary in the lifelong process of justification. Unsurprisingly, unformed

1. For a more detailed account, see Alister McGrath, *Iustitia Dei: A History of the Christian Doctrine of Justification*, 3rd ed. (Cambridge: Cambridge University Press, 2005), 117–28.

2. See John Van Engen, "Faith as a Concept of Order in Medieval Christendom," in *Belief in History: Innovative Approaches to European and American Religion*, ed. Thomas Kselman (Notre Dame: University of Notre Dame Press, 1991), 31–36.

3. Thomas Aquinas, *Commentary on Saint Paul's Epistle to the Galatians*, trans. Fabian R. Larcher (Albany, NY: Magi, 1966), 156.

faith came to be identified with the sacrament of baptism, and the transition to a formed faith with that of penance: "Forming faith meant persuading people to put the faith into practice by way of charity or penance, and restraining or absolving them from mortal sin."[4] There were now two kinds of faith, for unformed faith is truly faith, but it is incomplete in important ways. It is the presence or absence of love that is crucial, for "when unformed faith becomes formed, it is not the faith itself that is changed, but the soul, the subject of faith; at one instant it has faith without charity, and at the next, faith with charity."[5]

The distinction between unformed and formed faith filled a gap by answering a question implicit in Augustine's Pauline exegetical grammar. Augustine had closely connected faith and love, arguing that faith is never given alone and is never unproductive. He had also ascribed to love many of the characteristic powers and benefits of faith. However, he had never fully clarified the relationship between the two, and the doctrine of faith formed by love provided such clarification. It became widely accepted within medieval theology. This left scope for the Reformers later to present the doctrine of faith formed by love as a distortion of Augustine's legacy and to turn Gal 5:6 into an exegetical battleground (see 7.4). For Augustine had never defined faith solely in terms of cognitive content or intellectual assent. The doctrine of faith formed by love raised in particularly acute form a question that the Reformers would ask in relation to many medieval clarifications of Augustine. Were they fully consonant with Augustine's vision, or did they represent an adherence to its letter in defiance of its Pauline spirit?

4.2. Traditions within Medieval Pauline Interpretation: Thomas Aquinas

Among the different appropriations of Augustine's Pauline exegetical grammar in the medieval period, several are significant as part of the context of the Reformation. They have all been carefully considered by scholars in relation to the development of Luther's thought. They are those of Thomas Aquinas, those of nominalist theologians admired by Luther's teachers at the University of Erfurt, and those of certain figures in the order of Augustinian friars to which Luther himself belonged, most notably Johann Staupitz (c. 1460–1524), Luther's superior and confessor. In the post-Reformation context, it was Aquinas who was to emerge

4. Van Engen, "Faith as a Concept of Order," 35.

5. *Summa Theologica* 31:131 (IIaIIae q. 65. a4 ad.4). This statement is also highlighted by Sun-young Kim, *Luther on Faith and Love: Christ and the Law in the 1535 Galatians Commentary* (Minneapolis: Fortress, 2014), 84.

as providing the most compelling alternative to the Reformers' Pauline exegetical grammar. Ultimately, an 1879 encyclical of Pope Leo XIII was to declare that Aquinas's theology is a definitive exposition of Catholic doctrine. In Luther's own time, however, Aquinas was simply one important theologian among others in the matrix of appropriations of Augustine from which Luther's radical alternative was to emerge.

Aquinas shared Augustine's Platonic view that created, contingent existence is a limited form of participation in the primary and absolute existence of God. This participation is severely disrupted and diminished by sin. Salvation is therefore a return to God that involves renewed participation in God. This salvific participation in the divine exceeds what would naturally be possible for human creatures without the distorting impact of sin, but it also stands in direct continuity with it. Saving grace perfects and does not destroy nature. On the basis of these doctrinal commitments, Aquinas responds powerfully to texts like Gal 2:19–20 ("I have been crucified with Christ; and it is no longer I who live, but it is Christ who lives in me") in which Paul speaks of union with Christ: "the love of Christ, which He showed to me in dying on the cross for me, brings it about that I am always nailed with him."[6]

Such an emphasis on union with the divine raised for Aquinas the question of the nature of grace. If grace enables the return of the Christian to God, is grace itself to be identified with the Holy Spirit? Augustine had never clarified whether this was the case or whether grace was something closely related to the Spirit but distinct from the Spirit. The ambiguity prompted discussion among medieval theologians about whether grace is uncreated (*gratia increata*)—that is, the Holy Spirit—or whether it is created (*gratia creata*). Concerned to maintain a proper distinction between God and still sinful Christians, Aquinas argued that the grace operative in ongoing justification is created. In this life, the Christian's final vision of God and final union with God is only anticipated.[7] Grace is therefore the gift of a created, permeating quality in the human soul that enables the journey of the justified person back toward God. It is a transforming habit (*habitus*) of love, which is received in initial justification.

However, this habitual grace does not become something that, once given, functions in a manner somewhat independent from its divine giver. For, operating with another medieval distinction that sought greater precision than had been offered by Augustine, Aquinas distinguished between habitual grace (*gratia gratum*

---

6. Aquinas, *Commentary on Saint Paul's Epistle to the Galatians*, 63.

7. See Joseph P. Wawrykow, *God's Grace and Human Action: 'Merit' in the Theology of Thomas Aquinas* (Notre Dame: University of Notre Dame Press, 1995), 167.

faciens) and external or actual grace (*gratia gratis data*). The receipt of habitual grace in initial justification requires God first to exercise external or actual grace, and for habitual grace to be effective the continued granting of external or actual grace is also necessary. Habitual grace is effective because it is enfolded within the broader structure of external or actual grace.

This means that human cooperation with divine grace remains dependent upon divine sustenance. Although human beings choose the means by which a good deed is performed, and execute the act, the end of the deed is determined by God. Good works are meritorious and enable the Christian to grow in righteousness, but the very possibility of such merit is itself an expression of divine grace. God's goodness is manifested in creation by the fact that God has graciously built into the structure of reality the possibility for God to be obligated to human beings in this way. Aquinas develops this idea by drawing upon yet another distinction within medieval theology, this time between two kinds of merit. There is congruous merit (*meritum de congruo*) in which, although the merit is real, God grants a reward that exceeds what a person strictly deserves, and there is condign merit (*meritum de condigno*), where there is an objective match between the value of a person's actions and the reward received.

For Aquinas, there was no possibility of fallen human beings achieving even congruous merit in initial justification. Yet God merits condignly, and since grace allows a degree of participation in the life of God, it is possible for those Christians who grow sufficiently in righteousness to come condignly to merit eternal life: "Insofar as the Holy Spirit makes us sons and daughters in the Son, our works truly deserve the inheritance that God gives us, namely our eternal sharing in his life."[8] When Aquinas considers the faith of Abraham in Rom 4, he interprets it within this structure. Abraham's acceptance of God's promises to him as true renders to God what is justly due to God. It is an act of justice, and therefore God sees the gift of faith that Abraham has received as righteousness, that is, as what it actually is.[9] However, this initial expression of faith is only the first act of justice wrought by the divine gift, for works of love will follow. Faith like Abraham's is but the beginning of the journey in growth of righteousness that by God's grace will ultimately result in the meriting of eternal life.

8. Matthew Levering, *Paul in the Summa Theologiae* (Washington, DC: Catholic University of America Press, 2014), 164.

9. See Bruce Marshall, "*Beatus Vir*: Aquinas, Romans 4, and the Role of 'Reckoning' in Justification," in *Reading Romans with St. Thomas Aquinas*, ed. Matthew Levering and Michael Dauphinais (Washington, DC: Catholic University of America Press, 2012), 219–21.

4.3. Traditions within Medieval Pauline Interpretation: Nominalism

Luther's teachers during his theological education at the University of Erfurt were nominalists. Their views about salvation took inspiration from positions earlier argued by Duns Scotus (1266–1308) and William of Ockham (c. 1287–1347) about the relationship between God and creation. Scotus and Ockham objected to the idea that the being of the creature depends upon participation in the divine. They rejected the view that God and humanity are part of the same extended chain of being. Instead, creation is something external to God: "That God wants something to be does not mean that he has to be present in it. . . . God's will can act from a distance to cause a being."[10] This refusal to accept that God is implicated in a chain of being guards against any possible implication that God acts in certain ways out of necessity. The existence of creation depends upon God's absolute will alone, and untrammeled divine freedom is preserved.

The consequences of this position for the nominalist appropriation of Augustine's Pauline exegetical grammar were defined by Gabriel Biel (c. 1420–1495). He strongly emphasized the biblical concept of covenant (*pactum*). If God is not implicated in a chain of being, then the reliability of divine behavior depends entirely upon promises that God has freely made. God has absolute power (*de potentia absoluta*), but God's promises form self-imposed constraints upon subsequent divine actions. The divine power that operates within these constraints is God's ordained power (*de potentia ordinate*).[11] Because God is committed to God's promises, once a divine promise has been made, a particular course of action will reliably follow.

This impacts justification, which depends upon God's faithfulness in responding to human actions in the ways God has promised. If people do *quod in se est* (what lies within them), which is to humble themselves before God and repent of sin, God has made a commitment to give the gift of grace. This is not a matter of condign merit (where the value of the deeds performed and their reward are equal), through which eternal life is merited, but instead of congruous merit (where the reward exceeds the value of the deeds performed), by which the sinner receives habitual grace in initial justification. The sinner has done something in no sense equal to the gift of grace, but the reward is appropriate because of the commitments made by God through God's promises.[12]

---

10. Sammeli Juntunen, "Luther and Metaphysics: What Is the Structure of Being according to Luther?," in *Union with Christ: The New Finnish Interpretation of Luther*, ed. Carl E. Braaten and Robert W. Jenson (Grand Rapids: Eerdmans, 1998), 149. Scotus and Ockham disagree radically on many other issues, including significant aspects of justification, but here they are in agreement.

11. On the origins of this distinction, see McGrath, *Iustitia Dei*, 150–58.

12. The term "nominalist" is potentially confusing, because it formally refers to a philosophi-

This means that although the growth in righteousness of the Christian toward the meriting of eternal life then unfolds in terms very similar to those described by Aquinas, nominalists did hold a different view of initial justification. For their belief in the capacity of fallen human beings congruously to merit the gift of habitual grace implies the ability to prepare for grace. Although damaged by sin, human beings retain an inclination toward good, and the human will can still choose the good despite the difficulty of doing so. The exegetical consequences of this become clear when Wendelin Steinbach (1454–1519), a disciple of Biel, commented on the faith of Abraham in Rom 4: "What St. Paul is claiming (and we must be careful not to miss his point or be thrown off by his incautious phraseology) is that Abraham merited the first grace of justification by his good works, preeminently by the good work of believing God with his unformed faith."[13]

Unsurprisingly this understanding of faith as itself meritorious means that when nominalists discuss predestination, they place considerable emphasis on God's foreknowledge of how a person will behave. God predestines, at least in part, because God knows that a person will respond to the gospel with faith. At this point, nominalists have clearly departed from Augustine and have been perceived by many as toppling over into semi-Pelagianism. Yet it is important to appreciate that nominalist theologians themselves felt not only that they had avoided Pelagianism but were explicitly concerned to do so. They emphasized the radical disjunction between the feeble moral reality of human deeds and the high meritorious value accorded to them by God as human beings act in response to God's promises. From their perspective, this ensured that the whole process was a matter of grace. The foreseen merits of the individual have significance only because God freely wills that they do so in an exercise of his ordained power. Further, the considerable tension between this account of initial justification and that offered by Aquinas went largely unnoticed in the late medieval context, for Thomas was widely misinterpreted as also affirming that a sinner can congruously merit initial justification.[14]

---

cal commitment—that is, Ockham's rejection of the idea that there are universal categories lying behind specific instances of being. This position rejects an inherently participatory account of being and therefore has affinities with the theological thought processes that led to the distinction between the absolute and ordained powers of God. However, it was perfectly possible to hold a nominalist soteriology without being nominalist in a philosophical sense and vice versa.

13. David C. Steinmetz, "Abraham and the Reformation," in *Luther in Context*, 2nd ed. (Grand Rapids: Baker, 2002), 36–38.

14. See John L. Farthing, *Thomas Aquinas and Gabriel Biel* (Durham, NC: Duke University Press, 1988), 150–80; Steinmetz, "Luther among the Anti-Thomists," in *Luther in Context*, 52–56; Heiko A. Oberman, "*Iustitia Christi* and *Iustitia Dei*: Luther and the Scholastic Doctrines of

4.4. Traditions within Medieval Pauline Interpretation: Some Augustinian Theologians

There is much scholarly literature that speaks of the existence of a school of theology in the early sixteenth century within the Augustinian order—typically termed the *schola Augustiniana moderna*—which may have exercised considerable influence upon the young Luther. Recent studies have in fact cast considerable doubt on the existence of something so well defined as a distinct school or movement.[15] Nevertheless, there clearly were individuals within the Augustinian order whose soteriological thought is of considerable interest because they stand at certain points closer to the Reformers' than do other Catholics. Despite this, they were unwilling to join the Reformers. This was not simply out of horror at the tearing apart of the church, although this was undoubtedly significant, but also because they ultimately remained wedded to Augustine's Pauline exegetical grammar. They could not break with it as the Reformers did.

Johann Staupitz is the classic example of such an individual. He responded to the trauma of Luther's break with Rome by resigning in 1520 as Vicar-General of the Augustinian order in Germany. He subsequently became a Dominican abbot. Staupitz utterly rejected the nominalist idea that individuals can congruously merit initial justification. Humility and repentance are not meritorious but are instilled in sinners by God as a consequence of initial justification. They are the fruits of grace. Predestination is the cause of initial justification, and here divine foreknowledge of faith plays no part, that is, merit of any sort is excluded. Sinners must indeed do what lies within them (*quod in se est*), but at this point, what lies within is "to accuse oneself as a sinner, to abandon all hope of making oneself righteous before God by one's own pious acts. Humility is not a virtue which the sinner offers to God in exchange for grace, but an embarrassed confession that the sinner has nothing whatever to exchange but his own sin."[16]

Viewed in relation to initial justification only, there is nothing here very distant from the views of Aquinas. Yet when Staupitz discusses the subsequent life of the baptized, significant differences emerge not only with the nominalists but also with Aquinas. Christians cooperate with grace, but this is not understood primarily in terms of a created habit of grace: "The Pauline doctrine is that sin-

---

Justification," in *The Dawn of the Reformation: Essays in Late Medieval and Early Reformation Thought* (Edinburgh: T&T Clark, 1986), 208.

15. See Eric L. Saak, *High Way to Heaven: The Augustinian Platform between Reform and Reformation 1292–1524* (Leiden: Brill, 2002), 683–735.

16. David C. Steinmetz, *Luther and Staupitz: An Essay in the Intellectual Origins of the European Reformation* (Durham, NC: Duke University Press, 1980), 73.

ners are made pleasing to God through election and then given the gift of love which makes their faith living and active. Staupitz does not use the metaphysical language of act and habit to describe this love, preferring rather to stress the bond of charity as a personal union of Christ with the Christian."[17] Staupitz seems here to come close to regarding all grace simply as uncreated (i.e., as the Holy Spirit) rather than created.[18]

Staupitz also seems effectively to reject the distinction between congruous merit (where the value of the deeds performed and their reward are equal) and condign merit (where the reward exceeds the value of the deeds performed) and to treat all merit as congruous: "Staupitz refuses, however, to allow the good works of the Christian to be regarded as merits of condignity, since only the works of Christ can claim to be merits in that sense. There is too great a disproportion between the inherent worth of the moral activity and the reward promised to such good deeds to permit anyone to think in terms of condign merit. Besides, the good works of the Christian are, in the last analysis, nothing more than the works of Christ in him."[19]

The disjunction between the actual worth of human deeds and the scale of the reward granted to them is not resolved primarily by appeal to God's covenanted pledge to accept such deeds (the nominalist solution). Nor is it dealt with primarily on the basis that despite this disjunction, God has graciously built the possibility of condign merit into the structure of reality (Aquinas's position). The gap is bridged rather by the work of the cross: "The Christian is just with a righteousness given him by Christ, while Christ becomes a sinner through his assumption of the guilt and weakness of the Christian. . . . God . . . accepts even imperfect contrition when it is grounded in the sufferings of Christ."[20] The Christian may not be able to do all that the Christian ought to do, but for the shortfall, the penitent Christian may rely on Christ: "Diminutive human repentance can reach heaven on the shoulders of the giant Christ."[21] The issue is no longer how the Christian may be transformed into a person pleasing to God. Election means that the person in Christ already is pleasing to God. The issue is rather how the Christian may be changed so that God becomes truly pleasing to the Christian and the center of his or her affections and desires.

---

17. Steinmetz, *Luther and Staupitz*, 106.
18. See McGrath, *Iustitia Dei*, 185.
19. Steinmetz, *Luther and Staupitz*, 107.
20. Steinmetz, *Luther and Staupitz*, 106–8.
21. Berndt Hamm, "Impending Doom and Imminent Grace: Luther's Early Years in the Cloister as the Beginning of His Reformation Reorientation," in *The Early Luther: Stages in a Reformation Reorientation* (Grand Rapids: Eerdmans, 2014), 19.

The powerful resonances between many of Staupitz's views and those later adopted by the Reformers should not blind us to the fact that his perspective remains wholly within Augustine's Pauline exegetical grammar. Justifying righteousness is "something Christ effects in the Christian by his presence and activity."[22] Staupitz preserves Augustine's understanding of the Christian life as a pathway of transformation along which progress is made as further grace is secured and justice increases. Faith itself is a divine gift and is granted without any prior human merit, but "this faith is in turn consummated in works of charity. Faith must be living and active rather than idle and dead. Faith is related to works as a beginning to the end, as a foundation to the building erected upon it, as the root of a plant to the fruit which it finally bears."[23]

Staupitz's point is simply that, given the inherent lack of worth of his or her deeds, the Christian who has received initial justification and who cooperates with grace must still rely on Christ's death for mercy. When the Council of Trent (1545–1563) discussed justification in 1546, a similar position was advocated by Girolamo Cardinal Seripando (1493–1563), general of the Augustinian Order. However, the purpose of the council was to respond to the rupture in the church triggered by Luther's protests. Unsurprisingly the reception of Seripando's ideas was influenced by the existence of the Reformers' radically alternative way of viewing salvation, and his ideas were rejected by a clear majority. His views were regarded as suspiciously close to those of the Reformers. Trent's decree on justification instead stressed the possibility that the person in Christ can fully satisfy the divine law and truly merit eternal life.[24]

4.5. Pauline Interpretation: The Eve of the Reformation

As this account of different traditions within it illustrates, the world of medieval Pauline interpretation contained significant disagreements. Yet these disagreements existed inside the Pauline exegetical grammar established by Augustine. What is surprising about Luther as a Pauline interpreter is not that he developed distinctive views or that these perspectives were controversial among Pauline

---

22. Steinmetz, *Luther and Staupitz*, 106.

23. Steinmetz, "Abraham and the Reformation," 41–43.

24. Daphne Hampson, *Christian Contradictions: The Structures of Lutheran and Catholic Thought* (Cambridge: Cambridge University Press, 2001), 56–96. For an account of Seripando's advocacy at Trent and of the earlier discussions between Catholic and Protestant theologians at the Colloquy of Regensburg (1541), see Anthony N. S. Lane, *Justification by Faith in Catholic-Protestant Dialogue: An Evangelical Assessment* (London: T&T Clark, 2002), 45–85.

interpreters. What is surprising rather is that this Augustinian friar came to hold positions that also conflicted with Augustine's Pauline exegetical grammar itself. It is the dismantling of an interpretative framework that had endured for over a thousand years and its replacement by another that makes the Reformation truly revolutionary in exegetical terms. It is time to turn to the story of how that took place and to the content of that revolution.

CHAPTER FIVE

The Reformers' New Pauline Exegetical Grammar: Context and Emergence

The story of how the Reformers' alternative Pauline exegetical grammar emerged out of the complex world of medieval interpretation inevitably centers on Luther's own exegetical and theological development. However, that development takes place in a context. Luther does not only exercise influence upon others but is himself influenced by other individuals and movements. Before discussing when and how Luther developed a new theology, it is necessary to explore significant aspects of his environment.

5.1. The Context of Humanism

As a university professor, prominent among the contextual influences upon Luther was humanist scholarship. Humanists argued for a renewed emphasis on the study of classical antiquity and placed a high value on the study of ancient languages. They also desired to reform the university curriculum in order to escape what was perceived as the sterile logic of medieval theology. The characteristic humanist emphasis was on a return *ad fontes* (to the sources) and on the importance of diffusing the wisdom found there as widely as possible. In this way, humanists hoped there might be a renewal of church and society.

Luther did not himself receive a humanist education, and the Reformation and Renaissance humanism must be distinguished as movements. For to be a humanist was certainly not necessarily to be a Reformer. Yet despite these qualifications, Luther's revolution in Pauline exegesis is unimaginable without the impact of humanism: "The Reformation 'scripture principle' belongs in this connection, with its mobilization of linguistic proficiency in Greek and Hebrew, ra-

49

tional textual criticism, academic education of ministers and the cultivation of literacy in the vernacular among the laity."[1] As part of a movement emphasizing a return to ancient sources, humanists often approached biblical interpretation with "a philological approach, arguing on the basis of grammatical rules, etymology, and classical usage."[2] It is unlikely that contemporaries would have found Luther's attack on the medieval tradition plausible had not humanism been so strongly present in the scholarly context.[3]

The humanist scholar closest to Luther was his younger faculty colleague at the University of Wittenberg, Philip Melanchthon (1497–1560). As we shall see, Melanchthon became an important Pauline interpreter in his own right, and it was sometimes he who mediated important exegetical developments to Luther. However, the great champion on the European stage of a humanist approach to biblical interpretation was Desiderius Erasmus (1466–1536). In 1516, in a single year, Erasmus had triumphantly published his *Novum Instrumentum* (Greek New Testament), the first part of his *Annotationes* (critical notes on the New Testament text), and an edition of the letters of Jerome (c. 342/347–420). There were critics who thought his work dangerous and who believed that the study of theology should be based exclusively on the Latin Vulgate, the Bible translation that had served the Western church for over a thousand years. Erasmus was nevertheless confident that his view would prevail, and he felt that a new golden age was dawning.[4] Through a return to the study of Scripture in its original languages, he sought for the church a spiritual revival based on a way of theologizing and a manner of life that related Christian truth to personal spirituality.[5]

Although he never denounced monasticism or the rites and ceremonies of the church, Erasmus's focus was on a lay piety that in matters of salvation emphasized faith combined with love of neighbor. He was an advocate of reform but one who "intended to rely on the gradual transformation of the spirits, attitudes, and be-

---

1. Berndt Hamm, "The Place of the Reformation in the Second Christian Millennium," in *The Reformation of Faith in the Context of Late Medieval Theology and Piety: Essays by Berndt Hamm*, ed. Robert J. Bast (Leiden: Brill, 2004), 290.

2. On humanism and the Reformation, see Erika Rummel, *The Humanist-Scholastic Debate in the Renaissance and Reformation* (Cambridge: Harvard University Press, 1995).

3. On the impact of humanism on the university curriculum and its implications for the study of Scripture, see Gillian R. Evans, *The Roots of the Reformation: Tradition, Emergence, and Rupture* (Downers Grove, IL: InterVarsity Press, 2012), 253–86.

4. See his letter from February 1517 to Wolfgang Capito: *CWE* 4:261–68 (no. 541).

5. On the controversial aspects of Erasmus's biblical scholarship, see Allan K. Jenkins and Patrick Preston, *Biblical Scholarship and the Church: A Sixteenth-Century Crisis of Authority* (Aldershot: Ashgate, 2007), 3–80, and also Christine Christ-von Wedel, *Erasmus of Rotterdam: Advocate of a New Christianity* (Toronto: University of Toronto Press, 2013), 79–164.

havior of his Christian readers, stimulated by the quiet voice of his writings and the preaching and works of his collaborators, high and low" (*CWE* 76:xxi). The advent of Luther, who burst onto the European stage following the posting of his Ninety-Five Theses against the sale of indulgences in Wittenberg on October 31, 1517, was a disaster for Erasmus. The resulting polarization of opinion undermined all hopes of quiet reform. Erasmus was caught between a status quo he wanted to change and a revolution he could not endorse.

On the one hand, Erasmus's philological work on the New Testament provided a textual basis for some of Luther's views. Erasmus interpreted grace (*charis*) in some New Testament texts (e.g., Luke 1:28, Rom 1:5) in ways difficult to reconcile with regarding it as an infused habit.[6] Similarly, he interpreted faith (*pistis*) in several key texts in a manner much closer to Luther's emphasis on unconditional trust in God than to the doctrine of faith formed by love.[7] On the other hand, Erasmus seems to have regarded these instances as translation issues relating to specific texts that did not imply any general rejection of traditional doctrines. There is also no evidence that Erasmus ever supported Luther's views on justification. In discussing the faith of Abraham in Rom 4, Erasmus will speak of this faith as trust (*fiducia*) but insist that it was a work (*opus erat*) by which Abraham merited justification (*mereretur iusti titutlum*) (*CWE* 77:678–80). In the 1520s, Erasmus was to criticize Luther very publicly in what became a bitter quarrel, but his exegesis was undoubtedly significant to the development of the Reformers' Pauline exegetical grammar. Despite his loyalty to Rome, Erasmus's biblical scholarship was posthumously consigned to the Index of Forbidden Books.[8]

5.2. Luther's Journey to Reformation

For his part, Luther's journey toward his break with Rome seems to have begun in earnest when he left Erfurt after being appointed as a professor at Wittenberg in 1512. It is only then that Luther began to react with some ferocity against nominalism. There is some disagreement over whether Luther's *Lectures on the Psalms* (*Dictata super Psalterium*), delivered in 1513 but revised for publication in

---

6. On Luke 1:28, see *ASD* VI-5:458–59 (368–404). No English translation yet exists of the *Annotations* on Luke. On Rom 1:5, see *CWE* 56:19.

7. See, for example, his comments on the phrase "from faith to faith" in Rom 1:17 at *CWE* 56:43–44.

8. The *Index librorum prohibitorum* was a catalog of publications deemed heretical or contrary to morality and therefore not to be read by Catholics. It went through twenty editions from 1559 to 1948 and was abolished in 1966.

1515–1516, represent an expression of nominalist soteriology or an incipient break with it.[9] However, such a break is clearly apparent by the time of Luther's *Lectures on Romans* (1515–1516). It is tempting to ascribe this development to Staupitz's influence over Luther during their earlier close relationship in Luther's years at the monastery at Erfurt (1505–1512). Certainly, Staupitz's views were in tension with those of Luther's nominalist teachers at Erfurt's university. Yet he and Luther had a relationship that was primarily pastoral and existed outside a formal educational setting. The degree to which Luther would have been directly exposed to Staupitz's perspectives on soteriology is not clear.[10]

What is very clear is that Luther's difficulties with nominalist soteriology were not solely or even primarily intellectual. They were also personal and pastoral. For despite his undoubted devotion to monastic practices, Luther despaired of his salvation. Nominalism taught him that if he did what lay within his power (*quod in se est*) to humble himself before God and to repent, he would receive grace. The difficulty that so troubled Luther was his inability to be certain that he had performed the acts of repentance within his power. What was enough, and could he trust the perceptions of his own conscience about what he had done? Luther's zeal and his spiritual struggles (his *Anfechtungen*) fed each other in an unhappy symbiosis. Unsurprisingly, to break out of his struggle, Luther had to reject the nominalist view that initial justification could be congruously merited.

This meant that Luther was rejecting an important commitment of the whole earlier medieval theological tradition as he understood it. For Luther's understanding of Aquinas was mediated through the nominalist misreading in which Aquinas, too, held that it was possible congruously to merit initial justification.[11] However, although not the focus of his personal struggles in the same way as nomi-

---

9. See the very different assessments reached by Alister E. McGrath, *Luther's Theology of the Cross: Martin Luther's Theological Breakthrough*, 2nd ed. (Oxford: Wiley-Blackwell, 2010), 115–20; and David C. Steinmetz, *Luther and Staupitz: An Essay in the Intellectual Origins of the European Reformation* (Durham, NC: Duke University Press, 1980), 78–95.

10. On the difficulty of determining the detail of Staupitz's influence, see Steinmetz, *Luther and Staupitz*, 27–34, 141–44. The whole argument of Berndt Hamm, *The Early Luther: Stages in a Reformation Reorientation* (Grand Rapids: Eerdmans, 2014), presupposes that the pastoral relationship between Staupitz and Luther would have been the means by which the theology of Staupitz was communicated clearly to Luther.

11. David C. Steinmetz, "Luther among the Anti-Thomists," in *Luther in Context*, 2nd ed. (Grand Rapids: Baker, 2002), 47–58. It is sometimes proposed that the Reformation rupture could have been avoided had Luther understood Aquinas's theology accurately. This is completely implausible. Luther's new theology does emerge in reaction against nominalism. However, his ultimate rejection of justification as a lifelong process of growth in righteousness strikes just as fundamentally against Aquinas.

nalism, Luther seems already to have had differences with Aquinas. For even in his earliest works (his marginal comments on Augustine and on Lombard's *Sentences* from 1509–1510), Luther seems doubtful about the role of created habits of grace in justification.[12] It is little wonder that, Augustinian friar as he was, Luther viewed himself as rejecting positions that distorted Augustine's true intentions.

Yet when Luther broke through to a new understanding of justification, the dam that burst swept away in its flood much more than simply nominalist soteriology. It also impacted Augustine's Pauline exegetical grammar. For Luther did not merely reach a position like that of Staupitz. He did not simply reject congruous merit in initial justification and emphasize that, in place of created habits of grace, the mercy of the cross plays a crucial role in countering the loss of justice entailed by the sins of the baptized. Luther instead reached a position where his despair over his salvation was answered and transformed to joyful certainty by moving altogether outside of the framework of justification as a lifelong process of growth toward a righteousness that would become his own. He could now be sure about his salvation because what was decisive was no longer who Luther was or who he might become but instead Christ and who he is: "In place of the two-way medieval Catholic path of gradual cooperation between God and humanity in salvation, there entered the new theme that God alone is effective."[13]

For Luther and for all those who later joined him in rejecting the idea of justification as a lifelong process of meritorious growth in righteousness, God encounters people in justification only outside of themselves. The righteousness they receive remains an alien righteousness. Justification is unconditional in the sense that acceptance by God is not in any way caused by the works of the believer, either those performed prior to baptism or those performed after it. The concept of merit is utterly rejected as inappropriate to Pauline exegesis. The righteousness granted to the believer in justification remains wholly and entirely that of Christ. This does not mean that the believer is unchanged. Those who are justified are accepted into holiness, which is the corollary of justification. For if justification is genuine, then good works will inevitably follow, and their absence could indicate

12. This means that Luther's misinterpretation of Aquinas ultimately made very little difference in relation to central soteriological issues. Luther was misinformed about Aquinas's true views concerning initial justification but also vehemently rejected Aquinas's commitment to infused habits of grace and the condign meriting of eternal life. See David Luy, "Sixteenth-Century Reception of Aquinas by Luther and Lutheran Reformers," in *The Oxford Handbook of the Reception of Aquinas*, ed. Matthew Levering and Marcus Plested (Oxford: Oxford University Press, 2021), 104–20.

13. Berndt Hamm, "Justification by Faith Alone: A Profile of the Reformation Doctrine of Justification," in *Early Luther*, 257.

only that faith is not real. However, while genuine holiness of life is in this sense essential to salvation, such holiness forms no part of the basis of the believer's acceptance before God. The salvation that is granted to believers from outside themselves is complete and perfect, for God judges those justified on the basis of the person and work of Christ alone.

It was by means of this new emphasis on the effectiveness of God alone that Luther addressed the uncertainty about salvation that caused him so much anguish. For as the Council of Trent (1545–1563) was to insist, if final divine judgment rests upon where an individual has reached in the process of increasing righteousness, then assurance of salvation is an appalling presumption. No one can know with certainty where they have reached in their own journey of justification.[14] While hope can be strong, complete assurance is possible only in relation to God's desire to forgive not in relation to the accomplishment of salvation. Uncertainty about salvation follows from viewing justification as a lifelong process. By contrast, in Luther's new perspective, justification now depended not upon the cooperation of Christians with grace but on the already perfectly accomplished saving work of Christ on their behalf. Full assurance of salvation is possible, and anything less is blasphemously to doubt divine promises and the effectiveness of Christ's sacrifice.

5.3. A Reluctant Rejection of Augustine

It is therefore clear that Luther found a rock upon which to stand only by leaving behind basic components of Augustine's Pauline exegetical grammar. In time, the extent of this break with Augustine was fully appreciated. Writing in 1551, Calvin quite calmly dismisses Augustine's interpretation of Rom 3:21 and Paul's phrase the "righteousness of God":

> I am well aware that Augustine gives a different explanation. He considers that the righteousness of God is the grace of regeneration and this grace is free, he states, because God renews us, unworthy as we are, by His Spirit. . . . But it is evident from the context that the apostle includes all works without exception, even those which the Lord produces in His own people. . . . The two propositions, that man is justified by faith through the grace of Christ, and yet that he is justified by the works which proceed from spiritual regeneration, are held to

---

14. Henry J. Schroeder, trans., *Canons and Decrees of the Council of Trent: Original Text with English Translation* (Saint Louis: Herder, 1941), sixth session, chapter 7.

be in the fullest agreement, because God freely renews us, and we also receive His gift by faith. But Paul suggests a very different principle, viz. that men's consciences will never be at peace until they rest on the mercy of God alone.[15]

It is precisely Augustine's insistence on justification as a lifelong process, his assertion that Christians are at least in part justified by the works that flow from regeneration, that must be rejected. Yet the extent of the break had not initially been so clear, not even to Luther himself. For one thing, both he and the Reformers generally held the greatest respect for Augustine as a theologian and as an interpreter of Paul. In his dispute with Pelagius, they unhesitatingly identify with Augustine. Further, for quite some time, Luther's protest was presented by him and by his allies as a recovery of Augustine. The medieval drive for clarification and precision in filling out the details of Augustine's Pauline exegetical grammar had resulted in appropriations of Augustine that could be rejected as distortions of Augustine's true intentions. In a letter of May 1517, Luther rejoices that "our theology and St. Augustine are progressing well, and with God's help rule at our university. . . . It is amazing how the lectures on the *Sentences* are disdained."[16]

This habit of claiming Augustine's support never left Luther. Luther was after all an Augustinian friar, a member of an order that self-identified as true heirs of Augustine and true followers of his religion.[17] Even as late as 1545, when Luther wrote his famous account of his "Reformation discovery" of the true interpretation of the "righteousness of God" in Rom 1:17, he was still eager to point out that he and Augustine agree on the main point. Paul means by the "righteousness of God" not the formal righteousness by which God justly punishes sinners but "the righteousness with which God clothes us when he justifies us." However, Luther immediately must go on to admit that Augustine expresses this "imperfectly" and fails to "explain all things concerning imputation clearly."[18] The claim that Luther's exegesis represents a recovery of Augustine is no longer entirely successful.

---

15. *Comm. Rom.* 3:21, *CNTC* 8:71. Calvin published the first edition of his commentary on Romans in 1540, but the quotation above was not included until the 1551 edition.

16. *LW* 48:41–42 (letter no. 41). The *Sentences* were the standard textbook of scholastic theology produced by Peter Lombard (c. 1096–1160) that were the mainstay of theological education throughout the remainder of the medieval period.

17. The collective identity and ethos of the Augustinian Order is explored in detail in Eric L. Saak, *High Way to Heaven: The Augustinian Platform between Reform and Reformation 1292–1524* (Leiden: Brill, 2002), 584–675. Despite excommunication by Rome in January 1521, Luther did not bring himself to put off the Augustinian habit until October 9, 1524.

18. *LW* 34:337. There are indications in Luther's *Table Talk*, as recorded by Veit Dietrich, 1531–1533, that Luther did recognize his differences with Augustine. See no. 85 and no. 347 in *LW* 54:10, 49–50.

The reality of Luther's engagement with Augustine, and that of other Reformers, is that Augustine's work was honored and respected where it granted insight into Scripture. His exegesis was used at many points to correct the perceived faults of medieval interpreters. Yet where Augustine's positions were deemed exegetically unconvincing, there was a recognition that even the greatest patristic authorities have an authority subordinate to the word itself.[19] In relation to that authority of the word, what the Reformers had done was to evaluate various aspects of Augustine's Pauline exegesis quite differently. Augustine's passionate emphasis on the priority of divine grace they considered consistent with Paul's teaching, and they intensified it even further. Augustine's emphasis on meritorious cooperation with divine grace they rejected as unbiblical. This pattern leaves considerable room for debate over the Reformers' relationship with Augustine. In breaking with his Pauline exegetical grammar, did the Reformers betray Augustine's principal theological concerns? Or was their rejection truer to those concerns than the many approving medieval appropriations of his Pauline interpretation?

This somewhat tangled relationship with Augustine and his legacy is one of the factors that helps to obscure exactly when Luther made the transition from rejecting nominalist soteriology to something even more radical. His 1545 account seems to present his "Reformation discovery" as a dramatic and definitive moment of revelation. This may in fact retrospectively simplify a longer process of which it was the culmination, for the event is difficult to date. Luther himself seems to place the discovery in 1519, well after his protest against indulgences, and this has seemed implausibly late to many scholars.[20]

Yet while it would indeed be unlikely as a date for Luther's break with nominalist soteriology, it fits well as a date at which he moved decisively beyond Augustine's Pauline exegetical grammar. It is plausible as the point at which Luther ceased to conceive of justification as a process of human cooperation with grace but instead began to regard it as wholly an act of God in which believers receive

---

19. Timothy J. Wengert, "Philip Melanchthon and Augustine of Hippo," in *Philip Melanchthon, Speaker of the Reformation: Wittenberg's Other Reformer* (Burlington, VT: Ashgate Variorum, 2010), 235–67, demonstrates that Melanchthon held a very similar attitude: "We drink from the streams of Augustine. Or, rather, we are led by him to the sources [*ad fontes*] that are purer than any writings of human beings" (254). In a laudatory 1545 preface to an edition of "The Spirit and the Letter," Melanchthon awkwardly notes the differences on justification between Augustine and the Wittenberg Reformers: "But elsewhere he often states that human beings are justified through grace when the Holy Spirit is given who enkindles love in our hearts. This explanation is not complete" (260).

20. Lyndal Roper, *Martin Luther: Renegade and Prophet* (New York: Random House, 2017), 87–88.

the alien righteousness of Christ. For it is only in November 1520 with the publication of the tract *The Freedom of a Christian* that a summary of a radically new theology appeared for the first time.[21] Not long afterward, in January 1521, Luther was excommunicated by Pope Leo X (1475–1521). The breach had become irreparable.

21. Heiko A. Oberman, "Headwaters of the Reformation," in *The Dawn of the Reformation: Essays in Late Medieval and Early Reformation Thought* (Edinburgh: T&T Clark, 1986), 43–44: "For all those who could read either Latin or German, the *De libertate Christiana* presents without explicit polemics the platform of the new theology ranging from *iustificatio sola fide* to the priesthood of all believers and the distinction between law and gospel."

CHAPTER SIX

The Reformers' New Pauline Exegetical Grammar:
The Human Plight

As we have seen, the Reformers' fundamental break with an Augustinian account of justification begins with Luther. Without Luther's personal struggles, the rejection of justification as a lifelong process of growth toward a righteousness inherent to the Christian is inconceivable.

6.1. Exegetical Struggle and New Communities of Interpretation

Yet Luther is such a consequential figure precisely because he was not ultimately an isolated one. He succeeded in spawning communities of interpretation who shared a new Pauline exegetical grammar. As dispute raged about Scripture's teaching concerning salvation, texts became battlegrounds marked by fierce exegetical combat. While new accounts of broad theological themes like justification were crucially important, the conviction of their truth depended upon the plausibility of the exegetical positions adopted in relation to features of multiple individual texts.

This was especially so on the Protestant side, where Scripture was granted authority over against the tradition of the church. What is typical or endlessly repeated in early Protestant exegesis is therefore only the more significant for its characteristic nature. It is here that we see emerge the specific components of a new Pauline exegetical grammar through the forging of a new consensus about the meaning of key Pauline terms. Given that the Reformers' Pauline exegetical grammar underpinned their account of salvation in this way, it can helpfully be viewed in terms of the soteriology to which it was crucial. If that soteriology is outlined in summary form, then we can identify the work done by shared interpretations of key Pauline terms. It will then be possible to trace in more detail the exegetical arguments on which these shared interpretations of key terms rested. In this chapter, we will follow this procedure for the Reformers' distinctive account of the human plight. In the next chapter, we will explore what they taught about the remedying of that plight through the person and work of Christ.

6.2. The Human Plight in Summary

For the Reformers, humanity's fundamental problem, which results in alienation from God, is sin. As we have seen, sin had been identified by Augustine with misdirected desires that prefer lesser goods above the highest good, which is God. Medieval interpreters embraced this view of sin but engaged in debate about how it should be appropriated in more precise terms. There were two aspects of these discussions against which the Reformers reacted with considerable force. One was the definition of original sin as a privation of original justice, that is, the loss of the supernatural gift that before the fall enabled human nature to will what God wills. This "lack of a certain quality in the will" (*LW* 25:299) seemed to make sin merely the absence of something good and was perceived as simply too passive to capture what the Reformers heard Paul saying about the active nature of sin.

The other was how Paul's term "flesh" (*sarx*) was to be interpreted. Augustine had regarded the misdirected desires about which it speaks as indicative of a disordering of the whole person. Yet again and again he described sexual desire as the characteristic expression of the flesh. Augustine was a thinker for whom sexual desire had significant psychological components, but his descriptions of the flesh lent themselves to later medieval interpretations that explained it primarily in terms of bodily desires luring the soul into complicity with sin. According to the Reformers, sin must instead be understood as an active inclination of the will against God. Paul's term "the flesh" denotes the whole of a human being in rebellion against God. It is not simply that sin has captured the body and its desires. Sin does not only disrupt healthy hierarchies between mind and body, and between reason or the will and other parts of the soul, so that the lower will not obey the higher. Instead, sin also captures the higher faculties. The whole person is captive unless set free by God.

Unsurprisingly therefore when concupiscence (misdirected desire) rears up in the lives of the baptized, the Reformers continue to regard it as fully sinful in nature. Augustine's distinctions between suggestion, inclination or desire, and consent, may be helpful in describing how sin often works. However, his view that concupiscence is now not fully sinful unless consent is given is rejected. This divergence of perspective about sin among the baptized relates directly to different concepts of justification. For given Augustine's understanding of justification as a lifelong process, to regard concupiscence as fully sinful would leave little hope for the growth of justifying righteousness. Yet from the Reformers' perspective, concupiscence can be truly sinful without threatening justification. It must be resisted, but acceptance by God in justification depends entirely on receiving the already perfect righteousness of Christ.

Since sin concerns the whole of the person in rebellion against God, for human beings even to recognize their captivity and their need of Christ is a matter of divine revelation. The instrument of this revelation is God's law. Here the Reformers build on Augustine's insight that the law tells human beings the truth but cannot empower them to obey the truth. They build on it by addressing very directly the most obvious objection to Augustine's position, which is that the Old Testament portrays the law as given by God to instruct Israel in how to live and demands that it be obeyed. The Reformers develop a formal distinction between this purpose or use of the law, which they term its political or civic use, and the law's role in justification. The law's civic use relates to its role in restraining sin and ensuring harmony in human society. This is valuable in its own sphere but is completely distinct from the law's principal or theological use, which is to demonstrate to people their sin and provoke them to seek the grace of Christ. It is this theological use of the law of which Paul speaks in key texts where he discusses justification.

This development of the theological use of the law had profound consequences for the part played in salvation by the conscience. The necessity for the law to reveal to people their captivity to sin and need of Christ means that the human problem is no longer conceived exclusively as the inability to desire the good. It is also the inability of the conscience reliably to identify the good. The conscience is therefore unable to move people toward God. The confused consciences of those to whom conviction of sin has not yet been granted may even tell them that they are fulfilling the law and stand as righteous before God. Perhaps especially if they lead upright lives by human standards, individuals may fail to grasp the crucial distinction between the civic and theological uses of the law. They have civic righteousness but tragically confuse it with justifying righteousness.

By contrast, those who are convicted about sin may well experience a period of guilt and despair as they grapple with the reality of their position before God. However, the psychological dimensions of this struggle, and its severity or duration, are of little ultimate importance. For a despairing conscience is no more inherently trustworthy or able to save than a robust one. The conviction of sin accomplishes little if it stops simply with the recognition of sin and with despair. It is productive only if it turns people's attention away from the nuances of their inner condition and outward toward Christ and his mercy. People need to be assured not just that they are sinners but that God's purpose in Christ is to save them and that, if they trust in God's promises, their salvation is certain.

6.3. Sin

With regard to sin (*hamartia*), it is Luther himself who develops what was to become the characteristically Protestant position. He does this first in his *Lectures on Romans* (1515–1516), and despite their nonpublication in the sixteenth century,[1] the exegetical arguments he develops there became ubiquitous. Luther rejects what he regards as erroneous medieval elaborations of Augustine's teaching, but the impact is not in any simple way a return to Augustine's position. For Luther offers an intensified, hyper-Augustinian perspective on the impact of sin in which fallen human nature is not so much seriously wounded as wholly corrupted. The reason for this radical perspective is how Luther perceives original sin. In his discussion of Rom 5:12 (where Paul says that death entered the world through sin), Luther insists that it is "a total lack of uprightness and of the power of all the faculties both of body and soul and of the whole inner and outer man" (*LW* 25:299).

Luther here takes sides in a long-running debate over whether Augustine had intended to distinguish between concupiscence (misdirected desires) and original sin or to identify them with each other. Luther opposes those who took the former view and who followed Anselm (c. 1033–1109) in defining original sin as the privation or loss of original justice. Luther chooses instead to follow Peter Lombard's understanding of Augustine, in which original sin is concupiscence. However, Luther defines concupiscence much more radically than Lombard's identification of it with the sensuality of the body.[2]

Original sin has for Luther the character of "a sick man whose mortal illness is not only the loss of health of one of his members, but it is, in addition to the lack of health in all his members, the weakness of all of his senses and powers,

---

1. Luther did not lecture on Romans again since Melanchthon took over this task upon his arrival at Wittenberg in 1518. Only Luther's own manuscript and a single copy of it survived, the latter somewhat ironically in the Vatican Library. It was rediscovered by Johannes Ficker, with initial publication in 1908 and inclusion in the *Weimarer Ausgabe* of Luther's works in 1938. For details, see *LW* 25:ix–xiv. The views Luther expresses in the lectures about the nature of sin remain typical throughout his career, but in other important respects, for example, the nature of justification, their early date makes controversial the question of whether they reflect Luther's mature perspective on Paul.

2. Phillip W. Rosemann, *Peter Lombard* (Oxford: Oxford University Press, 2004), 114.

culminating even in his disdain for those things which are healthful and in his desire for those things which make him sick."[3] It is this sense of original sin as completely rampant misdirected desire that gives rise to Luther's new and famous description of sin as "the person turned in upon the self" (*homo incurvatus in se*).[4] This original sin "lives and commits all sins and is the real essential sin which does not sin for an hour or for a while; rather no matter where or how long a person lives, this sin is there also."[5]

The distinction between mortal sins (serious sins committed deliberately) and venial sins (minor sins committed with less self-awareness) is therefore redundant, since all actual sins are the practical expression of this fundamental underlying captivity in which human beings are cut off from God. Similarly rejected is the view that for the baptized misdirected desire is only the tinder of sin (*fomes peccati*), a spark that can ignite sin but is not itself sin unless consent is given. This rejection can be seen clearly in Luther's interpretation of Rom 7, where Paul discusses the struggle with sin. Paul's argument is complex, and there is a long history of debate over whether he discusses a struggle with sin in his life prior to his conversion, or whether 7:14–25 places this struggle in his life as a believer. Luther, somewhat unusually, hears not only vv. 14–25 as a discussion of Paul's struggle with sin as a believer but all of Rom 7:7–25.[6] Luther therefore naturally understands covetousness (Rom 7:7), the essence of misdirected desire, as sin even in Paul's Christian life. Luther is prepared to allow that God may mercifully decline to impute the guilt of desires to which assent is not given, but, apart from such divine mercy, "we ourselves are this weakness, therefore it is guilty, and we are guilty until this weakness ceases and is cleansed."[7]

In 1515–1516 this qualification about the imputation of guilt allows Luther to remain for the time being within an Augustinian framework of justification. God's mercy in not imputing the guilt that would accrue from misdirected desires still allows the Christian to grow in grace. Yet viewed retrospectively, Luther's insis-

---

3. *LW* 25:300. Neither Augustine nor Lombard is explicitly mentioned here, but the editors draw attention to the connection. See their n. 13 on the same page.

4. *LW* 25:345. See also *LW* 25:291.

5. *LW* 52:152. This is from *Gospel for New Year's Day* (1521/1522), one of a series of sermon guides designed to aid preachers published as the *Kirchenpostille*.

6. See *LW* 25:327. "From this passage on to the end of the chapter the apostle is speaking in his own person and as a spiritual man and by no means merely in the person of a carnal man."

7. *LW* 25:340. L'ubomír Batka, "Luther's Teaching on Sin and Evil," in *The Oxford Handbook of Martin Luther's Theology*, ed. Robert Kolb, Irene Dingel, and L'ubomír Batka (Oxford: Oxford University Press, 2014), 239, identifies Luther's interpretation of the Hebrew terms underlying Paul's quotation of Ps 32:1 in Rom 4:7 as also of particular significance in Luther's identification of concupiscence as sin.

tence that concupiscence is sin even in the baptized points forward toward a different framework in which the believer receives Christ's righteousness. Already Luther's famous twofold designation of the believer as both righteous and a sinner is appearing on the horizon.

Luther's all-encompassing definition of original sin also results in a distinctive response to Paul's insistence that as regards the flesh, he is in slavery to sin (Rom 7:14, 25). Luther does not accept that Paul here refers to a contest between different parts of a person in which sin disrupts the healthy hierarchies between soul and body, and between reason/the will and the other parts of the soul, so that the lower parts refuse to obey the higher. Flesh is not to be identified primarily with the lower parts of the person. Paul's contrasts between the inner and the outer person and the mind and the bodily members (7:22–23) do make it clear that sin has its characteristic sphere of operations. Nevertheless, the term flesh does not refer primarily only to one part of a person: "The apostle does not wish to be understood as saying that the flesh and the spirit are two separate entities, as it were, but one whole, just as a wound and the flesh are one. . . . The flesh is itself an infirmity or wound of the whole man who by grace is beginning to be healed in both mind and spirit. For who imagines that in a sick man there are these two opposing entities? For it is the same body which seeks health and yet is compelled to do those things which belong to its weakness" (*LW* 25:339–41).

The same insistence that the term "flesh" designates the whole person in opposition and rebellion against God appears in Luther's first *Commentary on Galatians* (1516–1517/1519). Paul's diverse list of the works of the flesh at Gal 5:19–21 prompts Luther to comment that "flesh is understood not only in the sense of lustful desires but as absolutely everything that is contrary to the spirit of grace . . . by flesh the whole man is meant . . . the inward and the outward man, or the new man and the old, are not distinguished according to the difference between soul and body but according to their dispositions" (*LW* 27:367).

This has radical consequences for the life of the church. Since sin infects the whole person and the flesh is not necessarily typified by sexual or other bodily desires, there cannot be a higher religious life that corresponds to the higher parts or faculties of a person. When Paul says that sin once lay dead apart from the law (Rom 7:8), Luther does not completely dismiss Augustine's view that Paul's statement is a reference to childhood, before the attainment of reason, and before the arrival of sexual desire. However, Luther's own opinion is that Paul is speaking of those who burn with great zeal for the law but who are unable to recognize their own sin. Luther has particularly in mind those who covet the religious life and feel that nothing else will please God. They fail to see that God has called them to other things and that "whatever is coveted besides God, even if one covets it for the sake of God, becomes a sin" (*LW* 25:337). On this view, not only is the ascetic life not necessarily effective in battling sin. It is also possible for it to become an expression of sin.

Other Reformers later repeatedly make the same exegetical points as Luther on the basis of the same Pauline texts. In relation to Rom 7, they typically do not join Luther in taking 7:7-13 as Paul's reflections on his life as a Christian. Yet the nature of coveting in 7:7 as the paradigmatic sin—in relation to which the law turned out to bring death—makes it difficult for them to accept that, even after baptism, it can ever be regarded as anything less than real sin.[8] The list of the works of the flesh in Gal 5:19-21, referred to above in relation to Luther's exegesis, is also cited frequently. Calvin notices the inclusion of both jealousies and envying and slyly turns a favorite scholastic authority against scholastic theology (the approach to theology that dominated in European universities prior to the rise of humanism) by observing that Aristotle "tells us that none but low and mean persons are envious, whereas he ascribes jealousy to lofty and heroic minds." Calvin goes on to say that "it should be observed that he [Paul] reckons heresies among the works of the flesh, for it shows clearly that the word flesh has a wider reference than sensuality, as the Sophists imagine. What produces heresies but ambition, which resides not in the lower senses but in the highest seat of the mind?" (*Comm. Gal.* 5:19, *CNTC* 11:104).

There is also repeated appeal to Rom 8:6-7, where Paul speaks twice of "the mind of the flesh" (*to phronēma tēs sarkos*), which is unable to submit to God's law, and contrasts it with "the mind of the Spirit" (*to phronēma tou pneumatos*). It is difficult to read Paul here as contrasting the mind shaped by the Spirit with the mind overwhelmed by sensual desire since there is no real hint of a division between the higher and lower parts of a person. The contrast is instead between those "in the flesh" and those "in the Spirit" (8:9), and the Reformers interpret it as differentiating between the whole person lost in sin and the whole person in Christ.

Melanchthon writes in *Loci Communes* (1521) that since the mind of the flesh cannot submit to the law, "it follows, therefore, that all works of men, however praiseworthy they are externally, are actually corrupt and are sins worthy of death."[9] Heinrich Bullinger (1504-1575) concludes a discussion in which he has

---

8. Heinrich Bullinger, "Sermon IV," in *Bullinger's Decades: The Third Decade*, ed. Thomas Harding, Parker Society 8 (Cambridge: Cambridge University Press, 1851), 122: "For although there be some which think that such motions, diseases, blemishes, and affections of the mind are no sins, yet God, by forbidding them in this law, doth flatly condemn them." Despite the use of the title "Sermon," the *Decades* are in fact exegetical discussions intended as resources for preachers, not sermons that were preached.

9. Philip Melanchthon, "Loci Communes Theologici," in *Melanchthon and Bucer*, ed. Wil-

cited Rom 8:6–8 with the reflection that "God requireth at the hands of those that worship him such kind of righteousness as is altogether sound and absolutely perfect, not in the outward deed alone, but also in the inward mind and settled purpose of the heart."[10] The component of action in human deeds may be genuinely good when assessed from a human perspective, but motivation matters and the flesh will ensure that it shares in corruption when assessed from the divine perspective.

Romans 8 is also significant for the degree to which it makes the Holy Spirit central to the discussion. It is the Spirit who makes it possible to fulfill the law, and Melanchthon uses this to make a general point based on the pattern of Paul's argument in Romans: "The apostle continually carries on his argument as follows: 'The flesh could not fulfill the law; therefore there is need of the Spirit to fulfill it.' If we should use the word 'flesh' for only part of a man, how will Paul's argument stand? For it could be eluded in this way: 'Even if the flesh could not keep the law, yet some better part of man could have done so, and thus there would have been no need for the Spirit to fulfill the law.'"[11]

Since Paul makes it clear through the phrases "the Spirit of God" and "the Spirit of Christ" (8:9) that in view here is indeed the Holy Spirit, "it necessarily follows that you call 'flesh' whatever in us is foreign to the Holy Spirit."[12] Later in his *Commentary on Romans* (1540), Melanchthon will similarly insist that "*flesh* should be understood of whatever is in man without the Holy Spirit, namely, not only the desires of the senses, but also reason and will without the Holy Spirit."[13] Peter Martyr Vermigli (1499–1562) will say succinctly that "whatsoeuer is in us besides the spirite and grace, is called fleshe."[14] Although flesh is not an external force and remains something in human beings, there is a powerful sense that the dilemma of humanity is not so much how to choose right actions but how to be under the right lordship. Once believers are justified under the lordship of Christ, then, like good trees, they will naturally bear good fruit.

When sin still does appear in the Christian life, some Reformers continue to find helpful Augustine's distinctions between suggestion, inclination or desire,

---

helm Pauck (Philadelphia: Westminster, 1969), 39. *Loci Communes* is Melanchthon's influential theological textbook. This translation is of the 1521 first edition.

10. Bullinger, "Sermon IV," *Third Decade*, 124.

11. Melanchthon, "Loci Communes Theologici," 37.

12. Melanchthon, "Loci Communes Theologici," 38.

13. Philip Melanchthon, *Commentary on Romans*, trans. Fred Kramer (Saint Louis: Concordia, 1992), 170. This is the second of three major commentaries on Romans by Melanchthon (1532, 1540, and 1556). Only the commentary of 1540 is available in English translation.

14. Peter Martyr Vermigli, *Most Learned and Fruitful Commentaries upon the Epistle of S. Paul to the Romanes*, trans. Sir Henry Billingsley (London: John Daye, 1568), 162a.

and consent. Bullinger makes use of them as an explanation of how sin works in the very same discussion as he insists that for the component of outward action alone to be good does not suffice to make a deed righteous.[15] Yet these distinctions now appear in an entirely different framework. While assent to a misdirected desire may mark an increase in the seriousness of a sin, it does not form the frontier between something that is truly sinful and something that is not. Such desires are truly sinful, but the consequences of the sins of the believer are no longer remedied by a compensatory accumulation of righteousness through meritorious good deeds. As Luther comments, those who are truly godly "do not minimize sin; they emphasize it, because they know that it cannot be washed away by any satisfactions, works, or righteousness, but only by the death of Christ" (*LW* 27:75–76).

6.4. The Law

The central features of the Reformers' understanding of the law (*nomos*) develop early and are shared by all. When Paul says that the law "brings knowledge of sin" (Rom 3:20), or that it was "added because of transgressions" (Gal 3:19), he means that the law reveals to human beings their sin. In his *Lectures on Romans* (1515–1516), when discussing 3:20, Luther comments that if the law prompts people to do good they otherwise would not have chosen, "then man understands how deeply sin and evil are rooted in him, which he would not have understood if he did not have the Law and had not attempted to work in accordance with it. . . . Hence, to say, 'Through the Law is the knowledge of sin' is the same as saying: 'Through the Law is the knowledge of sinners'" (*LW* 25:240–41).

In his first *Commentary on Galatians* (1516–1517/1519), Luther correlates Gal 3:19, where Paul says that the law was added because of transgressions, with Rom 5:20, where Paul says that sin came in order to increase the trespass. The excess of transgression serves a revelatory function: "The Law was laid down for the sake of transgression, in order that transgression might be and abound, and in order that thus man, having been brought to knowledge of himself through the Law, might seek the hand of a merciful God. Without the Law he is ignorant of his sin and considers himself sound" (*LW* 27:269). Paul's subsequent statement concerning imprisonment under the law until faith came, and his description of the law as a "disciplinarian" or "guardian" (*paidagōgos*) until Christ came (Gal 3:23–24) is interpreted in a similar vein. The law may well restrain sin, but the point is not that

---

15. Bullinger, "Sermon IV," *Third Decade*, 121–22.

in doing so it teaches delight in the good. Rather, it frustrates the desire to sin and through that frustration shows human beings the truth that they are sinners.

Similar pieces of exegesis from other Reformers could be documented almost endlessly. Calvin says of Rom 3:20 that "the law convinces us of sin and salvation" (*Comm. Rom.* 3:20, *CNTC* 8:70), and of Gal 3:24 that "the law, by displaying the righteousness of God, convinced them of their own unrighteousness ... it gave them no rest until they were constrained to seek the grace of Christ" (*Comm. Gal.* 3:24, *CNTC* 11:66). Melanchthon comments on Paul's statement that "the power of sin is the law" (1 Cor 15:56) by saying that "sin would not confound and terrify us unless it were shown to us by the law."[16] Bullinger brings together a medley of texts from Romans to show that "the proper office of Moses, and the principal use and effect of the law, is to show to man his sin and imperfection."[17]

In understanding the central purpose of the law as the revelation of humanity's true position as sinners before God, the Reformers were repeating and emphasizing a theme earlier explored by Augustine. Where they went beyond his reflections was that they did not simply deal with the law on the basis of individual texts. They also began to articulate a formal distinction between different uses of the law: "Luther's treatment of the law under the concept of *usus* was clearly without precursors in all the tradition."[18] Luther had not employed the concept at all in his first *Commentary on Galatians* (1516–1517/1519). It appears for the first time in a sermon on Gal 3:23–39 in his *Weihnachtspostille* (Christmas Sermons) for 1522,[19] and it is employed frequently in his later *Commentary on Galatians* (1531/1535).[20] The way in which Luther employs the concept does vary, but he typically speaks of a double or twofold use of the law (*duplex usus legis*). The second use is the principal or theological use, that of the revealing of sin. The first is a political or civic use. At Gal 3:19 Luther is clear that Paul is discussing the theological use of the law only, but Luther nonetheless takes the opportunity to describe the civic use: "God has ordained civic laws, indeed all laws, to restrain transgressions. Therefore every law was given to hinder sins. Does this mean that when the Law restrains sins, it justifies? Not at all. When I refrain from killing or from committing adultery or from stealing, or when I abstain from other sins, I do

---

16. Melanchthon, "Loci Communes Theologici," 80.

17. Bullinger, "Sermon VIII," *Third Decade*, 239.

18. Bernhard Lohse, *Martin Luther's Theology: Its Historical and Systematic Development* (Edinburgh: T&T Clark, 1999), 270.

19. Martin Luther, "New Year's Day," in *Advent and Christmas Season*, vol. 1 of *Luther's Epistle Sermons*, trans. John Nicholas Lenker (Minneapolis: Luther, 1908), 267–310 (esp. 271–72).

20. See Gerhard Ebeling, "On the Doctrine of the *Triplex Usus Legis* in the Theology of the Reformation," in *Word and Faith*, trans. James W. Leitch (Philadelphia: Fortress, 1963), 69–72.

not do this voluntarily or from the love of virtue but because I am afraid of the sword and of the executioner.... Therefore restraint from sins is not righteousness but rather an indication of unrighteousness" (*LW* 26:308).

The thought that the law exists not for the righteous but for the lawless and disobedient (1 Tim 1:9) may well be in the background here. Certainly Melanchthon later directly refers to it in his *Commentary on Romans* (1540), both when he adds a locus on the effects of the law (Rom 5) and when he expounds Rom 3:20. As with Luther, Melanchthon accepts that Paul is not directly discussing the law's political use, but he feels he must comment on it to prevent the possible false inference that the discipline involved in this use is justifying.[21] The purpose of the civic or political use of the law is strictly limited to saving human society here and now from social chaos. As Calvin puts it, "This constrained and forced righteousness is necessary for the public community of men, for whose tranquility the Lord herein provided when he took care that not everything be tumultuously confounded" (*Institutes* 2.7.10 [359]).

Despite the unanimity of the Reformers on the central significance of Paul's statements about the law, there are two other issues where they do not all agree. The first is the hermeneutic of law and gospel developed by Luther. The medieval tradition had generally understood the terms "law" and "gospel" "as a description of two phases of salvation history, with the gospel of Christ replacing the law which foreshadowed it."[22] Luther instead emphasized that they contrast divine command and divine promise. Law is "that word of God which sets forth the Creator's demand for human performance," and gospel is "the promise of God which re-creates sinners as God's children and restores the loving, trusting relationship between them and their Lord."[23]

There was precedence for this in the Pauline exegesis of Augustine, but Luther went further than Augustine. Whereas Augustine had applied the distinction in the interpretation of individual texts, Luther articulated it as a formal principle of biblical interpretation to be applied in all reading of Scripture. The Old and New Testaments each contain both law and gospel, but in different proportions, with law predominating in the Old Testament and promises in the New Testament. The law-gospel distinction first appeared, around the same time as the different uses of the law, in an Advent sermon for 1522.[24] Its application became universal

---

21. Melanchthon, *Commentary on Romans*, 98, 140–43.

22. Robert Kolb, *Martin Luther: Confessor of the Faith* (Oxford: Oxford University Press, 2009), 50–51.

23. Kolb, *Martin Luther*, 51.

24. Martin Luther, "Third Sunday in Advent," in *Gospels: Advent, Christmas, and Epiphany*

within the Lutheran tradition, but it was not adopted as a general hermeneutic within other Protestant traditions.

The other issue concerning the law where there was not unanimity among the Reformers was its role in the Christian life. Luther did not clarify this issue in his own interpretative work, but Melanchthon proposed a third use of the law as binding for Christian conduct. This appeared in substance in *Loci Communes* (1535) but was not expressed using the term "third use" until the 1543 edition.[25] Melanchthon argues that "the law must be preached to the regenerate to teach them certain works in which God wills that we practice obedience . . . the divine ordinance remains that those who have been justified are to be obedient to God."[26]

Unsurprisingly this provoked anxiety about whether such statements were consistent with rejection of obedience to the law as a cause of justification. The situation was ultimately clarified for Lutheranism by article 6 of the Formula of Concord (1577), which accepts the third use of the law but considers it to apply to believers only insofar as they are still unregenerate. The law restrains the sins of believers and reveals their sin, so acting as a spur to ever-closer union with Christ. Yet obedience, understood positively as something willingly rendered on the basis of renewal, remains exclusively the province of the Spirit.[27]

This account of the place of the law in the Christian life was insufficiently positive for Calvin. He insisted that the law must be understood in the context of the grace of God's covenant with Abraham. The law retains an abiding validity as the expression of God's will for human behavior, and it both instructs believers in the content of this divine will and encourages them to persevere in pursuing righteousness.[28] The law is now a positive guide for those aiming to live life participating in Christ to the glory of God: "through Christ the teaching of the law remains inviolable; by teaching, admonishing, reproving, and correcting, it forms us and prepares us for every good work [cf. II Tim. 3:16–17]" (*Institutes* 2.7.14 [363]).

Sermons, vol. 1 of *Luther's Church Postil*, trans. John Nicholas Lenker (Minneapolis: Lutherans in All Lands, 1905), 87–113 (esp. 96–103).

25. Ebeling, "On the Doctrine," 65–69. Although all accept that Luther did not use the term or formally propose a "third use" of the law, there is continued discussion of whether the substance of the concept is present in his work.

26. Philip Melanchthon, *Loci Communes 1543*, trans J. A. O. Preus (Saint Louis: Concordia, 1992), 74. This is the third major edition of *Loci Communes*. The second edition of 1535 has never been translated into English.

27. Robert Kolb and Timothy J. Wengert, eds., *The Book of Concord: The Confessions of the Evangelical Lutheran Church* (Minneapolis: Fortress, 2000), 502–3.

28. For an overview, see Günther H. Haas, "Ethics and Church Discipline," in *The Calvin Handbook*, ed. Herman J. Selderhuis (Grand Rapids: Eerdmans, 2009), 332–44 (esp. 335–40).

This emphatic insistence on the law as a positive guide to Christian obedience became an identity marker distinguishing the Reformed tradition from Lutheranism, where the law merely revealed and restrained the sins of Christians.

Despite this difference, however, Calvin does not interpret key texts where Paul discusses the law's soteriological role in a significantly different way from Luther. For Calvin, Paul always tells the truth about the law, but he sometimes highlights one aspect of its nature exclusively. At Gal 3:19 Calvin finds only the theological use of the law but comments that "the law has many uses, but Paul confines himself to one which serves his present purpose.... [T]his definition of the use of the law is not complete and those who acknowledge nothing else in the law are wrong" (*Comm. Gal.* 3:19, *CNTC* 11:61). At Rom 8:15, where Paul contrasts a spirit of bondage with that of adoption, Calvin sees a contrast between law and gospel but also says that "although the covenant of grace is contained in the law, yet Paul removes it from there, for in opposing the Gospel to the law he regards only what was peculiar to the law itself, viz. command and prohibition, and the restraining of transgressors by the threat of death. He assigns to the law its own quality, by which it differs from the Gospel" (*Comm. Rom.* 8:15, *CNTC* 8:168–69).

In these texts Paul focuses on what distinguishes the law from the rest of Scripture and what is unique to the law. The law abstracted in this way from the promises of the covenant "is the bare law (*nuda lex*),"[29] but a full account also requires attention to the law in the context of covenant promises. When this is done, a fuller, more rounded picture of the law emerges. Christ fulfills all the law's requirements, and his righteousness is received in faith by believers. Therefore, while the law may still exhort and chide Christians, their relationship to it is fundamentally different from what it had been when their disobedience ensured that it functioned as a curse (Gal 3:10).

Now as believers the law "may no longer condemn and destroy their consciences by frightening and confounding them.... What Paul says of the curse unquestionably applies not to the ordinance itself but solely to its force to bind the conscience" (*Institutes* 2:7:14–15 [362–63]). Freed from its role as a curse, in the life of believers, "through Christ the teaching of the law remains inviolable; by teaching, admonishing, reproving, and correcting, it forms us and prepares us for every good work [cf. II Tim. 3:16–17]" (*Institutes* 2.7.14 [363]). In this way, Calvin is able to offer an account of the law that he feels is canonically consistent. Pauline statements about the law's abrogation (e.g., Rom 7:6) can cohere with Christ's teaching that he did not come to abolish the law (Matt 5:17–18).[30]

---

29. I. John Hesselink, *Calvin's Concept of the Law* (Allison Park, PA: Pickwick, 1992), 91.

30. Calvin alludes to both of these texts in the discussion in *Institutes* 2.7.14.

6.5. The Conscience

Few aspects of the Reformers' Pauline exegesis have been less well understood in contemporary Pauline scholarship than the relationship between their convictions about sin and the law and those they held concerning the conscience. The enormous influence of Stendahl's work (see 2.3), and that of interpretations of Luther as a champion of the individual conscience (see 2.5), has been crucial as the context for such misunderstanding. For this context has promoted a set of erroneous assumptions about the place of the conscience in the Reformers' Pauline interpretation. It is frequently assumed that if Luther's *Anfechtungen* have been projected back onto Paul, then the Reformers must have believed Paul to have experienced similar struggles prior to his Damascus Road experience. If they believed Paul, the passionate and devoted Pharisee, to have struggled with a guilty conscience, then the Reformers must have believed such struggles to be typical of Judaism. Further, their view that the principal or theological use of the law is to bring conviction of sin confirms this. For if this is the law's principal function, then the Reformers must suppose guilt to be characteristic of a religion in which law observance is central.

Yet if we examine what the Reformers say about the key texts (Gal 1:11–17, Phil 3:4b–6) employed by Stendahl to demonstrate Paul's robust conscience, there is a surprise in store. For they, too, interpret these texts as indicating that Paul's conscience was robust prior to his Damascus Road experience. Of course, the Reformers do not share the historical-critical goals of modern interpreters. They are not attempting to achieve an accurate historical description of the nature of Second Temple Judaism. Their concerns are instead explicitly Christian and theological, but what they say is nevertheless clear, with particular significance placed upon Paul's statement in Phil 3:6 that he was "blameless" (*amemptos*) as regards righteousness under the law.

In his *Commentary on Galatians* (1531/1535), Luther expounds Gal 1:13–14 by means of Phil 3:5–6. Paul's words imply that if even he, with all his reasons for confidence in the flesh, had to be justified by faith, the Galatians would be foolish to trust those urging circumcision upon them. For the record of these influencers as regards the righteousness of the law is less impressive than Paul's own. Going on to discuss Gal 1:15–17, where Paul recounts God's grace in calling him to be an apostle, Luther places an exposition in Paul's own mouth:

> It is as though he were saying: "I did not deserve this; for I was zealous for the Law of God, but without judgment. In fact, my foolish and wicked zeal so blinded me that, with the permission of God, I fell into even more abom-

inable and outrageous sins. I persecuted the church of God; I was an enemy of Christ. . . . But the abundant grace of God, who calls and shows mercy, pardoned and forgave all those blasphemies. And in place of these horrible sins of mine, which I then regarded as a service most pleasing to God, He gave me His grace and called me to be an apostle." (*LW* 26:69)

Even in the last months of his life, in January 1546, when preaching on the story of Paul's conversion in Acts 9, Luther still insists that Paul was trying to do good when he persecuted the church. Paul's deeds were prompted by true zeal for the law and his native land: "he thought he was doing right and pleasing God."[31] In a similar vein, when preaching on Gal 1:11–14, Calvin argues that Paul's persecution of the church "does not mean that he did not strive to live in all holiness and perfection for he shone as a mirror of great integrity. Indeed, he refers to himself as 'blameless' ('*irreprehensible*,' Phil. 3:6), and not without good cause. Rather, he is saying that he was blind enough to consider himself justified in God's sight simply because there was no spot in him which men could reproach him for."[32]

Paul's preconversion life is thus a kind of paradigm of the Reformers' view of sin. His major sins are not the consequence of bodily desire but in fact stem from his deepest religious impulses and devotion. Sin infects his higher faculties as well as his lower ones. His sin springs also from his commitment to the law and demonstrates the inability of the law to justify. It is this that explains the otherwise shocking manner in which Paul speaks of the law. Vermigli asks of Phil 3:6, "If we could obtain righteousness by this means, should such profitable things be counted as losses, such precious and holy things as vile, and matters acceptable and pleasing to God as dung?" (RCSNT 11:75). As an obedient Jew, the preconversion Paul does have a different kind of righteousness, but it corresponds for the Reformers only to the civic or political use of the law.

Calvin comments of Phil 3:6 that "there is a twofold righteousness of the law. The one is spiritual—perfect love to God and our neighbors: it is contained in doctrine, and never existed in the life of any man. The other is literal—such as appears in the view of men, while nevertheless, hypocrisy reigns in the heart, and there is in the sight of God nothing but iniquity" (*Comm. Phil.* 3:6, CNTC 11:271). If the spiritual righteousness of the law were possible, it would justify, but the literal

---

31. *LW* 58:370. On this sermon, see also Bruce Corley, "Interpreting Paul's Conversion—Then and Now," in *The Road from Damascus: The Impact of Paul's Conversion on His Life, Thought, and Ministry*, ed. Richard N. Longenecker (Grand Rapids: Eerdmans, 1997), 10.

32. John Calvin, *Sermons on the Epistle to the Galatians*, trans. Kathy Childress (Edinburgh: Banner of Truth, 1997), 71–72 (sermon 5).

blamelessness before the law of which Paul speaks cannot do so. Paul the Pharisee can honestly claim this blamelessness before human beings, but it did not save him from the sin of persecuting the church. Luther structures the argument of his *Commentary on Galatians* (1531/1535) using a similar distinction. There is an earthly, active righteousness of the law that produces good works, but it is not righteousness in the sight of God. There is also a heavenly, passive righteousness that is not performed but is received by faith and creates a new person (*LW* 26:4–12).

Paul's condition before his Damascus Road experience was thus not one of spiritual struggle and despair. Rather, he confuses justifying righteousness and the righteousness of the law, mistaking them as the same thing. Paul thinks that through his zeal for the law, he stands blameless before God, but in fact sin controls his life. Unsurprisingly, the Reformers take this false consciousness as typical of Judaism, and they interpret Paul's phrase the "works of the law" in this way. These works are *not* identified with the theological use of the law in revealing sin. They are *not* those that drive a person to repentance. Instead, argues Luther, these works are identified by those who perform them "in themselves as being sufficient for righteousness and salvation. . . . [T]hey think they are fulfilling the Law and thus are righteous. . . . [T]hey do not dispose themselves to seek righteousness, but rather boast as if through these works it were already in their possession" (*LW* 25:241).

This way of hearing Paul has profound consequences for the Reformers' perspective on the relationship between the law and conscience. As Luther outlines them in his *Prefaces to the Old Testament* (1523), the upright person confusing justifying with civic righteousness and attempting to fulfill the law in his or her own strength has one of three possible human relationships with the law. There is also the blatant sinner willfully disregarding the law, and there is also the sinner in the process of being driven to Christ by the realization that the law demands impossible things.[33] Even in the last instance, where people correctly perceive their true position before God, to stay there permanently would be to fall into the sin of blasphemous despair of God's mercy. Further, this theological use of the law is a matter not simply of conscience but of revelation. In none of these three attitudes toward the law is the human conscience ultimately an appropriate and reliable guide to the human situation.

To identify the Reformers as heroes of the conscience, advocating obedience to it as a straight path to true experience of God is therefore a serious distortion.

---

33. *LW* 35:245–46. The confusion between justifying righteousness and civic righteousness arises because the former would require complete obedience to the law, and Judaism fails to recognize that such perfect obedience is impossible. The textual basis for this view is provided by Gal 3:13, where Paul says that Christ redeems believers from the curse of the law, a curse that falls upon those who do not do *all* that the law commands.

The theological use of the law may manifest itself in a guilty conscience, but this is not because the fallen human conscience is equipped reliably to identify right from wrong. Instead, even repentance is not a human work but a divine gift: "Real preparation for grace is not the preparation sinners make through their contrition and confession but the preparation God has made by his election, calling, and gifts. Contrition is the fruit of grace not its presupposition."[34] The conscience itself is quite unable to move a person toward God and is thereby condemned and moved to the margins, not made central.

The drama of justification is about God's truth breaking in from outside, not about human beings finding truth by listening to an inner voice. For Luther, "the conscience was a battlefield on which the forces of good and evil carried on spiritual warfare.... [T]he basic question of human existence was not, 'Who am I?,' but rather 'Whose am I? To whom do I belong?' By listening to the 'alien word' of God's promise in Scripture we are delivered from the burden of introspection and self-justification."[35] The conscience is therefore only reliable insofar as it is instructed by Scripture.

This is true for the Reformers not only in the experience of justification itself but also in the discipleship of the Christian life. Paul writes at Rom 14:23 that those who eat meat while doubting that they should do so stand condemned since "what does not proceed from faith is sin." Vermigli responds to this by refusing to identify faith with conscience in any simple or straightforward way: "If I were to grant that in this passage faith means conscience, I suppose we should also add that the conscience should not be believed unless it is instructed by the word of God. For there are many who have such a superstitious conscience that, whether they obey it or not, they sin most severely."[36]

Any idea that the Reformers took the spiritual struggles of Luther and projected them backward onto Paul is therefore completely misguided. It is true that in some later Protestant traditions, the theological use of the law gave rise to the expectation that a subjective experience of guilt was an essential preparation for conversion.[37] Yet this experience of guilt is not identified with Paul, whose experi-

---

34. David C. Steinmetz, "Luther against Luther," in *Luther in Context*, 2nd ed. (Grand Rapids: Baker, 2002), 10.

35. Timothy George, "Modernizing Luther, Domesticating Paul: Another Perspective," in *Justification and Variegated Nomism II*, ed. Donald A. Carson, Peter T. O'Brien, and Mark A. Seifrid (Grand Rapids: Baker, 2004), 444.

36. Peter Martyr Vermigli, *Predestination and Justification: Two Theological Loci*, trans. and ed. Frank A. James III, Peter Martyr Library 8 (Kirksville, MO: Sixteenth-Century Essays and Studies, 2003), 106.

37. On conscience and conversion, see Stephen J. Chester, "Romans 7 and Conversion in the Protestant Tradition," *ExAud* 25 (2009): 135–71.

ence is instead one of sudden grace. It is also true that there is a partial exception in Melanchthon's exegesis of Rom 7, which he interprets in a significantly different way from Luther. Melanchthon takes Paul's statement that apart from the law sin is dead (7:8) to speak of a time as a Pharisee when Paul mistakenly believed that he was satisfying the law and was righteous. However, Paul's statement that sin revived when the commandment came (7:9–10) refers to anxiety caused by the law, such that if Paul "had not heard the voice of the Gospel, he also would have perished in such terrors."[38]

This transition for Paul from false assurance to terror in the face of sin and the law does potentially seem to fit into Melanchthon's understanding of the order of salvation, "in successive stages consisting of the law, the gospel, and the necessary renewal of the Holy Spirit."[39] Yet Melanchthon does not explain when for Paul the second stage happened, and his focus is on the move from fear to comfort experienced by believers as they transition from law to gospel. Even if Melanchthon did intend to imply that Paul was prepared for his conversion by a struggle with his conscience, this view was not influential. For it is not prominent in subsequent Protestant interpretation. If later interpreters do hear Rom 7:9 in a way similar to Melanchthon, the coming of the law and the conviction of sin is identified with the moment of Paul's conversion itself, not with preparation for it.[40] It is only with the rise of historical-critical scholarship in the nineteenth century that a prior psychological struggle with the law was proposed. An explanation from within history was now sought for an event that previous generations had explained through direct divine intervention.

---

38. Melanchthon, *Commentary on Romans*, 157.

39. Lohse, *Martin Luther's Theology*, 179.

40. See Bruce C. Hindmarsh, *The Evangelical Conversion Narrative: Spiritual Autobiography in Early Modern England* (Oxford: Oxford University Press, 2005), 143.

CHAPTER SEVEN

The Content of the Reformers' Pauline Exegetical Grammar: Salvation in Christ

J ust as with Reformers' perspective on the plight of fallen humanity, it is helpful to present their convictions about salvation in Christ in summary form before exploring in more detail the exegetical arguments on which they were founded.

7.1. Salvation in Christ in Summary

Any such summary must recognize that although they regard human captivity to sin as enormously deep, for the Reformers the immensity of the divine mercy made available in Christ is infinitely greater. Paul's repeated statements that human beings are not justified by the "works of the law" are taken to indicate complete and exclusive reliance upon this divine mercy for salvation. Not only does Paul eliminate any role for the "works of the law" as a cause of justification, but he intends the phrase to be understood in the broadest possible terms. It does not designate ceremonial aspects of the law only but refers to the whole law. Further, this reference to the whole law encompasses deeds performed on the basis of the law in all times and places. It is not to be interpreted with reference only to works performed prior to faith. It also excludes works of love performed by the baptized from any role in justification. Those who believe are justified solely through Christ's person and work.

This makes redundant both the Augustinian understanding of grace as something infused into believers, and the medieval elaboration of that understanding in terms of created habits of grace. No longer do believers cooperate with grace in order to grow in justice through meritorious good works. Instead, in key Pauline texts concerning justification, grace denotes a divine disposition. It is the divine favor or mercy that consists in God's desire to forgive sins on the basis of Christ's saving sacrifice. Such divine favor is gratuitous, conditioned by nothing outside of God, including human actions. As such, grace is external to the believer, and it is total. There is nothing provisional or partial about divine grace, and, for this reason, assurance of salvation is possible even though, in this life, the obedience of believers to God's will remains incomplete. Such assurance does not depend on the actions of the believer.

Although grace itself is no longer a divine gift that makes possible obedient human actions, believers are not left unchanged. For divine grace is nevertheless the indispensable basis of the gift of faith. Faith is the means by which Christ and his saving benefits are received, and it is therefore justifying. Faith includes historical and doctrinal knowledge of Christ's person and work, but it is always most fundamentally a disposition of trust in God's promises as exemplified in the Pauline Letters by the biblical example of Abraham. This committed trust in God's promises does not need to be formed by love in order to be alive. It is either inherently active and alive, or it is not faith. Yet faith justifies not because it leads to good works or is itself meritorious, but because it looks away from the self and looks instead to Christ.

In doing so, faith receives an alien righteousness that comes to the believer from outside. It is through faith and only through faith that this alien righteousness may be received, and it is in this sense that the Reformers claim that justification is by faith alone. The trust involved in faith is trust in Christ's person and saving work, so faith is always focused on Christ. Precisely because faith receives Christ and his saving benefits, it may sometimes itself appropriately be described as a kind of righteousness. However, such a description is appropriate only on the basis of this reception and never because of the merits of the believer. The Reformers intend their contrast between relying on Christ and relying, even in part, on who the believer becomes to be a stark one.

7.2. Not by Works of the Law

The greatest concentration of the phrase "works of the law" comes in Gal 2:16: "yet we know that a person is justified not by works of the law but through faith in Jesus Christ, so that we might be justified by faith in Christ, and not by doing the works of the law, because no one will be justified by the works of the law."[1] In

---

1. As well as the three uses here in Gal 2:16, the phrase also appears in Rom 3:20, 27, 28; Gal 3:2, 5, 10.

their interpretation of the phrase, the Reformers speak with one voice. They insist that by the "works of the law," Paul intends the whole law, including its ethical aspects, and not merely ceremonies. This was a crucial point, for if Paul meant to say that justification was not by means of the ceremonial aspects of the law, then he does not exclude other types of obedience from justification. This exegetical point could impact even translation. As early as 1525, William Tyndale's New Testament excludes interpretation of the phrase in terms of ceremonies alone by rendering it into English as the "dedes of the lawe."[2]

Often this feels like a straightforwardly confessional divide, with the Reformers insisting that the phrase "works of the law" means the whole law, and their Roman opponents that it means ceremonies. Later in the century, the *Rhemes New Testament* (1582), the first ever English translation sanctioned by Rome, includes a marginal note to Gal 2:16 insisting that "when justification is attributed to faith, the workes of charitie be not excluded, but the works of Moyses law: that is, the ceremonies, sacrifices and sacraments thereof principally."[3]

However, the Reformers' position that the phrase "works of the law" refers to the whole law was certainly not novel. It was a minority position in medieval exegesis, but it was certainly acceptable since it had been held by Augustine. On this view, Paul was taken to be excluding any role for human obedience in initial justification, but the works of the baptized still contributed to justification as a lifelong process of growth in righteousness. If in contrast, medieval exegetes understood "works of the law" to refer to ceremonies, they took Paul to be excluding the ceremonies of the Mosaic law from both initial and lifelong justification. This also does not exclude the works of the believer and the sacraments of the church from playing a part in justification as a lifelong process. Nor does it necessarily contradict Augustine's insistence that human obedience does not cause initial justification but means simply that Paul's use of the phrase "works of the law" does not comment on that issue.

Yet their insistence that Paul intends the phrase to refer to the whole law remains vital to the Reformers. For if it refers only to the ceremonies of the Mosaic law, then any general exclusion of works from justification becomes implausible. In contrast, if it does refer to the whole law, then debate can follow over whether Paul intends to reject any causal role whatsoever for human obedience in justifica-

---

2. Luther A. Weigle, ed., *The New Testament Octapla: Eight English Versions of the New Testament in the Tyndale-King James Tradition* (New York: Nelson, 1962), 1058. Tyndale was not followed by the Geneva Bible (1560) or by the King James Version (1611), the two most influential Protestant translations into English.

3. *The Rhemes New Testament* (Rhemes: John Fogny, 1582), 499.

tion or whether he intends to exclude it from initial justification only. To interpret "works of the law" in terms of the whole law did not by itself demonstrate that Paul intended the broader exclusion, but it was essential to the Reformers' position. If "works of the law" refers to ceremonies, then they must be wrong. Sixteenth-century interpreters of Paul could agree with the Reformers about the meaning of the phrase "works of the law" and still disagree with them over justification and salvation, but they could not embrace the Reformers' teaching on justification and salvation while rejecting their understanding of "works of the law."[4]

The total exclusion of works from any causal role in justification had not been clear in Luther's *Lectures on Romans* (1515/1516). Yet by the time of his first *Commentary on Galatians* (1516–1517/1519), Luther argues that works result from righteousness rather than lead to it: "he who wants to be saved must despair altogether of all strength, works, and laws" (*LW* 27:223). Luther draws this conclusion from his assertion that by the "works of the law," Paul intends the whole law. If even the Ten Commandments do not justify, then no law can do so. Luther also draws attention to what he regards as the implausibility of a division within the divine law. The apostle cannot be arguing that ceremonies are now obsolete as regards justification but that the ethical aspects of the law remain involved, for "just as the ceremonial law was good and holy at that time, so it is good and holy now; for it was instituted by God Himself" (*LW* 27:223).

A similar point is made again in the later *Commentary on Galatians* (1531/1535). Luther comments that "the ceremonial law was as much the divine law as the moral laws were. Thus circumcision, the institution of the priesthood, the service of worship, and the rituals were commanded by God as much as the Decalog was" (*LW* 26:138). If all parts of the law are equally worthy in their own nature, then one part cannot have been removed from a role in justification while another remains relevant. In his *Commentary on Galatians* (1548), John Calvin also refuses to find anything inherently wrong with the Jewish practices of Paul's opponents: "The use of ceremonies for edification was free so long as the believers were not

---

4. An interesting partial exception is Martin Bucer. See Edwin Tait, "The Law and Its Works in Martin Bucer's 1536 Romans Commentary," in *Reformation Readings of Romans*, ed. Kathy Ehrensperger and R. Ward Holder (New York: T&T Clark, 2008), 62: "Bucer interprets the 'works of the law' mentioned in Rom. 3:20 as the ceremonies of the OT law. In this he takes his stand with the bulk of the patristic tradition and with contemporary Catholics over against Augustine in the early church and contemporary evangelicals such as Melanchthon. But he does not regard this as a restriction of Paul's critique of the law—rather, Bucer argues that Paul is focusing on the ceremonial law because this was the part of the law in which his opponents were trusting. . . . The 'works of the law' in question (the ceremonial *mitzvoh*) cannot justify *because* the whole law cannot justify."

deprived of their liberty.... Paul was worried not so much about ceremonies being observed as that the confidence and glory of salvation should be transferred to works" (*Comm. Gal.* 2:16, *CNTC* 11:36, 39). The same basic point is made even more forcefully by Peter Martyr Vermigli when lecturing at Oxford in the early 1550s: "Is it not good and laudable conduct to worship God with certain fixed rites which he has commanded?"[5]

The position that the phrase "works of the law" refers to the whole law therefore has important consequences. It is a mistake to understand the Reformers' polemic against the rites of the Roman Catholic Church as based upon any general dislike of ceremonies. Their polemic is more focused, rejecting such ceremonies on the grounds that, in contrast to the true sacraments of baptism and Lord's Supper, God did not institute them, and they are the fruits of mere human invention. Calvin drives the point home when he comments that Paul's opponents "at least were able to say that they were not introducing their own ideas or traditions.... The Papists, however, have no such foundation, for all their rituals have arisen according to the will of men."[6]

This stands in contrast to the position of Erasmus, who, in the process of arguing for a different kind of reform from within the Roman church, did adopt a more general critique of ceremonies. Erasmus regarded piety as "an internal quality and independent of the external observance of rites."[7] He viewed Paul's opponents in Galatia as failing to understand that the time of the transitory law has passed now that Christ has come. They cling to obsolete ceremonies and risk bringing confusion to the Galatian believers: "If they perceive that these ceremonies are being observed by the chief apostles, those who are somewhat superstitious will conclude that without these ceremonies the faith of the gospel is not enough for attaining salvation" (*CWE* 42:104).

As Erasmus developed it, this interpretation of "works of the law" could invite "cogent analogies with ecclesiastical life in the sixteenth century,"[8] with much potential for criticism of the sacramental system in the name of true inner piety. By declining to interpret Paul's phrase in this way, the Reformers

---

5. Peter Martyr Vermigli, *Predestination and Justification: Two Theological Loci*, trans. and ed. Frank A. James III, Peter Martyr Library 8 (Kirksville, MO: Sixteenth-Century Essays and Studies, 2003), 118.

6. John Calvin, *Sermons on the Epistle to the Galatians*, trans. Kathy Childress (Edinburgh: Banner of Truth, 1997), 115 (sermon 8).

7. Erika Rummel, *Erasmus* (London: Continuum, 2004), 39.

8. Robert D. Sider, "Historical Imagination and the Representation of Paul in Erasmus' Paraphrases on the Pauline Epistles," in *Holy Scripture Speaks: The Production and Reception of Erasmus' Paraphrases on the New Testament*, ed. Hilmar M. Pabel and Mark Vessey (Toronto: University of Toronto Press, 2002), 100.

denied themselves any general criticism of ceremonies despite its potential utility for their own criticism of the sacramental system. This highlights the fact that what was principally at stake for them in the interpretation of the phrase "works of the law" was a correct understanding of justification. The insistence that Paul intends by the phrase the whole law matters so much to them because it enables their rejection of a causal role in justification for human cooperation with divine grace.

That they take Paul's focus to be on the whole law is also partly what leads the Reformers to pay little attention to issues of Jewish practice in their exegesis of Gal 2. If the apostle is concerned to eliminate law observance entirely as a cause of justification, then his primary concern cannot be with Jew-gentile relationships in the church at Antioch. It is instead with a theological question concerning the whole law and the basis of human relationships with God. Therefore, the significance of the quarrel that Paul recounts in the church at Antioch over eating with gentiles (2:11–14) is that it raises for him the issue of the nature of justification that he addresses in 2:16. Calvin articulates with some care the way in which one leads to the other:

> Many will be thinking, "What! The issue at stake is the ceremonial law. Why, then, does Paul throw himself right into the middle of the battle by raising issues such as righteousness, man's salvation and the forgiveness of sins? . . ." Well, to speak even of one of the ceremonies of the law involves discussing the role and function of the law. . . . He [Paul] not only gave his attention to what the Jews believed concerning eating pork . . . he considered why they believed such things. They claimed that the observance of the law was vital to salvation, and this was a yoke upon the conscience that Paul found intolerable.[9]

In arguing for this emphasis, Calvin employs what is initially a somewhat surprising argument. Paul's focus must be on the whole law and its inability to justify since "context" shows that this is what is meant. Yet context, the fact that the antitheses of Gal 2:16 are prompted by Paul's recounting of the dispute at Antioch about eating practices, might be thought one of the strongest arguments for the opposite view. How can Calvin claim context in his own support? Calvin's point is that "almost everything Paul adds relates to the moral rather than the ceremonial law" (*Comm. Gal.* 2:15, *CNTC* 11:38). Context for Calvin is not the circumstances of the dispute at Antioch but the rest of the argument of Galatians, where, especially in 3:10–29, Paul offers general contrasts between the law and faith. Paul does come "at length to the specific question of ceremonies" (*Comm. Gal.* 2:15, *CNTC* 11:39), by

---

9. Calvin, *Sermons on Galatians*, 162–64 (sermon 11).

which Calvin presumably refers to the renewed discussion of circumcision from 5:2 onward. However, in the meantime, the other things that Paul says about the law do not appear to relate to ceremonies alone.

This was a vital point in relation to literary analysis of Galatians. For 2:16 was widely taken as a kind of thesis statement for the letter, the implications of which are unpacked by the rest of Galatians. As the introductory notes to Gal 2 in the Geneva Bible (1560) were to claim, 2:16 is "the principal scope" of the letter, the term "scope" indicating the aim, intent, or central purpose of the text.[10] If the scope concerns ceremonies, then the subsequent argument of the text should reflect this. Its failure to do so was one of the main indications for early Protestant interpreters that they were correct to understand the phrase the "works of the law" in terms of the inability of the law in its entirety to justify.

Of great importance in supporting this analysis was Gal 3:10. Here Paul asserts that all who rely on the works of the law are under a curse, for, as Deut 27:26 states, "Cursed is everyone who does not observe and obey all the things written in the book of the law." The Reformers' opponents typically interpreted Paul's use of this text by again making a distinction within the law and concluding that the curse applies only to those who commit mortal sins.[11] In contrast, the Reformers emphasized the use of the word "all" so that everyone who does not perfectly perform the whole law falls under the curse. Perfect obedience would justify, but there are none who are perfectly obedient, and so all are under the curse. As Bullinger expresses it, "Now unless we do by the deeds of the law understand the morals, as well as the ceremonials, I do not see how his proof can hang to that which went before. For he saith expressly, 'In all the things which are written in the book of the law to do them.' Now who knoweth not that the ceremonials were not written alone, but that the morals were written also?"[12]

If Paul's emphasis is on obedience to all that the law commands, then he must intend universal antitheses between the entire law and faith and not restricted ones between ceremonies and faith. From the Reformers' perspective, to say that justification is not by works of the law is to say that meritorious human deeds do not number among its causes.[13]

---

10. *The Geneva Bible: A Facsimile of the 1560 Edition* (Peabody, MA: Hendrickson, 2007), 87 verso. This translation was prepared by English exiles in Geneva during the reign of Queen Mary (1553–1558), but subsequent editions were printed in England. On the term "scope," see Gerald T. Sheppard, "Between Reformation and Modern Commentary: The Perception of the Scope of Biblical Books," in William Perkins, *A Commentary on Galatians*, ed. Gerald T. Sheppard (New York: Pilgrim, 1989), xlviii–lxxvii.

11. *Rhemes New Testament*, 503, has a marginal note to this effect.

12. Heinrich Bullinger, "Sermon VIII," in *Bullinger's Decades: The Third Decade*, ed. Thomas Harding, Parker Society 8 (Cambridge: Cambridge University Press, 1851), 248.

13. Brian Lugioyo, *Martin Bucer's Doctrine of Justification: Reformation Theology and Early*

7.3. Grace

The Reformers understand grace (*charis*) not as something infused into human beings but as a disposition in God determining God's actions toward people of faith. Grace is God's favor (*favor*) or mercy (*misericordia*) and, as such, a shorthand for the divine desire to forgive sins on the basis of Christ's saving sacrifice. In his exegesis, Melanchthon comments that the word means "gratuitous mercy—the remission of sins and imputation of righteousness" (Rom 5:2) and "simply the forgiveness of sins, or God's favour" (Col 1:2).[14] Hundreds of similar comments could be collected from a wide variety of early Protestant interpreters. There is also a clear impact on translation. In 1525, Tyndale uses "favour" to translate *charis* six times, especially at crucial points in Rom 4 and 5.[15] Such favor is understood as free (*gratis*), which the Reformers take to mean that God's gracious disposition is not in any respect caused by factors external to God such as meritorious human deeds.

This does not mean that all occurrences of the word "grace" in the Pauline Letters are to be understood in the same way. The Reformers are aware that in Koine Greek the term possessed a wide range of meanings, and they feel no need to force its usage into a linguistic straitjacket. Bullinger even draws attention to the semantic range of "grace" and provides a brief survey of other meanings:

> The word "grace" is diversely used in the holy scriptures, even as it is in profane writings also. For in the Bible it signifieth thanksgiving, and also a benefit, and alms; as 2 Cor viii. Moreover, it signifieth praise and recompence, as in that

---

Modern Irenicism (Oxford: Oxford University Press, 2011), 37–102, demonstrates that Bucer again provides a partial exception. He conceives justification both as declarative and effective, and the latter embraces the works of the believer. Such works are a secondary effective cause of justification enfolded within the primary cause of God's electing grace: "the works of a believer are accepted by God as worthy of merit not because they are so in themselves but because, first, God has decreed them to be such and, second, they are his very works in the believer" (95). Bucer thus remains much closer to Augustine's exegetical grammar than do the other Reformers, but he, too, breaks in significant ways with medieval appropriations of Augustine. Bucer has no place for habits of grace, ascribing the works of the believer to the activity of the Holy Spirit. He also insists that God's rewards always remain fundamentally disproportionate to the reality of believer's works. They are rewarded only because God has covenanted to do so.

14. Philip Melanchthon, *Commentary on Romans*, trans. Fred Kramer (Saint Louis: Concordia, 1992), 124; Melanchthon, *Paul's Letter to the Colossians*, trans. D. C. Parker (Sheffield: Almond, 1989), 31–32.

15. Rom 4:4, 16; 5:2, 15, 17; 11:6. In 1534 Tyndale replaces "favour" with grace in all instances except Rom 4:4 and 4:16. The Great Bible (1539) 1540 also uses "favour" at 4:4 and 4:16, while the Geneva Bible (1560) uses it at 4:4 alone.

place where the apostle saith: "If, when ye do well, ye are afflicted, and yet do bear it; that is praiseworthy before God." It doth also signify faculty and licence; as when we say, that one hath gotten grace to teach and execute an office. For the apostle saith that he received grace; and immediately, to expound his own meaning, he addeth, to execute the office of an apostle. Moreover the gifts of God are called grace, because they are given gratis, and freely bestowed without looking for of any recompense.[16]

Only after this does Bullinger go on to discuss justifying grace as divine favor or mercy. Yet alongside such recognition of diversity in meaning stands a passionate insistence that, in key texts relating to justification, the term refers to gratuitous divine favor. The textual basis for this is above all Rom 3:24, where Paul says that all who believe are justified by God's grace "freely" (*dōrean*, the accusative form of *dōrea*, another Greek noun meaning "gift" but here used as an adverb and translated by the Vulgate as *gratis*). It is this qualification or further defining of grace that the Reformers find significant in ruling out human cooperation with grace in justification. In his treatment of grace in *Loci Communes* (1543), Melanchthon comments that "this exclusive particle means that reconciliation is given for the sake of the Son of God, the Mediator, and not because of our worthiness, not because of our merits, not because of our virtues or deeds."[17]

A decade later, Martin Chemnitz (1522–1586) provides a brief philological analysis of the adverb and suggests that it appears in Rom 3:24 precisely in order to counter alternative possible definitions of "grace." He points to the Septuagint version of Gen 39:4, where "the text says of Joseph: 'He found grace in the sight of Potiphar.' But there is the added note 'because he was a prosperous man,' that is, on account of the eminent gifts which he noticed in Joseph he loved him and made him great."[18] Potiphar's grace, Chemnitz argues, was based on qualities possessed by the recipient. Therefore, it is the addition of "freely" that shows that at Rom 3:23 Paul is *not* thinking of grace in this way. The grace that justifies depends not at all on who the recipients are or become but is instead entirely gratuitous.

Such exegetical conclusions were incendiary in a context where infused grace and human cooperation with it were central to traditional soteriology, and the sacramental system was one of the principal means by which such grace was

16. Heinrich Bullinger, "Sermon I," in *Bullinger's Decades: The Fourth Decade*, ed. Thomas Harding, Parker Society 9 (Cambridge: Cambridge University Press, 1851), 6–7.

17. Philip Melanchthon, *Loci Communes 1543*, trans J. A. O. Preus (Saint Louis: Concordia, 1992), 92.

18. Martin Chemnitz, *Examination of the Council of Trent*, vol. 1, trans. Fred Kramer (Saint Louis: Concordia, 1971), 496.

mediated. It also marks a point where, despite their recovery of Augustine's exegesis in so many subsidiary matters, the Reformers decisively broke with him. Their views about grace therefore represent a fundamental rupture in the history of Pauline reception.

The origins of this rupture lie in the work of someone who did not approve of it. For it was Erasmus, in the *Annotations* published to accompany his 1516 edition of the Greek New Testament, who noted at Rom 1:5 that "grace" can have various meanings, including "sometimes 'favour,' for example, 'you have found *gratiam* [favour] with God'" (*CWE* 56:19). This reference to Luke 1:30 and the annunciation to Mary was explosive since the Vulgate did not here speak of Mary as "favored one" or "beloved" but as "full of grace" (*gratia plena*) (*ASD* VI-5:458–59 [368–404]). In the hands of Erasmus, a text that in the Vulgate appeared to speak of the Virgin as having received a superabundance of infused grace spoke instead of God's favor toward her.

Erasmus himself regarded this and similar instances as translation issues and did not intend to question traditional doctrine. The breadth of possible meanings of "grace" meant that to question the validity of a traditional translation in one text was not to make a general assertion about its meaning in every place. Further, it could be argued that divine favor might lead to infused grace being granted. Yet neither the Reformers nor Erasmus's traditionalist critics were convinced by these qualifications. Worse, Erasmus left another significant hostage to fortune in his *Annotations* on Rom 5:16 and 5:20. For here Erasmus distinguishes between Paul's use of the terms "gift" (*charisma*) and "grace" (*charis*). In his view, they should be translated into Latin using different terms, but the Vulgate used *gratia* (grace) for both. "Gift" should instead be translated using *donum* (gift), "unless we suppose that 'gift' and 'grace' are entirely the same."[19]

This distinction between "gift" and "grace" was appropriated by Melanchthon in a lecture series on Romans delivered at Wittenberg in 1520.[20] He employed it to question the traditional view of grace, arguing that to regard grace as infused makes it into a gift when for Paul grace and gift are not the same. Romans 5 shows that they are closely connected and that grace motivates and leads to divine gift, but they are distinct. Unlike gift, grace remains as something in God and not in human beings. Of particular significance for Melanchthon is Rom 5:15, which Erasmus

---

19. *CWE* 56:170. On 5:20, see *CWE* 56:172.

20. I rely here upon Rolf Schäfer, "Melanchthon's Interpretation of Romans 5.15: His Departure from the Augustinian Concept of Grace Compared to Luther's," in *Philip Melanchthon (1497–1560) and the Commentary*, ed. Timothy J. Wengert and M. Patrick Graham (Sheffield: Sheffield Academic, 1997), 79–104.

had not commented upon but which seemed to invite the drawing of a distinction between grace and gift. For Paul speaks of "the grace of God and the free gift in the grace of the one man, Jesus Christ." In his theology textbook, *Loci Communes* (1521), Melanchthon states simply that "Paul in Rom 5:15 distinguishes 'grace' from the 'gift of grace'. . . . He calls grace the favor of God in which he embraced Christ and because of Christ, all the saints. Therefore, because he favors, God cannot help pouring out his gifts on those on whom he has had mercy."[21] Melanchthon will continue to refer to the verse in all subsequent editions of the textbook and to propose this interpretation in all editions of his *Commentary on Romans*.

Melanchthon's radical appropriation of Erasmus's philological analysis was then passed on to Luther who abruptly changed his own exegetical position. For while Luther had long been skeptical about created habits of grace, he did adhere to the general view that grace is something present in the Christian. In 1515–1516, when lecturing on Romans, Luther had specifically identified the grace and the gift of 5:15 with each other: "But 'the grace of God' and 'the gift' are the same thing, namely the very righteousness which is freely given to us through Christ" (*LW* 25:306). In his first *Commentary on Galatians* (1516–1517/1519), despite already having developed the view that works are in no sense the basis of righteousness, Luther's comments on Gal 3:7 reveal an explicit rejection of grace as favor: "For just as God loves in very fact, not in word only, so, too, He is favorably disposed with the thing that is present, not only with the word" (*LW* 27:252). God's favor is something present in the believer and not solely a disposition in God.

Yet in his tract *Against Latomus* (1521), Luther makes explicit use of Rom 5:15 and adopts the distinction between grace and gift:

> A righteous and faithful man doubtless has both the grace and the gift. Grace makes him wholly pleasing so that his person is wholly accepted, and there is no place for wrath in him anymore, but the gift heals from sin and from all his corruption of body and soul. . . . Everything is forgiven through grace, but as yet not everything is healed through the gift. The gift has been infused. The leaven has been added to the mixture. It works so as to purge away the sin for which a person has already been forgiven, and to drive out the evil guest for whose expulsion permission has been given. (*LW* 32:229)

It is therefore clear that, on this crucial point, the primary agent of change was not Luther himself. The flow of influence was from Erasmus to Melanchthon to

---

21. Philip Melanchthon, "Loci Communes Theologici," in *Melanchthon and Bucer*, ed. Wilhelm Pauck (Philadelphia: Westminster, 1969), 87–88.

Luther. Yet once the Wittenberg Reformers had developed their new understanding of grace, it became universal within early Protestant exegesis. Throughout the rest of the sixteenth century and long afterward, Rom 5:15 and its distinction between grace and gift were cited as evidence against understanding grace as infused and for understanding grace as divine favor.[22] For Luther, it even became a benediction with which to end a letter: "May the grace and the gift be with you."[23]

7.4. Faith

The Reformers argue that in many Pauline texts concerning justification, the Greek noun "faith" (*pistis*) bears the sense of "trust" (*fiducia*) in response to God's promises. In trusting divine promises, sinners accept that they come before God empty-handed and that their hope is based entirely upon gifts of God that can come to them only from outside themselves. In this sense, faith is primarily receptive. However, it is not passively receptive. Faith is *active* and impacts every aspect of a person's existence. As Luther famously defined faith in the *Preface to Romans* (1522) of his German Bible: "It kills the old Adam and makes us altogether different men, in heart and spirit and mind and powers; and brings with it the Holy Spirit. O it is a living, busy, active, mighty thing, this faith" (*LW* 35:370).

By contrast, faith (*fides* in Latin) was understood in medieval interpretation primarily as intellectual assent to the truth of the gospel. It was this understanding that established the necessity for faith to be formed by love in order to justify (see 4.1). For it seemed obvious that intellectual assent alone does not justify, and therefore unformed faith, which consists of such assent, needed the shaping and forming power of love. Only then could it be truly alive and justifying. However, once faith was defined by early Protestant exegetes as trusting and active, the restriction of the sense of the term to intellectual assent disappeared. Along with it disappeared also the necessity for faith to be formed by love. As Melanchthon expresses it, "Obviously, when Paul says, 'since we are justified through faith, we have peace with God' [Rom 5:1], he speaks of a faith which brings comfort and peace to

---

22. Calvin and Peter Martyr Vermigli provide examples from the early Reformed tradition. For Calvin, see *Comm. Rom.* 5:15, *CNTC* 8:115 and for Vermigli, *Most Learned and Fruitful Commentaries upon the Epistle of S. Paul to the Romanes*, trans. Sir Henry Billingsley (London: John Dayc, 1568), 115b. At the very end of the sixteenth century, William Perkins, *A Commentary on Galatians*, ed. Gerald T. Sheppard (New York: Pilgrim, 1989), 7, still relies upon Rom 5:15 to sustain a distinction between grace and gift.

23. *LW* 49:264–67 (letter no. 202). The letter is to Nicholas Hausmann, pastor at Zwickau, and probably dates from early February 1530.

the heart. This peace is not just knowledge, for the devils know, and it causes them to tremble and flee from Christ; they are certain that God will punish them."[24]

Thus, the Reformers and their opponents agree that Jas 2:19 ("Even the demons believe—and shudder") demonstrates that a knowledge of the historical truth of the gospel alone does not save. But whereas this leads one side to the conclusion that faith must be formed by love, it leads the other side to the conclusion that faith is not to be understood exclusively in terms of historical knowledge. There must instead be a significant emphasis upon trust. For his part, Erasmus again tried to steer a middle course. He did not in any direct way attack traditional doctrine, yet he did note very clearly the semantic range of the Greek noun and the fact that in the New Testament it often bears the sense of "trust."[25] It was difficult for his readers to hear this as a ringing endorsement of faith formed by love, and his work provided the Reformers with ammunition for their arguments about the nature of faith as trust.

There were to be some differences of emphasis among the Reformers concerning the nature of faith. Interpreters in the emerging early Reformed tradition, such as Bucer and Calvin, wished to place some emphasis on the content of what is believed alongside the trust that faith expresses.[26] Faith is also knowledge. Calvin's famous definition of faith in the *Institutes* brings the two together: "faith is a firm and certain knowledge of the divine benevolence towards us, which founded on the truth of the free promise in Christ, is both revealed to our minds and sealed on our hearts through the Holy Spirit" (*Institutes* 3.2.7 [551]). Here trust is a very important aspect of faith as knowledge (*cognitio*), but faith is not simply equated with trust. Space is thus created for understanding faith not only in relation to God's saving activity but also in relation to God's creative and providential activity.[27] Convinced that faith relates in this way to the whole of the Christian life, Calvin argues that "faith lays hold of regeneration just as much as forgiveness of sins in Christ" (*Comm. 1 Cor.* 1:30, *CNTC* 9:46). If Luther and Melanchthon can insist that faith is not solely historical knowledge, so Calvin can insist that it is not solely

24. Philip Melanchthon, *Melanchthon on Christian Doctrine*, trans. Clyde L. Manschreck (New York: Oxford University Press, 1965), 158. This is a translation of the 1555 German edition of *Loci Communes*.

25. See especially *CWE* 56:43–44 for Erasmus's comments on the phrase "from faith to faith" (Rom 1:17).

26. Bucer again adopts a position distinct from that of other Reformers. His understanding of faith is shaped by his insistence that mental convictions determine affections and actions. Right knowledge will lead to right actions, and faith will lead to deeds of love, and so from Bucer's perspective, there is only limited validity to the distinction between knowledge and trust as different aspects of faith. See Lugioyo, *Martin Bucer's Doctrine*, 87–90.

27. See the discussion in Barbara Pitkin, *What Pure Eyes Could See: Calvin's Doctrine of Faith in Its Exegetical Context* (Oxford: Oxford University Press, 1999), 9–40.

trust. All agree, however, that it is trust that stands at the forefront in key Pauline texts concerning justification.

This key conviction about the nature of justifying faith emerged from Luther's work. It is not a major emphasis in either the *Lectures on Romans* (1515–1516) or the first *Commentary on Galatians* (1515–1516/1519). Yet by the time of *The Freedom of a Christian* (September 1520), Luther expresses a rich and multifaceted concept of faith. In doing so, he makes restricted but significant use of what was to become the Reformers' primary biblical resource concerning faith: the figure of Abraham (Rom 4, Gal 3). In believing God's promises, Abraham considers and confesses God to be truthful and in so doing gives God the worship that is God's due. Faith justifies because in trusting God's promises, it acknowledges and honors God for who God is. Faith lets God be God. In this way, Abraham "grew strong in faith as he gave glory to God" (Rom 4:20).

How influential an aspect of Protestant concepts of faith this was to become can be illustrated from the exegesis of Calvin. He is typical of many in making this aspect of faith paradigmatic of true worship: "No greater honour can be given to God than by sealing His truth by our faith. On the other hand, no greater insult can be shown to Him than by rejecting the grace which He offers us, or by detracting from the authority of His Word. For this reason the main thing in the worship of God is to embrace His promises with obedience. True religion begins with faith" (*Comm. Rom.* 4:20, *CNTC* 8:99).

Abraham's faith soon also became significant in other ways. Paul's insistence that Abraham was justified while uncircumcised (Rom 4:10), prompts Luther to argue in his *Preface to Romans* (1522) that "if the work of circumcision contributed nothing to his righteousness, though God had commanded it and it was a good work of obedience, then surely no other good work will contribute anything to righteousness" (*LW* 35:374). Luther construes Paul's argument not merely as chronological—that is, Abraham was justified before he was circumcised, which might arguably restrict Paul's exclusion of works to initial justification. Luther also construes it as qualitative—that is, if such a preeminent work as circumcision does not justify, then no other works whatsoever can contribute to justification.[28] Such exegetical arguments provide the basis of the Reformers' characteristic insistence that justification is by faith *alone*. For them Paul's contrasts between faith and works exclude any cooperation between them in justification. As Calvin puts it, "We have to ascribe either nothing or everything to faith or to works."[29]

---

28. Paul's Greek actually speaks of Abraham "being in circumcision" or "being in uncircumcision" with his justification occurring when in a state of uncircumcision, and so Luther's qualitative point is more exegetically defensible than most English translations might suggest.

29. *Comm. Gal.* 2:16, *CNTC* 11:40. See also *LW* 26:137.

A further significant aspect of Abraham's faith is the incredible nature of the divine promise to him of a son. Abraham received what was not possible humanly speaking. He walked by faith and not by sight (2 Cor 5:7): "Abraham is justified not because he believes this or that promise of God but because he stands ready to believe *any* promise of God, no matter how violently it may contradict the judgments of his own prudential reason and common sense. Abraham's faith is not so much an act (e.g., believing that Sarah will become pregnant in spite of her advanced years) as a disposition (e.g., believing that whatever God promises, however startling, he is able to perform)."[30]

This emphasis on faith as believing in defiance of reason or common sense demonstrates that faith trusts however discouraging its circumstances. When commenting on Gen 15:6 in 1536, Luther noted that "in this passage no mention is made of any preparation for grace, of any faith formed through works, or of any preceding disposition. This, however, is mentioned: Abraham was in the midst of sins, doubts, and fears, and was exceedingly troubled in spirit" (*LW* 3:20–21). And as Calvin was to say, again of Rom 4:20, "Our circumstances are all in opposition to the promises of God. . . . What then are we to do? We must close our eyes, disregard ourselves and all things connected with us, so that nothing may hinder or prevent us from believing that God is true" (*Comm. Rom.* 4:20, *CNTC* 8:99).

That faith trusts divine promises in this way, in spite of experiences that appear to contradict them, leads to an emphasis on the certainty of faith or assurance. Sin and death may lead people to doubt salvation, but faith tells those who believe that they are justified. It produces confidence that God is not wrathful in attitude toward them but benevolent. This assurance stands in sharp contrast to the insistence of the Reformers' opponents that it is only possible to be certain that God will justify the elect but not to be certain whether one numbers among them (see 5.2).

For the Reformers' opponents, such uncertainty expressed appropriate humility about how much one had grown in justice. By contrast, the Reformers viewed it as indicative of a failure to treat the promises of God contained in Scripture as reliable. Paul's asserts that the Spirit enables believers as children of God and heirs of a divine inheritance to cry "Abba! Father!" (Rom 8:15–17; Gal 4:6–7). Yet how can such a cry be consistent with uncertainty about justification? "For whoever doubts the grace of God toward him this way must necessarily doubt the promises of God and therefore the will of God, as well as the birth, suffering, death, and resurrection of Christ. There is no greater blasphemy against God than to deny

---

30. David C. Steinmetz, "Abraham and the Reformation," in *Luther in Context*, 2nd ed. (Grand Rapids: Baker, 2002), 41.

the promises of God and God Himself, Christ, etc."[31] The relevance of this strong emphasis on trust and assurance to the struggles of the sixteenth century was clear. Those who staked all on the truth of the evangelical gospel in defiance of the power and prestige of the Catholic Church were trusting God as Abraham had trusted God.

Yet having insisted both that justifying faith has the character of trust, and that such faith is inherently active, the Reformers had to explain the relationship between faith and works. If faith justifies and faith is active, might there remain a causal role for works in justification precisely when works express trust? In his *Commentary on Romans* (1540), Melanchthon addresses this directly: "Although a work by a believer has its praise, is necessary obedience, and becomes righteousness, it nevertheless does not possess worth so that a person may have remission of sins on account of the work itself and be righteous, that is, accepted to eternal life before God. It is necessary that a person first have forgiveness of sins and justification. Afterward, the obedience which has been begun is found pleasing, and is worship of God."[32]

This embodies what was to become the principal Protestant method of relating faith and works. Works are inseparable from faith, and their absence demonstrates the absence of justification, but nevertheless works are not an effective cause of justification. As Luther puts it in the *Preface to Romans* (1522), although works do not justify, "good works emerge from faith itself. . . . [I]t is impossible to separate works from faith, quite as impossible as to separate heat and light from fire" (*LW* 35:369–71). Elsewhere he uses organic images, emphasizing works as the fruit of faith and ubiquitously quoting Matt 7:17, "every good tree bears good fruit." When Paul speaks of "faith working through love" (Gal 5:6), he is not indicating the need for faith to be formed by love in order to justify. Instead "he attributes the working itself to faith rather than to love. . . . He makes love the tool through which faith works" (*LW* 27:29).

The Reformers thus both place considerable emphasis upon what faith does and insist that this activity is not in any sense a cause of justification. It is not any human quality inherent to faith that enables it to justify. Faith is not a virtue or a work that deserves God's approval. What makes faith justifying is instead its christological focus. Bullinger expresses this clearly in the *Second Helvetic Confession* (1566), "because faith receives Christ our righteousness and attributes everything

---

31. *LW* 26:385. In this quotation, Luther has so welded together faith as trust in God's promises and faith as assent to the historical truth of the gospel that to doubt the promises is also to doubt the historical truth.

32. Melanchthon, *Commentary on Romans*, 109.

to the grace of God in Christ, on that account justification is attributed to faith, chiefly because of Christ and not therefore because it is our work."[33] As in the *Apology of the Augsburg Confession* (1530), faith can sometimes be described as "the very righteousness by which we are reckoned righteous before God,"[34] but this is always and only because it receives Christ and his saving benefits. The faith of Abraham prefigures the faith of those "who believe in him who raised Jesus our Lord from the dead, who was handed over to death for our trespasses and was raised for our justification" (Rom 4:24–25).

Since faith is not a human work or virtue, justification requires a looking away from the self and outside of the self to Christ alone. The righteousness reckoned to believers (Rom 4:3; Gal 3:6; Gen 15:6) is an alien righteousness that is not the believer's own.[35] This reckoning is frequently described using the noun "imputation," and it is in understanding how this takes place that differences among the Reformers do begin to emerge. Some, like Luther and Calvin, characteristically argue that faith unites the believer with Christ and that in the context of this union, the righteousness of Christ is given directly to the believer. In contrast, Melanchthon characteristically does not stress union with Christ in explaining imputation but instead offers a relational account. The superabundant righteousness of Christ's life and saving death pleads effectively for sinners before God the Father, where it is set over and against divine wrath against sin. As we shall see in chapters 10–14, this difference is of great exegetical and theological significance. Nevertheless, the Reformers do all insist with complete unanimity that it is the receiving by faith of an alien righteousness from outside of themselves that brings those who believe into right standing before God.

As a result of this christological focus on their understanding of faith, the Reformers are profoundly conscious of the ecclesial context of justification. If Protestant interpreters in later eras sometimes came to provide rather individualistic accounts of Paul's soteriology, this is not true of the Reformers. Since faith justifies because it trusts God's promises and appropriates Christ and his saving benefits, then justification by faith cannot be understood other than in the context

33. Arthur C. Cochrane, ed., *Reformed Confessions of the Sixteenth Century* (Louisville: Westminster John Knox, 2003), 256.

34. "Apology of the Augsburg Confession," in *The Book of Concord: The Confessions of the Evangelical Lutheran Church*, ed. Robert Kolb and Timothy J. Wengert (Minneapolis: Fortress, 2000), para. 86.

35. On the alien nature of the righteousness received through faith, see Berndt Hamm, "What Was the Reformation Doctrine of Justification?," in *The Reformation of Faith in the Context of Late Medieval Theology and Piety: Essays by Berndt Hamm*, ed. Robert J. Bast (Leiden: Brill, 2004), 179–216.

of the church as Christ's body. And once justification is understood in an ecclesial context then it is also related to the sacraments. Luther notes of Christ that we "rely upon his righteousness, life, and blessedness. And through the interchange of his blessings and our misfortunes, we become one loaf, one bread, one body, one drink, and have all things in common. O this is a great sacrament, says St. Paul, that Christ and the church are one flesh and bone."[36] To receive Christ in justification by faith is necessarily also to become one body with all believers and for this communion with Christ and his church to be expressed through baptism and the Lord's Supper.

36. *LW* 35:58. The tract from which the quotation comes is *The Blessed Sacrament of the Holy and True Body of Christ, and the Brotherhoods* (1519).

CHAPTER EIGHT

Setting the Record Straight: The Reformers' Contributions to the New Perspective on Paul

N ow that we have explored the content of the Reformers' Pauline exegetical grammar, we can compare their interpretations to those characteristic of the New Perspective on Paul (NPP).[1] For several decades any comparisons made between the two were almost always negative about the Reformers' exegetical legacy. NPP interpreters regarded this legacy as one to escape from (see 1.1). However, in recent years, a more nuanced approach has begun to develop in which the Reformers' legacy can be evaluated in more complex ways, avoiding either uncritical reverence or straightforward rejection based upon false assumptions about their views.[2]

8.1. The NPP and the Reformers: Charting a More Complex Relationship

In attempting a more nuanced assessment, it is important to identify accurately the different elements in the relationship between the Reformers' Pauline exegesis

---

1. I have not used the analogy of an exegetical grammar in relation to the NPP. The analogy seemed less apt than in relation to either the Reformers or Augustine because the unity of the NPP operates across a much narrower range of exegetical issues. On the question of the nature of Second Temple Judaism and Paul's relationship to it, the impact of the NPP has run very deep. It is no longer possible credibly to portray Judaism as a religion of works-righteousness. Yet in other respects, what has emerged is a variety of newer perspectives, which might more appropriately be pictured as a loose constellation of related interpretations of Paul. Kent L. Yinger, *The New Perspective on Paul* (Eugene, OR: Wipf & Stock, 2011), 27–38, entitles a chapter, "The NPP Spreads and Mutates: Varied Forms of the NPP."

2. See, for example, *Reformation Readings of Paul: Explorations in History and Exegesis*, ed. Michael Allen and Jonathan A. Linebaugh (Downers Grove, IL: InterVarsity Press, 2015).

and that of the NPP. To achieve this, we will now explore and demonstrate in more detail the four key claims made at the outset of this part of the book (see 3.1):

1. There are important respects in which NPP interpretations in fact continue to depend in important ways on exegetical positions developed by the Reformers.
2. NPP interpreters in varying ways intensify some aspects of the Reformers' Pauline interpretation at the expense of others.
3. NPP interpreters sometimes simply make false assumptions about the Reformers' Pauline exegesis.
4. There are nevertheless some crucial areas where the NPP is truly in conflict with the Reformers' exegetical legacy.

This chapter will be devoted to the first two of these claims, with chapter 9 focused on the third and the fourth.

Exploring and demonstrating these claims matters because it is only through accurately understanding the relationship between the NPP and the Reformers' Pauline exegesis that it is possible to stage a discussion of what the Reformers have to offer for Pauline interpretation today. For the different criticisms of the Reformers' Pauline exegesis offered from within NPP scholarship were mutually reinforcing and together produced the general dismissal of their legacy. It is by demonstrating that these criticisms present much too simplistic a picture of the relationship between the Reformers' exegesis and the NPP that space can be cleared for a more nuanced approach to the Reformers' exegetical legacy. Given the usual perception of the relationship between the Reformers' exegetical legacy and the NPP as an antithetical one, the NPP itself turns out to be surprisingly close to that legacy in some significant ways.

8.2. Continued Dependence: Pauline Anthropology

The continued influence of exegetical positions developed by the Reformers upon contemporary interpreters is seen nowhere more clearly than in the treatment of Paul's anthropology, especially his use of the term "the flesh" (*sarx*) and its relationship to "sin" (*hamartia*). As we have seen (6.3), the Reformers strongly insist that "the flesh" refers not to part of a human being but to the whole person as he or she stands in opposition to God through sin: "*flesh* should be understood of whatever is in man without the Holy Spirit."[3] The term "the flesh" therefore does not represent

---

3. Philip Melanchthon, *Commentary on Romans*, trans. Fred Kramer (Saint Louis: Concordia, 1992), 170.

the lower component of anthropological hierarchies, either within the soul or between the soul and the body. It is striking that disagreements in recent scholarship about what Paul means by "the flesh" often take place *within* this fundamental understanding developed by the Reformers, an understanding that seems uncontroversial to many contemporary scholars but was not so in the sixteenth century and that marked a rejection of much medieval exegesis of the term.

In his influential 1988 monograph on Galatians, *Obeying the Truth*, John Barclay offers an analysis of "the flesh" in line with the concerns of the then recently emerged NPP. In doing so, Barclay takes issue with the previously dominant understanding of the term offered by Rudolf Bultmann. Barclay objects to Bultmann's emphasis on the flesh as that which is visible and outward, objects to Bultmann's focus on the transformed self-understanding of the individual as central in soteriology, and objects to Bultmann's commitment to defining the flesh in a way that reflects a Reformation critique of works-righteousness.[4] In its place, Barclay offers an understanding of Paul's term that locates its meaning within an apocalyptic dualism. Living according to the flesh is characteristic of human existence under the present evil age in contrast to the new age inaugurated by the death and resurrection of Jesus: "the flesh" is "what is merely human, in contrast to the divine activity displayed on the cross and in the gift of the Spirit."[5]

Paul includes the Jewish tradition to which he had formerly been devoted within the realm of what is merely human. Yet he makes this radical move because the Jewish tradition now belongs on the previous side of the turn of the ages effected by the coming of the Messiah rather than because of any critique of works-righteousness. Yet while Barclay can critically note that "Bultmann's interpretation drew on the Augustinian and Lutheran emphasis on man's sinful self-reliance (*cor incurvatum in se*)," he also notes the implication of his own position that "Paul is not concerned here with a 'fleshly' part of each individual (his physical being or his 'lower nature') but with the influence of an 'era' and its human traditions and assumptions."[6] This can be compared to Luther's assertion that "by flesh the

---

4. John M. G. Barclay, *Obeying the Truth: Paul's Ethics in Galatians* (Edinburgh: T&T Clark, 1988), 197–98. Without retreating from his earlier criticisms, Barclay has now offered an evaluation of Bultmann's anthropology that pays more attention to what he considers to be its strengths. See John M. G. Barclay, "Humanity under Faith," in *Beyond Bultmann: Reckoning a New Testament Theology*, ed. Bruce W. Longenecker and Mikeal C. Parsons (Waco, TX: Baylor University Press, 2014), 79–100. However, Barclay has also continued to assert and elaborate the interpretation of "the flesh" offered in *Obeying the Truth*. See Barclay, *Paul and the Gift* (Grand Rapids: Eerdmans, 2015), 426–27: "'the flesh' represents the environment of all human agency untransformed by the Spirit.... [E]verything is either beholden to God-in-Christ or beholden to human tradition (1:10–11), either 'new creation' or *passé* cosmos (6:14–15), either Spirit or flesh (3:3)."

5. Barclay, *Obeying the Truth*, 206.

6. Barclay, *Obeying the Truth*, 195, 213.

whole man is meant.... [T]he inward and the outward man, or the new man and the old, are not distinguished according to the difference between soul and body but according to their dispositions" (*LW* 27:367).

There are some important differences between what these two statements affirm about the nature of "the flesh," notably between Luther's emphasis on the flesh as the total disposition of the unredeemed person and Barclay's broader focus on an era and its traditions (although a contrast between Paul's gospel and human traditions and assumptions is scarcely antithetical to Luther's theology more broadly). However, the two are identical in what they deny. Even as Barclay parts company with the way in which Bultmann developed and intensified the Reformers' attitude toward works, his own alternative proposal ultimately relies on the Reformers' rejection of anthropological hierarchy as the appropriate context within which to understand Paul's statements about the flesh.

Barclay is far from alone in this respect. N. T. Wright asserts that Paul's anthropological terms "sometimes appear to designate different 'parts' of a human being, but, as many have pointed out, it is better to see them as each encoding a particular way of looking at the human being *as a whole* but *from one particular angle*."[7] The significant point is not that there are no differences in detail between the positions of these contemporary scholars and those of the Reformers but rather that a commonplace conclusion in contemporary scholarship (note Wright's phrase "as many have pointed out") is an expression of the same exegetical conclusions as those reached by the Reformers.

In developing his view of "the flesh," Barclay was influenced by Ernst Käsemann, who had placed such terms in an apocalyptic context. Käsemann did so as part of his reaction against Bultmann's focus on the individual, reasserting the significance of the cosmic level of Paul's thought (see 2.6). Paul's pitting of the flesh against the Spirit in Gal 5:16–17 speaks in relation to the human being of "that reality, which, as the power either of the heavenly or the earthly, determines him from outside, takes possession of him and thereby decides into which of the two dualistically opposed spheres he is to be integrated."[8] Christ is God's invasion of the present evil age in order to liberate humanity and to bring new creation, with the cross as an act of cosmic warfare. The bondage from which Christ liberates human beings is so all-encompassing that even their acts of piety are no more than aspects of this bondage.

It is very clear that Käsemann, and those like Barclay who came after him, are saying something significantly different from the Reformers, who do not under-

---

7. N. T. Wright, *Paul and the Faithfulness of God* (Minneapolis: Fortress, 2013), 1:491.

8. Ernst Käsemann, "On the Subject of Primitive Christian Apocalyptic," in *New Testament Questions of Today* (London: SCM, 1969), 136.

stand the terms "sin" and "the flesh" as themselves denoting external forces but rather understand them as forces in human beings. Nevertheless, the Reformers do understand the corruption and human failure involved in sin as total, and as extending even to piety, and they do regard the condition of the human being as one of captivity. Luther for one goes even further and does not hesitate to speak of the present age as evil (Gal 1:4), because "whatever is in this age is subject to the evil of the devil, who rules the entire world" (*LW* 26:39). Luther's sense of the profound nature of this evil is one of the characteristic features of his theology that led him to reject the view that human beings can prepare themselves for grace. For Luther, the freedom given in creation has been so wholly lost through sin that what is necessary is the radically new beginning from outside that he believes is granted through union with Christ and the receipt of his alien righteousness. It is this deep sense of the captivity of human beings to sin that grants Luther's theology its own apocalyptic dimension (see 2.6).

Yet despite the existence of differences between the apocalyptic patterns of thought in Luther and Käsemann (who as a Lutheran theologian was scarcely unfamiliar with Luther), the latter is inconceivable without the former. This point can be brought into sharp relief by comparing Luther's willingness to speak of the reign of the devil with the patristic interpretations of Gal 1:4 (Christ "gave himself for our sins to set us free from the present evil age") followed by the medieval Western church. Faced with dualist heresies that posit two creators, these interpretations avoid any hint that nature is evil and insist that the present age is evil because it is populated by people who choose to commit evil actions. Augustine comments that "the present world is understood to be evil because of the evil people who live in it, just as we also say that a house is evil because of the evil people who live in it."[9]

In contrast, Luther's thoroughgoing insistence on humanity's bondage to sin and the reign of the devil establishes new trajectories in the history of interpretation.[10] Thus, while in recent discussion of Paul's anthropology there is a sharp rejection of Bultmann's particular way of appropriating Reformation insights, some of the most prominent alternative proposals rely just as heavily on exegetical positions first developed by the Reformers. However significant the other differences between the Reformers' exegesis and that of dominant voices within contemporary scholarship, here the Reformers' influence continues even when it is not fully recognized.

---

9. Augustine, *Augustine's Commentary on Galatians: Introduction, Text, Translation, and Notes*, trans. Eric A. Plumer (Oxford: Oxford University Press, 2003), 129 (3.3).

10. On the reception history of Gal 1:4, see John K. Riches, *Galatians through the Centuries* (Oxford: Blackwell, 2008), 77–82.

8.3. Intensification: The Apocalyptic Paul

While Käsemann's assertion of an apocalyptic dimension in Paul's theology has been very widely accepted in recent scholarship, much more controversial has been the intensification of his ideas in the work of J. Louis Martyn and others (see 2.6). This intensification has led to the emergence of the "apocalyptic Paul," a distinctive approach to interpreting the apostle in which the term "apocalyptic" is understood to capture the essential nature of his theology.[11] This stands in contrast to the approach of other interpreters who accept that Paul's theology is apocalyptic in important respects but who prefer the term "covenantal" as a description of its essential nature.

For Martyn, Paul's argument in Galatians excludes continuity between the history of Israel and what God has done in Christ: "Paul says [Gal 3:14] that the blessing of Abraham has *come* to the Gentiles (*genētai eis*), not that the Gentiles have been granted the possibility of entering the blessed family of Abraham. . . . the gospel is about the divine invasion of the cosmos (theology), not about human movement into blessedness (religion)."[12] God's invasive (apocalyptic) act of new creation cuts across all that has gone before so that, although God is now enacting through Christ the covenant made with Abraham, this invasive act cannot be described as "covenantal" as if it constitutes the climactic episode within an unfolding story. Rather, Paul speaks of a series of apocalyptic antinomies or contrasts previously characteristic of the fundamental structures of the cosmos but now abolished through the death of Christ, prominent among them the contrast between circumcision and uncircumcision.[13]

Nor should any emphasis be placed on what human beings do to respond to the gospel. Justification (for which Martyn prefers the term "rectification") is "no more God's response to human faith in Christ than it is God's response to human observance of the law. God's rectification is not God's response at all. It is the *first* move; it is God's initiative, carried out by him in Christ's faithful death."[14] In order to avoid any possibility of misconstruing justifying faith as a human possibility, Martyn is insistent that Paul speaks of faith primarily in relation to Christ's faithful

---

11. For discussion of the movement, see Jamie Davies, *The Apocalyptic Paul*, Cascade Library of Pauline Studies (Eugene, OR: Cascade, 2022).

12. J. Louis Martyn, *Galatians*, AB 33A (New York: Doubleday, 1997), 349. Martyn is prepared to allow that Paul is more circumspect in Romans about the relationship between Israel and the gospel.

13. J. Louis Martyn, "Apocalyptic Antinomies," in *Theological Issues in the Letters of Paul* (Edinburgh: T&T Clark, 1997), 111–24.

14. Martyn, *Galatians*, 271, commenting on Gal 2:16.

obedience. Paul's disputed genitive phrases (*pistis Christou*, Rom 3:22, 26; Gal 2:16 [×2], 20; 3:22; Phil 3:9), usually translated in English Bibles as if it is an objective genitive construction, "faith in Christ," is in fact a subjective genitive construction that should be translated as the "faithfulness of Christ."[15] Paul still speaks clearly of the significance of human faith in justification but it is to be understood as a participation in the faithfulness of Christ.

Martyn pays no direct attention to the exegesis of the Reformers, but it is not difficult to discern a reflection (via the theology of Karl Barth) of their own critique of human religiosity and their own emphasis on the soteriological priority of divine initiative.[16] Yet this element has become so highly developed as to limit what can be said on the basis of Paul's texts concerning the Reformers' equally emphatic emphasis on the active nature of human faith and its crucial role in appropriating Christ and his saving benefits. It is one thing to insist with the Reformers on the gifted nature of human faith but quite another so to fear any compromise of divine initiative as to be unable to say much concerning the nature of the gift.[17]

Thus, the very intensification of one motif or interpretative element leads to the diminution of another out of a sense of the paramount importance of preserving the former in its purest possible form. Here is an example of what John Barclay, drawing on the work of the literary critic Kenneth Burke, terms the "perfecting" of a concept. It is pushed to "an end of the line extreme, developing its meaning to the maximum, exploiting the concept to its fullest possible extent . . . much like we might speak of a terrible concatenation of events as a 'perfect storm' or a complex and extremely inconvenient obstacle as a 'perfect nuisance.'"[18]

An even stronger example of this *intensification* of divine initiative by an apocalyptic interpreter of Paul can be found in the work of Douglas Campbell. Campbell rejects a model of Paul's soteriology that he terms "Justification Theory" in favor of his own emphasis on the liberating divine initiative in Christ that breaks human bondage to sin.[19] "Justification Theory" (which is Campbell's own label for trajecto-

---

15. In principle, parallel issues can arise in English. The sentence "Robert did it for the love of Mary" could mean either that Robert performed the action concerned because of Mary's love for him (subjective genitive) or his love for Mary (objective genitive).

16. Barclay, *Paul and the Gift*, 147–50, traces the influence upon Martyn of both Barth and Käsemann.

17. Martyn, *Galatians*, 275–77, does not ignore human faith or deny its importance but is left with little to say about faith *exegetically* except to deny its human origin.

18. John M. G. Barclay, "Pure Grace? Paul's Distinctive Jewish Theology of Gift," *ST* 68 (2014): 5. For a fuller discussion of "perfecting" a concept, see Barclay, *Paul and the Gift*, 66–78.

19. Barclay, *Paul and the Gift*, 171–73, suggests that Campbell is unique in insisting on all six of the possible perfections of the concept of grace he identifies.

ries in Pauline interpretation that he regards as erroneous, not a theory developed or argued for by other scholars) is focused on the individual and takes a conditional approach to salvation while holding a prospective epistemology (a prior human awareness of sin prompts repentance and faith). In contrast Campbell focuses on the corporate level of Paul's thought and takes an unconditional approach to salvation while holding a retrospective epistemology (the divine gift of faith reveals the depth of human bondage to sin). The characteristic features of Justification Theory represent a catastrophic misinterpretation of Paul, in contrast to the healthy interpretative pathway represented by the characteristic features of Campbell's apocalyptic approach. Tension is inevitable between Justification Theory and Campbell's alternative, which emphasizes "divine initiative over against human choice and couples that with a liberative and transformational view of salvation."[20]

Campbell does pay considerable attention to the Reformers in his work but remains puzzled by their failure entirely to fit the pattern of his own strong contrasts. From Campbell's perspective, they appear on both sides of the great divide that he has constructed. Among the Reformers, only Melanchthon is consistent, and misguidedly so, appearing on the wrong side of all of Campbell's contrasts.[21] Campbell identifies Luther as the ultimate source of the errors of Justification Theory, arguing that Luther misconstrues important aspects of what Paul says about God's response to the failure of humanity to obey God's commands. Luther hears God respond with a more generous offer of salvation in which the punishment due to sinners is redirected onto Christ in his death, and the more manageable condition of faith (an act of belief) replaces the requirement for complete obedience. However, Luther is also contradictory, undoing his own interpretation of Paul through his strong emphasis on human depravity and bondage to sin.[22] Similarly, Calvin falls into the same errors but fails to notice that his own "commitments to depravity, to election, and to Christian regeneration by the Spirit" stand in severe tension with them.[23]

On Campbell's account, any element of conditionality or hint of human choice can lead only to a radical misunderstanding of Paul's teaching. All elements in the thought of Paul and his interpreters that could entail the risk of such contra-

---

20. Douglas A. Campbell, *The Deliverance of God: An Apocalyptic Rereading of Justification in Paul* (Grand Rapids: Eerdmans, 2009), 4.

21. Campbell, *Deliverance of God*, 258–60.

22. Campbell, *Deliverance of God*, 250–58, 264–70. For a defense of Luther's consistency in response to Campbell, see Graham Tomlin, "Luther and the Deliverance of God," in *Beyond Old and New Perspectives on Paul: Reflections on the Work of Douglas Campbell*, ed. Chris Tilling (Eugene, OR: Wipf & Stock, 2014), 23–33.

23. Campbell, *Deliverance of God*, 261–64, 270–76.

diction must be eliminated. In order to achieve this, Campbell posits the unlikely construal of Rom 1:18–3:20 largely as a "speech-in-character" representing not Paul's own position but that of an opponent whose arguments he is attempting to demolish. In presenting his view, Campbell feels he is rescuing the best insights of the Reformers from their own inconsistencies: "the solution that I am aiming toward is deeply Protestant if not Lutheran."[24]

Yet what is happening is not that Luther and Calvin are reading Paul in a grossly inconsistent manner. Instead, they simply do not read Paul in the conditional, prospective, and individualistic manner that Campbell suggests. Indeed, in many respects, their insistence on faith as gift, and on grace in opposition to works, is intended to oppose many of the soteriological emphases to which Campbell objects. He simply misunderstands important elements of their exegesis of Paul's texts. Campbell's intensification or perfection of divine initiative in salvation leaves him unable to hear any different notes in Paul, or in the Reformers' exegesis of Paul, as anything other than its contradiction. When the insights of the Reformers are intensified or perfected in such a manner, it is a matter of judgment as regards whether their interpretations of Paul are being reflected or rejected or in some measure both.

8.4. Intensification: The Covenantal Paul

In contrast to the apocalyptic Paul, N. T. Wright instead locates the apocalyptic dimension of the apostle's thought within the overarching category of covenant and insists that Paul understood himself as an actor within a single continuous story stretching forward from the creation of the world and the call of Abraham.[25] God entered into a covenant with Abraham's family to bless the world through that family, and what God has done in Christ is understood by Paul within that story. The people of Israel departed from their covenant obligations and ended up in exile, with even those Jews later resident in the land of Israel reminded by Roman occupation that the exile was not over. It continued in the sense that disobedience still estranged Israel from God and provided a barrier to blessing.

Yet rather than such failure providing the last word in Israel's story, there has been a surprising and definitive new plot twist. Through Messiah Jesus, the covenant has been fulfilled, the curse of continuing exile broken, and the family of

---

24. Campbell, *Deliverance of God*, 934.

25. See Wright, *Paul and the Faithfulness of God*, 1:114–39. As Yinger, *New Perspective on Paul*, 27, comments, Wright's version of the NPP is characterized by the setting of Paul's theology "within the larger biblical story (narrative) of God's work with Israel."

Abraham radically redefined so that the gentiles are included. Yet because Messiah Jesus has accomplished these things as Israel's representative, it remains the case that God will save the world through, and only through, Israel. In contrast to the claims of Martyn, Galatians is therefore about *"the definition of the community* as the people who are already declared to be in the right, declared to be part of God's single family, the true children of Abraham." It is the theme of covenant that "forms the essential and non-negotiable context within which the writings of Paul (especially Romans and Galatians, where Abraham plays such a central role, and Romans and 1 Corinthians 15, where Adam plays such a central role) demand to be read."[26]

As he expounds his argument, Wright pays some attention to the relationship between his own exegesis and that of the Reformers, identifying contemporary rejection of his own position as a kind of hangover from earlier Protestant backward projections of works-righteousness onto Second Temple Judaism:

> Part of the protestant retrojection has been the idea of *a necessary break in the narrative*. Instead of the "great church" rumbling along, gathering all kinds of accumulated baggage and heresy, and insisting that everyone simply go along with it, we have the Reformers (with all the energy and breezy arrogance of the Renaissance's "new learning and new ignorance") claiming to represent a new moment, a radical discontinuity, a clean break. That vision, of the previous dark narrative and the new bright intervention, is then played out in protestant visions of individual conversion; but, more particularly, in the corporate self-awareness of a protestant church history which disclaimed continuity with its immediate past and claimed, instead, a distant continuity with much earlier periods and their texts, namely the Bible and the Fathers.[27]

Wright's statements both reflect and profoundly misunderstand the significance of the Reformers for the current discussion of continuity or discontinuity between Paul's gospel and the story of Israel. In relation to the individual, the Reformers certainly do hear in Paul's texts a radical discontinuity. The depth of human depravity does indeed mean that only a radically new beginning in conversion can grant life through the righteousness of Christ. Yet at the corporate level, there can be no "clean break" for the Reformers in the sense that Wright alleges. They are as concerned as he is to assert a single divine plan to which God has been consistently faithful. This emphasis on continuity is more easily visible

---

26. Wright, *Paul and the Faithfulness of God*, 2:795, 971.
27. Wright, *Paul and the Faithfulness of God*, 1:141.

in a Reformed hermeneutic that emphasizes the continuing relevance of the law for Christian living and places considerable theological weight upon the category of covenant.[28] As already noted (see 3.2), Calvin believed that even in the worst times, God had maintained the covenant and a living church through the preservation of baptism and other vestiges of true catholicity.[29]

Yet even a Lutheran hermeneutic of law and gospel does not deny such continuity but instead configures it in a dialectical manner, discerning tension between divine demand and divine promise in both Old and New Testaments rather than a more straightforward progression between two eras of salvation history (see 6.4). Luther asserted that "it is impossible for the Church to err, even in the smallest article" (*LW* 33:85), something that, once he was persuaded that the Roman church was in error, could only and inexorably lead to the conclusion that it was not the true church. His assertion is not that of someone who regards continuity as a dangerous denial of grace but rather, as he goes on to explain, that of someone convinced that God's people persist throughout history as a faithful remnant sustained by divine grace. What is disputed is the true identity of the people of God and the form of its survival, not the persistence of that people. In the context of sinful humanity, the persistence of the church is a fragile but miraculous testimony to a continuity of divine purpose that "typically cuts against the grain of human history and is independent of human processes of development or descent."[30]

None of this removes other areas of tension between Wright's Pauline exegesis and that of the Reformers. They profoundly disagree over the meaning of the phrase "works of the law," the construal of justification, and Wright's denial that Abraham and his family stand among the ungodly (Rom 4:5).[31] Yet none of this concerns the issue of continuity at the corporate level of the people of God. Here Wright's deep concern with the importance of covenant for understanding Paul mirrors and

---

28. Wright, *Paul and the Faithfulness of God*, 1:499, does later identify the Reformed tradition with acceptance of a single continuous divine plan but without really explaining how this is consistent with his earlier identification of all Protestant traditions with a necessary break in the narrative.

29. Diarmaid McCulloch, "Calvin: Fifth Latin Doctor of the Church?," in *Calvin and His Influence 1509–2009*, ed. Irena Backus and Philip Benedict (Oxford: Oxford University Press, 2011), 37–38.

30. John M. G. Barclay, review of *Paul and the Faithfulness of God*, by N. T. Wright, *SJT* 68 (2015): 238. Barclay, *Paul and the Gift*, 413: "The relation of past human history is not that of the partial to the complete, or the beginning to the end; it is the relation of potential to actual, anticipated to realized, frustrated to enacted. . . . [T]he Christ-gift is both entirely *congruous* with the promise of God and wholly *incongruous* with the prior conditions of human (including Israelite) history."

31. Wright, *Paul and the Faithfulness of God*, 2:1004.

intensifies the same emphasis in the exegesis of Calvin. It is certainly true that in exegesis of texts where Paul comments on the significance of Abraham in relation to justification by faith (Rom 4, Gal 3), Wright emphasizes covenant to the exclusion of other themes in a way that Calvin does not. It is certainly also true that there are important differences in the accounts of justification offered and that Wright has been much criticized on this basis from within the Reformed tradition.[32]

However, there is also now at least one scholarly monograph treating Wright's account of justification as an evolution within the Reformed tradition. Wright is in fundamental continuity with Calvin not only in asserting that justification is forensic but also that it is received through union with Christ: "the Judge rules favorably for believers who are brought into union with Christ by faith."[33] It might also be added that for all the exegetical differences in handling Paul's use of the figure of Abraham, and therefore also in the nature of justification, both Wright and Calvin strongly connect Paul's covenantal language with familial imagery.[34] Wright prefers the rhetorical strategy of placing his insights in contrast to the work of earlier interpreters,[35] especially the Reformers, but this represents only part of the reality of the relationship between his work and the Reformed tradition. Wright's elimination from his Pauline exegesis of some very significant aspects of how that tradition typically interprets Paul in fact results from his dramatic intensification of that same tradition's emphasis on covenant as an important Pauline theme.

32. See especially, John Piper, *The Future of Justification: A Response to N. T. Wright* (Wheaton, IL: Crossway, 2007).

33. Jonathan Huggins, *Living Justification: A Historical-Theological Study of the Reformed Doctrine of Justification in the Writings of John Calvin, Jonathan Edwards, and N. T. Wright* (Eugene, OR: Wipf & Stock, 2013), 216.

34. See Stephen J. Chester, "Faith and Family: Calvin, the Figure of Abraham, and the New Perspective on Paul," in *Reformatorische Paulusauslegungen*, ed. Stefan Krauter and Manuel Nägele (Tübingen: Mohr Siebeck, 2023), 479–502.

35. In his endorsement of Huggins's monograph, Wright describes his discussion alongside Calvin and Jonathan Edwards as "an alarming honor."

CHAPTER NINE

Setting the Record Straight: The Reformers and the New Perspective on Paul in Tension

U nsurprisingly, two areas of criticism of the Reformers' Pauline interpretation that have been especially significant in its recent evaluation are their perceived views about (1) the introspective conscience and (2) the works of the law. The connection drawn by Stendahl between the Reformers and portrayals of Paul struggling with his inability to obey the law prior to his Damascus Road experience (see 2.4) fed directly into later New Perspective on Paul (NPP) scholarship. For example, N. T. Wright writes that "the standard assumption, since Augustine at least, and especially since Luther, was that Paul had been laboring under the problem of a guilty conscience, aware of his own inability to meet the inexorable demands of the Law, and unable to find peace with his maker."[1] On this view, experiences of a guilty conscience in subsequent Christian history, like that of Luther, have been erroneously projected back onto Paul.

Similarly, it has been widely perceived within NPP scholarship that the Reformers' interpretation of Paul's rejection of justification by works of the law as aimed against works-righteousness (see 2.4) reflects an anachronistic backward projection by the Reformers of the controversies of their own time and place. James Dunn writes that "Martin Luther understood Paul's reaction against Judaism in light of his own reaction against medieval Catholicism. The degeneracy of a Catholicism that offered forgiveness of sins by the buying of indulgences mirrored for Luther the degeneracy of a Judaism that taught justification by works."[2]

---

1. N. T. Wright, *Paul and the Faithfulness of God* (Minneapolis: Fortress, 2013), 2:747–48.

2. James D. G. Dunn, "New Perspective View," in *Justification: Five Views*, ed. James K. Beilby and Paul R. Eddy (Downers Grove, IL: InterVarsity Press, 2011), 179–80.

9.1. The NPP and the Reformers: Untangling the Key Issues

That these two major areas of criticism have indeed been mutually reinforcing can be illustrated by the reception of the work of forerunners of the NPP like Stendahl (see 2.3). His views and those of others like him were decidedly those of a minority until E. P. Sanders's reevaluation of Second Temple Judaism made it appear unlikely that Paul's critique of the works of the law was a rejection of works-righteousness. In particular, Sanders's reinterpretation of Judaism appeared to validate Stendahl's critique of the introspective conscience. For if Judaism emphasized grace, and works-righteousness was alien to it, then how could a deeply committed Pharisee like Paul have been struggling with guilt stemming from his inability to obey the law? Stendahl must have been correct to reject this idea and correct to identify its error with interpretations of Paul that equate the works of the law with Jewish works-righteousness.

The issue of whether these two aspects of the Reformers' exegetical legacy are in fact connected in this way is therefore a significant one. If they are not, and important aspects of the Reformers' characteristic positions have simply been misunderstood, then the relationship between their exegetical legacy and the NPP will need to be rethought. This does not mean that the Pauline interpretation of the Reformers is correct in all respects. The NPP legitimately raises serious objections to their view of the relationship between Paul's gospel and Judaism. Indeed, it would be surprising if sixteenth-century interpreters, working before the development of the tools of historical-critical scholarship, were able to offer accounts of Second Temple Judaism fully credible today. Yet any accurate view of the Reformers' views about the conscience and about the works of the law results in a more complicated picture than NPP scholarship has been prepared to allow. It also results in the identification of strengths in the Reformers' exegesis of Paul that NPP scholarship has overlooked.

9.2. Erroneous Contrast: The Introspective Conscience

Stendahl's use of the theme of Paul's conscience to propose a break with the Reformers' exegetical legacy rests upon historical inaccuracy. Perhaps somewhat ironically, this inaccuracy is not primarily a matter of poor exegesis. What Paul says about his life before the Damascus Road, in both Phil 3:6 ("as to righteousness under the law, blameless") and Gal 1:14 ("I advanced in Judaism beyond many among my people of the same age"), is indeed difficult to square with the notion that he struggled with a guilty conscience. Stendahl makes appropriate use of Paul's texts to correct a misinterpretation.

The problem is that Stendahl's instincts about the source of that misinterpretation were significantly off target. Stendahl felt that "Luther was wrong for importing Augustine's theology and his own existential concerns into the theology of Paul."[3] Yet, as we have seen (6.5), Luther and other Reformers interpret the same texts in substantially the same way as Stendahl. They, too, think that prior to his Damascus Road experience Paul's conscience was robust. They also identify the phrase "works of the law" not with the revelation of sin but instead with the kind of false confidence that someone is fulfilling the law possessed by the preconversion Paul. Here the conscience errs in evaluating the self not as a sinner but as righteous, and it is an unreliable guide to where human beings stand before God. When Paul says that no one will be justified through "works of the law" because "through the law comes the knowledge of sin" (Rom 3:20), he is speaking of the need for a revelation of the true human situation.

Perhaps precisely because they perceive the human conscience as such an inaccurate guide, the Reformers have little direct interest in the psychological dimensions of how the law reveals sin. Their concern is rather that it does in fact do so and that individuals are prompted to recognize their need of Christ. Melanchthon comes closest to establishing an experiential sequence in which enduring a guilty conscience becomes a necessary prelude to faith as an intermediate stage of repentance between faith and an earlier false confidence in fulfilling the law. However, both Luther and Calvin insist that repentance is only fully present in the experience of faith and not merely as its prelude.[4]

Both some of Stendahl's own points and many of the inferences drawn from his arguments by himself and others are therefore wrong. The Reformers evaluate Paul's robust conscience as sincere but wrong (i.e., before he met the risen Christ, Paul thought that he was fully obeying God's will when in fact he was doing the opposite by persecuting the church). There is no tension between Paul's robust conscience and their conviction that it is impossible for human beings to fulfill the law, which thereby brings condemnation. The impossibility of fulfilling the law represents the truth of the human condition before God, but the robust consciences of those seeking justification through the works of the law represent a delusion.

There is also no necessary tension between their convictions about the law and the idea that Paul's theologizing about salvation moves from solution to plight. The Reformers' evaluation of Paul's robust conscience as sincere but wrong shows

3. R. Ward Holder, "Introduction—Paul in the Sixteenth Century: Invitation and a Challenge," in *A Companion to Paul in the Reformation*, ed. R. Ward Holder (Leiden: Brill, 2009), 6.

4. On all these points, see Stephen J. Chester, "Paul and the Introspective Conscience of Martin Luther," *BibInt* 14 (2006): 508–36.

that they consider Paul himself to have understood his plight before God only after he encountered Christ. The Reformers certainly do hold that the knowledge of sin is necessary to faith and repentance, but they do not treat an experience of guilt and self-loathing as a necessary preparation for a breakthrough to faith. Conviction of sin and faith do stand in relationship with each other, but it is not "that an awareness of sin always precedes a knowledge of the gospel. . . . Although experientially at times law precedes gospel and at other times gospel precedes law, theologically they are correlative to each other: each needs the other for a true understanding."[5]

Finally, if the Reformers do not consider that Paul as a Pharisee struggled with a guilty conscience, then neither can they take the experience of such a struggle to be typical of Jewish engagement with the law. They clearly do characterize Judaism as holding to justification by works, but they are not led to this conclusion by their perspective on Paul's conscience. Portrayals of Paul as a hero of the introspective conscience are simply not essential to the Reformers' views about his theology. Stendahl is right to object to portrayals of Paul struggling with guilt before his Damascus Road experience, but it simply does not follow that, if Paul possessed a robust conscience, justification must be focused on the inclusion of the gentiles in the people of God to the exclusion of any concern with works-righteousness.

This same point can be illustrated by examining NPP interpretations of the knowledge of sin. N. T. Wright states that "from Paul's perspective there was no chance that anyone, however devout, would in fact keep Torah perfectly: 'through the law comes the knowledge of sin.'" Wright here recognizes the basic exegetical point that for Paul a principal function of the law is to reveal human sinfulness. This function holds true for Wright even in Paul's own biography: "Torah declared that the devout Jew (his own former self) had in fact broken it—at the very moment when he was rightly clinging to it." In explaining the law's function in revealing sin, Wright places great emphasis on the law speaking specifically to the people of Israel as those under the law. He explains that for Paul the knowledge of sin signifies that the Jewish people "were themselves under the covenantal curse which Torah pronounced on those who broke it."[6]

This emphasis on Israel perhaps does less than full justice to Paul's statements that the law is the means by which the whole world is held accountable for sin

---

5. Graham Tomlin, "Luther and the Deliverance of God," in *Beyond Old and New Perspectives on Paul: Reflections on the Work of Douglas Campbell*, ed. Chris Tilling (Eugene, OR: Wipf & Stock, 2014), 29–30.

6. Wright, *Paul and the Faithfulness of God*, 2:1034–35.

(Rom 2:20), and that Jew and gentile alike are under sin (Rom 3:9). Yet the Reformers presumably could have accommodated even this point by arguing from the greater to the lesser: "If it is true that Paul here speaks of even God's holy law bringing knowledge of sin to Jews who are committed to faithful observance of Torah, how much more it must be true that Gentiles who attempt to establish their own righteousness before God through ethical behavior will find only knowledge of sin." This, of course, would be unacceptable to Wright, who puts the law's revealing of sin into a very different interpretative framework and goes on to speak of the sin revealed to Jews not as that of those attempting to establish righteousness through ethical behavior but as that of those treating torah as "*a badge of privilege*."[7]

The tension between Wright's position and that of the Reformers is therefore not actually about the knowledge of sin and the introspective conscience. Instead, it primarily concerns the interpretation of what Paul means by the phrase the "works of the law" and its implications for Paul's perceptions about the nature of Judaism and the nature of justification. In good NPP fashion, Wright interprets Paul's rejection of justification by works of the law in relation to issues of ethnic identity, whereas the Reformers focus on works-righteousness. The main issue is whether the Reformers are misguided in that focus. It is this debate about the "works of the law" and the nature of Second Temple Judaism, not imagined disagreement about the introspective conscience, that marks the fundamental divergence between the NPP and the exegetical legacy of the Reformers. That the Reformers do not project struggles with a guilty conscience onto Paul means that in this debate, the dice can no longer be loaded by supposing that the Reformers must be wrong about the works of the law because they are wrong about the conscience. The former must instead be debated only on its own merits.

9.3. The Heart of the Matter: The Works of the Law and the Whole Law

That there is a fundamental divergence between the exegetical legacy of the Reformers and the NPP concerning the nature of the "works of the law" is indisputable. Yet even here, it is important to clarify the precise nature of the disagreement. Dunn articulates concisely the contrast between interpreting Paul's phrase in terms of works-righteousness or in terms of ethnocentrism: "the boasting which Paul condemned had more to do with pride in ethnic privilege than with pride in self-achievement.... Separateness to God (holiness) was understood to require separateness from the (other) nations as two sides of the one coin." Yet alongside

7. Wright, *Paul and the Faithfulness of God*, 2:1034.

this important contrast, it is also vital to note a significant agreement. In their own time and place, the Reformers insisted, against those among their opponents who interpreted Paul's phrase as referring to the ceremonial aspects of the law only, that the "works of law" encompass all that the law requires. Similarly, Dunn writes that "I have no doubt that 'works of the law' refer to what the law requires, the conduct prescribed by the Torah; whatever the law requires to be done can be described as 'doing' the law, as a work of the law."[8]

This agreement makes it clear that, however significant the differences between them, Dunn's position on the "works of the law" is closer to that of the Reformers than it is to the strands of patristic and medieval interpretation that restricted its reference to ceremonies. The contrast between the Reformers and the NPP concerns not to what Paul's phrase refers—they agree that it refers to all the law requires—but instead the terms in which obedience to the whole law is properly characterized. Dunn's point is that to characterize it in terms of self-achieved works-righteousness is to misunderstand Paul. Instead, Paul is particularly concerned with those works of the law—such as circumcision, food laws, and Sabbath observance—that served as boundary markers separating Jews from gentiles.

In a situation like that which prompted Paul to write Galatians, where these boundary markers have become contentious in the life of the church (see especially Gal 5:1–6), they will take on particular significance. Reflecting on Gal 2, Dunn writes that "the issue which caused the first recorded statement of the great principle of justification by faith alone were the works of the law by which Judaism distinguished itself and kept itself separate from the (other) nations."[9] Paul's teaching on justification finds its foil not in works-righteousness but instead in an insistence on separation from gentiles that fails fully to recognize the radical breaking down of such boundaries wrought by the gift of Christ and the accompanying full inclusion of the gentiles in God's people. It is not that Paul's phrase refers to boundary-marking practices instead of to the whole law but rather that these practices function as important indicators of fidelity to the whole law.

That the debate takes this shape, with the reference of the "works of the law" to all that the law requires not in dispute, raises important questions. For it indicates that simply to debate whether Paul's teaching about justification finds it foil in works-righteousness or ethnocentrism is insufficient. If the phrase "works of the law" refers to the whole law and therefore denotes the Jewish commitment to an entire way of life swathed in obedience to divine commandments, can such obedience

---

8. James D. G. Dunn, "The New Perspective: Whence, What and Whither?," in *The New Perspective on Paul*, rev. ed. (Grand Rapids: Eerdmans, 2005), 14–16, 23–24.

9. Dunn, "New Perspective: Whence, What and Whither?," 28.

itself accurately be characterized in only one dimension? Must we simply debate between works-righteousness and ethnocentrism, as many have done since the rise of the NPP? Or might there be several dimensions to such obedience, so that to interpret the phrase "works of the law" with exclusive reference to only one of them is misleading? If this is so, then we should expect to find weaknesses in both positions and to discover that neither an exclusive emphasis on works-righteousness nor on ethnocentrism is able satisfactorily to account for all the available evidence.

In highlighting Jew-gentile relationships in the early church and their significance for understanding Paul's theology, Dunn certainly emphasizes something that forms a weakness in the Reformers' exegesis. For example, there is no sign in Luther's treatment of Gal 2 of any recognition of the potential significance of specific Jewish practices for understanding the conflicts that Paul addresses. Paul's statements about the works of the law and justification are interpreted entirely in terms of the conflict between theological ideas: "the issue here is nothing trivial for Paul; it is the principal doctrine of Christianity" (*LW* 26:106). For his part, Calvin suggests that Paul insightfully perceives differences over practice, such as observance of the food laws, as indicative of conflict over deeper soteriological principles. The former is symptomatic of the latter.[10] Yet given the importance of issues of practice to Jewish identity in the ancient world, this very distinction between practices and principles seems too easily to detach theological ideas from community life and the profound challenges involved in Jewish and gentile believers living together as the people of God.

In neglecting the significance of Jewish practice in this way, the Reformers fail to do justice to the significance of his first-century context for interpreting Paul's letters. Of course, unlike historical-critical interpreters, the Reformers were not seeking an accurate portrayal of Second Temple Judaism as a goal in its own right. Nor did they have access to the range of sources that allows contemporary scholarship to present more nuanced accounts of Second Temple Judaism. They were primarily concerned with how the gospel expressed in Paul's letters spoke to issues of pressing concern to them and their contemporaries. For this reason, they emphasize Paul's exclusion of self-earned righteousness in their interpretation of all texts where he discusses justification (and many others besides), and this feeds the analogy they draw between Paul's opponents and their own. Given the overwhelming evidence that circumcision, food laws, and Sabbath observance did serve in important ways to maintain boundaries between Jews and gentiles,[11]

---

10. John Calvin, *Sermons on the Epistle to the Galatians*, trans. Kathy Childress (Edinburgh: Banner of Truth, 1997), 162–64 (sermon 11).

11. On this boundary-defining function, see John M. G. Barclay, *Judaism in the Mediterranean Diaspora* (Edinburgh: T&T Clark, 1996), 428–44.

it is undeniable that, in drawing attention to the historical inadequacy of this procedure, the NPP represents a welcome advance.

Yet for all the differences between sixteenth- and twenty-first-century scholarly goals and procedures, it is part of the task of theological interpreters of Paul's texts to discern their contemporary relevance. Regardless of whether they acknowledge it, NPP scholars are also engaged in this task. Their own less prejudicial account of Second Temple Judaism arose precisely in a post-Holocaust context where it was a pressing contemporary need, and to understand Paul's objection to the works of the law in terms of a rejection of the exclusivity of his own ethnic tradition provides a significant theological resource for today's diverse global Christianity.[12] Recognition of this contemporary relevance should at one and the same time prompt an appreciation of NPP scholarship and cause us to ask whether it also interprets Paul's phrase in too monolithic a manner. If there are fatal weaknesses in characterizing obedience to the whole law exclusively in terms of works-righteousness, are there also weaknesses in characterizing it exclusively in terms of boundary markers and separation from gentiles?

9.4. The Heart of the Matter: The Works of the Law and Boundary Markers

Here it is significant that Dunn views Paul's polemic against works of the law as correcting a misunderstanding of what the law truly requires: "the 'works' which Paul warns against were, in his view, Israel's misunderstanding of what her covenant law required."[13] Yet if this is Paul's view, it is odd that he contrasts not only the works of the law with faith and grace but also the law itself (see, e.g., Gal 3:11; Rom 6:14, 15), treating the law and its works interchangeably.[14] Paul does not respond to the insistence that gentile converts must be circumcised by saying that this is to misunderstand the law but rather with the assertion that "if justification comes through the law, then Christ died for nothing" (Gal 2:21).

Paul has already identified Christ's death as necessary to the justification of Jews as well as gentiles (Gal 2:15–16), so his point here is not solely the chronological one that his opponents err in failing to appreciate that the ages have turned in the coming of the Messiah and the giving of the Spirit so that God's purpose is now to include the gentiles in his people. Paul clearly also intends to say, even if

---

12. In seeking to exploit this theological resource, it is essential to be aware of the danger of leaping from the frying pan of mischaracterizing Judaism as a religion of works-righteousness into the fire of implicitly mischaracterizing Judaism as a religion of misanthropic exclusivism.

13. James D. G. Dunn, *The Theology of Paul the Apostle* (Edinburgh: T&T Clark, 1998), 366.

14. John M. G. Barclay, *Paul and the Gift* (Grand Rapids: Eerdmans, 2015), 374, says of Galatians that "there is no material difference in this letter between 'works of the Law' and 'the Law.'"

such knowledge is only possessed retrospectively from the vantage point of faith in Christ, that the law never justified anyone since, if it could have done so, the saving death of the Messiah would not have been necessary. Paul does not denote by the phrase the "works of the law" a misunderstanding of the law's requirements but rather his conviction that the deeds required by the law, even when it is rightly understood, simply do not justify.[15]

Alongside Paul's treatment of the law and its works as interchangeable, a further objection to Dunn's position is the various occasions on which Paul appears explicitly to contrast the gospel he preaches with human ethical achievement. Paul contrasts working to receive wages with the nature of justification by faith as a gift (Rom 4:4–5). He argues that God's election of Jacob but not Esau before birth, and before either had done anything good or bad, demonstrates that election is not by works (Rom 9:10–13). When he lists his reasons for confidence in the flesh (Phil 3:4b–6), Paul includes his blamelessness in relation to righteousness under the law as one component of the righteousness of his own that he then goes on to contrast with righteousness by faith (Phil 3:9). For each of these texts, NPP exegetes provide alternative interpretations in which Paul contrasts his gospel not with ethical achievement but instead with ethnocentrism. Ultimately such debates can be pursued only through detailed exegetical argument, but none of these alternative interpretations have succeeded in establishing a consensus. NPP proposals also often contrast with each other as well as with more traditional alternatives,[16] and the details of these texts are not most naturally explained in relation to ethnocentrism.

Interpretation of the phrase "works of the law" within the NPP is therefore more successful at highlighting the inadequacy of interpretations focused exclusively on works-righteousness than it is in establishing ethnocentrism as an alternative exclusive focus. Yet if Paul's phrase does refer, as is widely recognized, to all that the law requires, then this should not be surprising. For although marking boundaries between Jews and gentiles is often crucial in Second Temple Judaism precisely as an expression of commitment to obedience, it is this broader commit-

---

15. That Paul's interchangeable treatment of the "works of the law" and the "law" itself makes it unlikely that he is criticizing a misunderstanding of the law is spelled out by Stephen Westerholm, *Perspectives Old and New on Paul: The "Lutheran" Paul and His Critics* (Grand Rapids: Eerdmans 2004), 297–340.

16. Thus, for example, Dunn, "New Perspective: Whence, What and Whither?," 47–49, argues that Rom 4:4–5 concerns only initial justification ("getting in") with Abraham as "the type of the ungodly-idolator-become-proselyte" (here 48) and intends to point out simply that Abraham's election did not depend upon a preexisting covenant faithfulness. In contrast, Wright, *Paul and the Faithfulness of God*, 2:1004, is so insistent that the focus of the chapter is solely on membership of Abraham's family as to deny that Abraham himself should be numbered among the ungodly.

ment to an entire way of life swathed in divine regulation that is itself peculiarly and characteristically Jewish. This can be illustrated by reference to the work of none other than E. P. Sanders, who emphasizes that "Judaism's most distinctive point . . . was the extension of divine law to all the areas of life. . . . This emphasis on correct action in every sphere of life, technically called 'orthopraxy,' is a hallmark of Judaism. Judaism, that is, required obedience to the law, which includes the sacrifices and offerings, but also much more."[17]

In Sanders's subsequent long discussion of observing the law, it clearly emerges that practices such as circumcision, the food laws, and Sabbath observance served to delineate Jews from gentiles. Yet there is also recognition of the theological significance of these practices (e.g., circumcision is a sign of Israel's election and of the covenant with Abraham; observance of the Sabbath either reflects the rest of God on the seventh day of creation or it commemorates the exodus from Egypt). And there is also considerable emphasis on the law's mandate of love for humankind, including the gentiles and those among their number who might specifically count as enemies of Israel. Jewish responses to gentile society varied, and while "some Diaspora Jews responded to their pagan environment, full of idolatry and sexual immorality (from their perspective), by cutting themselves off from too much contact with Gentiles. . . . [O]ther Jews, it must be emphasized, participated in numerous aspects of pagan culture, such as the theatre and games, quite cheerfully."[18]

Given such an account, we should conclude not simply that Jews could take very different positions over how much separation from gentiles was required by obedience to the law, or that there could be significant disagreement over how to practice individual commandments. We should note also that if the great Jewish distinctive is commitment to an all-embracing law itself, then the meaning of the law and its constituent commandments will be understood in various ways. A phrase like the "works of the law" may indeed refer simply to the conduct required by the torah, but that required conduct is itself complex and multifaceted. Neither the phrase itself nor the very wide range of mandated behaviors to which it refers are convincingly to be explained exclusively in relation to any single function or purpose: *"the phrase 'works of the law' refers to the distinctive way of life of the Jewish community, but without any necessary orientation towards boundary markers . . . there is no need to import a reference to 'boundary markers' every time Paul uses the term 'works.'"*[19]

17. E. P. Sanders, *Judaism: Practice and Belief 63 BCE–66 CE* (London: SCM; Philadelphia: Trinity International, 1992), 191.

18. Sanders, *Judaism: Practice and Belief*, 216.

19. Francis Watson, *Paul, Judaism, and the Gentiles: Beyond the New Perspective*, 2nd ed. (Grand Rapids: Eerdmans, 2007), 19.

The failing of NPP scholarship in relation to the works of the law is not its emphasis on their boundary-marking function, which is indeed significant, but rather its apparent inability to discern any other function or purpose. For an emphasis on the boundary-marking function of the works of the law and a concern to point out that human attempts at obedience do not justify are compatible. Precisely because the law to which Jews are committed is God's law, the boundary between Jews and gentiles is also the boundary between holiness and sinfulness (Gal 2:15). Inevitably the pinnacles of human ethical achievement all lie on the Jewish side of the boundary with Paul confident that he was himself an exemplary representative of the Jewish tradition (Gal 1:14–15; Phil 3:4–12). As Stendahl puts it, Paul regards himself as having been a very successful Jew "even when he thinks about it from his Christian perspective."[20] Given Paul's realization that, despite all this, Jews as well as Greeks are under sin (Rom 3:9), and that therefore even the very best of human life partakes of sinfulness, it is unsurprising that on occasions he insists that human ethical achievement does not justify.

For Paul to insist on this does not diminish the significance for his theology of the boundary-defining function of the works of the law. An insistence that justification is not by obedience and an insistence that it is not by maintaining separation from gentiles are not mutually exclusive possibilities. They are not precisely because Paul uses the phrase "works of the law" with reference to an entire nomistic way of life. In a context where righteous behavior was synonymous with a Jewish way of life defined by faithful obedience to the law and sinful behavior with a gentile way of life, the assertions that justification does not result from such obedience or from Jewish ethnicity naturally belong together.

This claim can be illustrated with reference to one of the most heavily disputed of Paul's uses of the phrase "works of the law" in Gal 2:16. NPP scholarship has rightly emphasized the relevance in the context (the crisis in Galatia over circumcision and the immediately preceding discussion of the incident at Antioch in 2:11–14) of the boundary-defining function of these works. Yet as Stephen Westerholm points out,

> Substantiating Paul's point is a verse in the Psalms that, in the Psalms, reads as follows: "Do not enter into judgment with your servant; for before you no-one living is found righteous"; Paul paraphrases: "by works of the law no flesh will be justified." Now, if Paul's point had been that circumcision and other "boundary markers" are not requirements for sitting at the table of God's people, it is not clear why he would even have thought of Psalm 143:2 let alone deemed it proof

20. Krister Stendahl, *Paul among Jews and Gentiles* (Philadelphia: Fortress, 1976), 13.

of his claim. The verse from the Psalms was the perfect one to quote, however, if he wanted to say that human beings (Jews like Peter and Paul no less than Gentiles like the Galatians) are sinners who can never be deemed righteous before God by anything they do: "before you no-one living is found righteous."[21]

The point is not that "anything they do" means that Paul's focus is not on the boundary-marking function of the works of the law but instead on human ethical achievement. Rather, it is that even as the boundary-marking function of works is highlighted, it is so as part of a wider nomistic way of life in which recognizing and even boasting in praiseworthy, obedient behavior is appropriate.[22] NPP scholarship often acknowledges this wider nomistic reference of Paul's phrase but even as it does so glides by its implications in order to concentrate only and in every text on the boundary-defining function of the works of the law. The Reformers were guilty of a similar but opposite error, rightly hearing from Paul a denial that justification can be received through human ethical achievement but, under the stimulus of their polemical context, taking all his contrasts between faith and the works of the law to speak of this single concern.

Because the law provides an entire way of life, when Paul denies that the works of the law justify, he sometimes does so in contexts where his focus is on separation from gentiles, sometimes in contexts where his focus is on human ethical achievement, and sometimes in contexts where the two jostle together. As John Barclay argues in his groundbreaking study *Paul and the Gift*, the reason for this is that Paul construes the Christ-gift as always incongruous, as always given to those who are unworthy of it. This is true of its Jewish recipients just as much as of its gentile recipients, and Paul's target is not as such either a principle of ethnic superiority or a principle of works-righteousness.

Paul is not attacking the mistaken notion that divine approval of Israel depended upon separation from gentiles or the mistaken notion that it is possible to earn salvation but more fundamentally insisting that God's grace in Christ disregards any and every dimension of human worthiness, including even observance of a nomistic way of life. The Christ-gift is not given because there is something about the recipients that makes them the fitting beneficiaries of it.

---

21. Stephen Westerholm, *Justification Reconsidered* (Grand Rapids: Eerdmans, 2013), 77. The same allusion is also found in Rom 3:20.

22. See the excellent discussion in Simon J. Gathercole, *Where Is Boasting? Early Jewish Soteriology and Paul's Response in Romans 1–5* (Grand Rapids: Eerdmans, 2002), 161–94. The critique of Jewish boasting in Paul's texts comes not because all boasting is wrong but because the perception of blameless obedience to the torah is a false one from Paul's perspective. If the boast were true, it would be valid.

"Paul has ruled out numerous qualifying criteria for divine selection: birth (natural rights of descent), status (comparative 'greatness'), and practice ('works'), all forms of symbolic capital humanly ascribed or achieved." Since all are "under sin" (Rom 3:9), grace can belong to no one, and "it is because grace belongs to no-one that it goes to everyone."[23]

The error of both NPP scholarship and the Reformers is therefore to mistake the principal possible expressions of human worthiness in Paul's context as a Second Temple Jew (ethnic identity, ethical achievement) for the underlying issue that these expressions embody. Paul talks about both and does so in order to make it clear that the Christ-gift is not conditioned by any aspect of human worthiness. The Reformers error is more pernicious in the sense that their suggestion that Paul's contemporaries were committed to works-righteousness paved the way for later prejudicial accounts of Judaism as a religion of legalism. Yet at least in the process of their assault upon theologies of merit and polemic against works-righteousness, the Reformers allowed Paul to mean what he appears to say in texts where a concern with human ethical achievement is expressed. And at least they insisted loudly, at length, and correctly that Paul's phrase "works of the law" refers to the whole law. Both the content of Paul's texts and the all-embracing nature of the law as a way of life within Judaism suggest a broader focus for the term "works of the law" than an exclusive concern with boundary-marking will allow.[24]

9.5. The Reformers' Exegetical Legacy: A Reevaluation

It was noted earlier (see 8.1) that the various criticisms of the Reformers' Pauline exegesis offered from within NPP scholarship were mutually reinforcing and together served to produce a general dismissal of their legacy. The reality of the relationship is much more complex, with some respects in which NPP exegesis depends upon the Reformers' exegetical legacy, other respects in which NPP scholars intensify one aspect of that legacy at the expense of others, and yet other respects in which they typically simply misunderstand the Reformers' work. Even in relation to an issue like the works of the law, where there are serious inadequacies in the Reformers' exegesis when assessed from today's perspective, NPP

23. Barclay, *Paul and the Gift*, 531, 572.

24. Relevant here also is Paul's contrasting of his gospel with gentile culture in 1 Cor 1:26–29. No one may boast before God on the grounds of education, power, or noble birth. The gentile context means that the works of the law are not under discussion, but across his letters, Paul sets the gospel against many and varied aspects of human worthiness. It would be a little unexpected if he contrasted it with human ethical achievement nowhere in his letters.

scholarship is better at correcting inherited error than at formulating a convincing alternative. The insistence that Paul's concern is always with the boundary-defining function of such works simply perpetuates the opposite error from that of the Reformers.

It is therefore a mistake to accept at face value criticism of the Reformers that is not founded upon detailed examination of their Pauline exegesis, and a mistake to leap from the presence of inadequacies in some aspects of their exegesis to the assumption that they have little to offer in general to Pauline interpreters in the twenty-first century. Sometimes, as with the phrase "works of the law," what they offer is a different vantage point from which it is possible to see weaknesses in NPP exegesis. To return now to the Reformers polemic against works-righteousness would be a profound mistake, but to hear their voices afresh as a much-needed corrective to dominant contemporary concerns is vital and necessary.

At other times, what they have to offer goes well beyond serving as a corrective. The Reformers' views about justification by faith and its relationship to other important aspects of Pauline theology have often been unfavorably assessed in recent scholarship. Yet, when accurately understood, the Reformers' positions on justification are often somewhat different from what their critics assume. Part 3 of this book (chapters 10–15) will explore justification by faith in the Pauline exegesis of the three most enduringly influential early Protestant interpreters of Paul: Martin Luther, Philip Melanchthon, and John Calvin. It will emerge that there are important aspects of their exegesis, especially in their discernment of the relationship between justification and the theme of participation in Christ, where the Reformers' exegesis offers insights that could profitably be incorporated into contemporary interpretation.

PART THREE

Justification by Faith and Union with Christ
in the Reformers' Exegesis

CHAPTER TEN

Martin Luther: Alien Righteousness and Life in Christ

T he claim that the Reformers have significant gifts to offer contemporary exegesis, especially in their understanding of Paul's teaching about justification by faith and its relationship with participation in Christ, is a controversial one. For, in recent scholarship, it has become customary to discern important weaknesses in Protestant accounts of justification that are perceived to reflect their influence. It is held to distort Paul's intentions if justification is understood in terms of "imputation," a traditional label used to denote the transfer of Christ's own righteousness to believers on account of their faith in his atoning death. If justification is understood in this way, exclusively as a legal (forensic) metaphor with the divine judge declaring innocent those who in their own nature remain guilty sinners (they are, to use Luther's famous phrase, "simultaneously justified and a sinner"), then a wedge is driven between declaring and making righteous, between justification as a once-and-for-all external act and regeneration as an internal lifelong process. This fails adequately to reflect Paul's emphasis on the transforming power of the gospel and makes justification into little more than a legal fiction or transaction in which God accepts faith in place of the obedience that human beings are unable to offer.

10.1. Setting the Stage: Justification by Faith and Union with Christ

Such criticisms initially appear substantiated by the ways in which the Reformers agree in important aspects of their understanding of justification (see 5.2, 5.3). In their reaction against medieval accounts of justification that stress the cooperation of Christians with infused divine grace, the Reformers insist instead upon the alien nature of the righteousness granted to believers through Christ. There is no sense in which human obedience is an efficient cause of justification, and the righteousness that believers receive in justification remains wholly and entirely that of Christ. It is received by faith through the preaching of the biblical word, with those who believe drawn out of themselves and into total reliance on the promises of God. People do not encounter God by looking inward but instead do so as the convicting power of the word turns them outward toward Christ and enables them to receive his righteousness through faith. Believers must experience ethical transformation, but such transformation does not form part of the basis of their justification before God. When the gift of faith is given, God's justifying declaration in the heavenly courtroom that sinners are righteous provides all that is required.

There are several exegetical points that can legitimately be made by those who doubt the adequacy of such an account of Paul's teaching. One is the apparent lack of texts in Paul's letters that speak of Christ's own righteousness being given to the believer (Paul speaks in Phil 3:9 of having a righteousness "from God" but not explicitly of Christ's righteousness being transferred to those who believe). Another is the emphasis Paul places in relation to justification on life (Abraham trusted in the one who gives life to the dead [Rom 4:17], Christ was raised to life for our justification [Rom 4:25], and Christ's righteous act results in justification and life for all [Rom 5:18]). The Reformers' account may perhaps explain how justification deals with the guilt of sin, but for many it is far from clear that it fits with the connections Paul makes between justification and the gift of new life in Christ.[1]

Another way of expressing this criticism is to say that the Reformers are unable to explain how justification achieves "participation in Christ" or "union with Christ." These labels designate a crucial set of Pauline vocabulary. Paul uses the phrase "in Christ" approximately eighty times in his seven undisputed letters alone and there is also an associated cluster of images such as being united with Christ (Rom 6:5), joined with Christ (Rom 12:9; 1 Cor 6:17), conformed to Christ (Rom 8:29; Phil 3:10, 21), putting on Christ (e.g., Rom 13:12, 14; Gal 3:27), and dying or being crucified with Christ (e.g., Rom 6:8; Gal 2:20). In many instances, these images appear in the same context as Paul's discussions of justification. If it is true that the Reformers leave the two disconnected, then the criticisms directed at them appear valid.[2]

1. For example, E. P. Sanders, *Paul* (Oxford: Oxford University Press, 1991), 49, speaks of Luther's emphasis on "fictional, imputed righteousness."

2. Richard B. Hays, *The Faith of Jesus Christ: The Narrative Substructure of Galatians 3:1–4:11*, 2nd ed. (Grand Rapids: Eerdmans, 2002), xxix: "the greatest weakness of the traditional post-Reformation understanding of 'faith' and 'justification' is . . . that it offers no coherent account of the relation between the doctrine of justification and *Christology*."

Unsurprisingly, therefore, New Perspective on Paul (NPP) scholars typically distance themselves from traditional Protestant explanations of justification as a forensic declaration in which Christ's righteousness is imputed to the believer. They focus instead either on the inclusion of the gentiles in God's people or on participation in Christ, or upon some combination of the two. For example, Campbell offers a participatory and liberative account of justification that contrasts with what he regards as the inconsistencies and internal contradictions of the Reformers' approach.[3] Wright also comments on the strangeness for those holding a traditional Protestant understanding of justification of his own account of it, which centers on covenant membership.[4]

Yet once again, the reality of the relationship is much more complex than all of this would suggest. The reasons are twofold. First, although the Reformers' common commitments in understanding justification are genuinely shared and genuinely of vital significance to them, these common commitments do not tell the whole story of their engagement with Paul's teaching about justification. For alongside such common commitments, there are also differences among the Reformers in how they understand justification. There is in fact not a single perspective on Paul's teaching about justification among the Reformers but several overlapping perspectives. To understand accurately what they say about justification, it is necessary to explore the Pauline exegesis of individual Reformers and to understand their different opinions in relation to each other. For this reason, the next several chapters (10–15) will focus on individual interpreters: Martin Luther, Philip Melanchthon, and John Calvin.

Second, the differences that emerge between these three figures largely concern the christological dimensions of justification. Contrary to the criticisms directed against them, the Reformers do not in fact fail to offer accounts of the relationship between justification and union with Christ. Although Melanchthon proves an exception, Luther and Calvin in different ways both make union with Christ central to their accounts of justification. Their insights may stand in tension with some aspects of NPP discussions of justification, but they also confirm and strengthen others. It is in the interplay between the shared commitments concerning justification common to them all and their more distinctive individual views about its relationship to union with Christ that the enduring value of the Reformers' explanations of Paul's teaching emerges. The Reformers have resources to offer to those interpreting Paul's teaching about justification in

---

3. Douglas A. Campbell, *The Deliverance of God: An Apocalyptic Rereading of Justification in Paul* (Grand Rapids: Eerdmans, 2009), 817.

4. N. T. Wright, *Paul and the Faithfulness of God* (Minneapolis: Fortress, 2013), 2:1129.

and for contemporary contexts precisely because in their exegesis they integrate Paul's statements about it with other crucial dimensions of his teaching, especially union with Christ.

10.2. Union with Christ: Apocalyptic Dualism

In relation to Luther, it is through the emergence in the late twentieth century of apocalyptic interpretations of his thought and of the Finnish interpretation (see 2.6) that crucial christological aspects of his teaching about justification have been highlighted. While there remains plenty of scope for debate about various significant aspects of these interpretative movements, their central respective claims—that Luther's thought exhibits an apocalyptic dualism, and that union with Christ is central to his theology—have become commonplaces.[5] Yet Luther's use of apocalyptic motifs and his insistence on union with Christ are often treated as distinct and not integrated with each other. In fact, their integration is vital to understanding Luther on justification, the doctrine that he regards as key to interpreting Paul and concern with which permeates his writings. It is only when the two are appropriately integrated that what Luther hears Paul say about justification becomes clear.

Luther's apocalyptic dualism is exhibited in his configuring in absolute terms of the gulf between those who are being saved and those who are perishing. As we saw when exploring the development of shared perspectives among early Protestant interpreters (see 6.3), Luther understands a fallen human being to be like "a sick man whose mortal illness is not only the loss of health of one of his members, but it is, in addition to the lack of health in all his members, the weakness of all of his senses and powers, culminating even in his disdain for those things which are healthful and in his desire for those things which make him sick." It is this sense of original sin as completely rampant misdirected desire that gives rise to Luther's new and famous description of sin as "the person turned in upon the self" (*homo incurvatus in se*).[6] The fallen human being therefore has no resources

---

5. For a discussion of debates between the Finnish school and its critics, see Stephen J. Chester, *Reading Paul with the Reformers: Reconciling Old and New Perspectives* (Grand Rapids: Eerdmans, 2017), 201–14. The Finns often do fail to grant sufficient attention to the alien nature of the righteousness given to believers, but they are correct that for Luther union with Christ is essential to justification itself. For a recent nuanced assessment, see Reinhard Flogaus, "Justification or Deification: Luther's Soteriology in Ecumenical Perspective," in *Theological Anthropology, 500 Years after Martin Luther: Orthodox and Lutheran Perspectives*, ed. Christophe Chalamat et al. (Leiden: Brill, 2021), 185–215.

6. *LW* 25:300, 345. See also *LW* 25:291.

to apply to salvation but is in bondage to the self, in love with sin, and incapable of loving God.

Given these convictions, it is unsurprising that Luther finds incredible medieval accounts of justification in which Christians cooperate with divine grace to produce a righteousness that is inherent to them. In such accounts, believers eventually stand before God on the basis of their own merits. Although such merits are possible only when rooted in the grace of God, and therefore possible only when united with Christ, they are truly a person's own. For Luther, this entirely misses Paul's point, which is that the depth of human captivity to sin is so great that what is needed is not the gradual healing of the self but its death. Luther finds an exegetical locus for this perspective in Gal 2:20, where Paul asserts that, having been crucified with Christ, he no longer lives but Christ lives in him. Far from being gradually changed into the likeness of Christ through cooperation with infused grace, Christians must leave behind their own lives for that of Christ:

> Christian righteousness is, namely, that righteousness by which Christ lives in us, not the righteousness that is in our own person. Therefore when it is necessary to discuss Christian righteousness, the person must be completely rejected. For if I pay attention to the person or speak of the person, then, whether intentionally or unintentionally on my part, the person becomes a doer of works who is subject to the Law. But here Christ and my conscience must become one body, so that nothing remains in my sight but Christ, crucified and risen. . . . By paying attention to myself . . . I lose sight of Christ, who alone is my righteousness and life. (*LW* 26:166)

Luther rams the point home again, cautioning that "when it comes to justification, therefore, if you divide Christ's person from your own, you are in the Law; you remain in it and live in yourself, which means that you are dead in the sight of God and damned by the law" (*LW* 26:168). For Paul to continue to live as Paul would be death for him, but to die and for Christ to live in him is life. The old person and the new creation, the self under sin and the individual in Christ, are opposite possibilities. To think at all of meritorious human cooperation in reaching the goal of righteousness is a delusion.

Luther thus makes union with Christ essential to salvation (Christ lives in the believer) and locates it within an apocalyptic dualism that answers the human plight. The depth of this plight means that to place any continued emphasis on the self is to miss Paul's point. Those who believe have transitioned from one life to another, which simply is the life of Christ. Therefore, union with Christ cannot be reduced to an aspect of this transition, even if, as in medieval soteriology, it is the aspect on which the whole transition depends, and that makes possible human merit. Rather, for Luther the person of Christ encompasses the whole of salvation. For this reason, to be united with Christ is simply to be identified with salvation just as justification by faith in Christ is simply to be identified with salvation. One cannot in Luther's view be partially united with Christ or partially righteous.

Luther, of course, knows that believers continue to sin. When commenting on Rom 7:25 ("with my mind I am a slave to the law of God, but with my flesh I am a slave to the law of sin"), Luther argues that Paul does not divide the self into two compartments. Instead, he says that there are two different servitudes that are both characteristic of the self: "Note that one and the same man at the same time serves the law of God and the law of sin, at the same time is righteous and sins! For he does not say: 'My mind serves the law of God,' nor does he say: 'My flesh serves the law of sin,' but: 'I, the whole man, the same person, I serve a twofold servitude.'"[7] In Luther's view, the flesh is not part of a person but the entire person as he or she stands in opposition to God through sin (see 6.3). Paul does not mean that part of a person has become good and stands in internal conflict with another part of a person that has yet to be healed. Paul is not speaking of gradually becoming righteous by cooperating with grace in order to subdue sin.

Instead, Paul means that the believer faces constant strife between two modes of existence occupying the same body. When the believer lives out of union with Christ (the Christ-life not the Paul-life), the Christian is then truly and wholly righteous because Christ is truly and wholly righteous. But when faith falters, and the Christian lives from the self (the Paul-life not the Christ-life), the Christian is then truly and wholly a sinner. Whereas the person apart from Christ, whatever he or she perceives to be the case, in fact has only the possibility of enslavement to sin; the believer also has the possibility of obedience to Christ. As the notion of a twofold competing servitude makes clear, the Christian daily dwells victoriously in Christ and under his lordship or falls back defeated into captivity to sin. It is within this apocalyptic dualism that Luther's designation of the sinner as "simultaneously justified and a sinner" is to be understood. He does not mean that believers are permanently stalled in a half righteous state, unable to grow toward maturity in Christ. Instead, he means that, in the present life, believers never escape from the struggle to live out of who Christ is, or from the temptation to turn back to living from the old self. The Christian lives on an apocalyptic battlefield.

---

7. *LW* 25:336. The NRSV rather obscures Luther's point by using the English personal pronoun "I" twice, once in respect to the mind and once in respect to the flesh. Paul's Greek uses the pronoun once emphatically at the outset (*autos egō*, "I myself") before describing the two aspects of the self's servitude.

10.3. Union with Christ: Christ's Presence in Faith

Having argued that it is essential for believers to live out of union with Christ, Luther must explain how this is possible. His answer is that it is accomplished by faith. The significance of faith in Luther's theology is most clearly exhibited in his exegesis of Galatians. Indeed, his interpretation of the term is key to Luther's development of a new theology. For if one reads through the famous *Commentary on Galatians* (1531/1535) alongside the less well-known *Commentary on Galatians* (1516–1517/1519),[8] it is the transformation in his concept of faith that forms the most significant development in Luther's understanding of the letter. The nature of faith receives little reflection in the earlier commentary, but by 1535 it is a major topic, and, each time Paul uses the word, it carries multiple connotations for Luther.

When commenting on Paul's use of Gen 15:6 in Gal 3:6 and the words "Abraham believed God," Luther understands faith as trust in God's promises. Abraham believed against reason that God would keep his promise that the aged Sarah would have a son. Similarly, Christians are called upon to embrace "the foolishness of the cross" (1 Cor 1:18–25), trusting in the effectiveness of Christ's death on their behalf, and so "faith slaughters reason and kills the beast that the whole world and all the creatures cannot kill" (*LW* 26:228). However, this is not all. In believing God's promises, faith also acknowledges God for who he is. It regards him as "truthful, wise, righteous, merciful, and almighty . . . as the author and donor of every good." God has been given his place by his creatures, his glory affirmed, and so "faith justifies because it renders to God what is due him; whoever does this is righteous" (*LW* 26:227).

Further, by this giving to God of his glory, faith "consummates the deity; and, if I may put it this way, it is the creator of the deity, not in the substance of God but in us" (*LW* 26:227). Luther goes so far as to compare faith, in its relationship with works, to the divinity of Christ in relation to his humanity:

> Let faith always be the divinity of works, diffused throughout the works in the same way that the divinity is throughout the humanity of Christ. Anyone who touches the heat in the heated iron touches the iron; and whoever has touched the skin of Christ has actually touched God. Therefore faith is the "do-all" (*fac totum*) in works, if I may use this expression. Thus Abraham is called faithful because faith is diffused throughout all of Abraham. When I look at Abraham

---

8. Luther's interpretation of Gal 1–4 in the 1531/1535 commentary appears in *LW* 26. His interpretation of Gal 5–6 and the whole of the 1516–1517/1519 commentary appear in *LW* 27.

doing works, therefore, I see nothing of the physical Abraham or of the Abraham who does works, but only Abraham the believer. (*LW* 26:266)

However, Luther does not understand the relationship between faith and the person of Christ simply as an analogy. In his previous comments on Gal 2:15–16, where Paul asserts that justification is by faith in Christ and not by works of the law, Luther emphasizes that Christ himself is present in faith. "Faith justifies because it takes hold of and possesses this treasure, the present Christ . . . the Christ who is grasped by faith and who lives in the heart is the true Christian righteousness" (*LW* 26:130). In an important passage, Luther uses another image: "Here it is to be noted that these three things are joined together: faith, Christ, and acceptance or imputation. Faith takes hold of Christ and has him present, enclosing him as the ring encloses the gem. And whoever is found having this faith in the Christ who is grasped in the heart, him God accounts as righteous."[9]

Thus, faith takes hold of Christ and has him present, and because the righteous one is present in faith, imputation is possible. When Luther says, "Christian righteousness consists in two things, namely, faith in the heart and the imputation of God," it is important to recognize that faith itself is to be identified with union with Christ. Luther makes clear, once again in his comments on Gal 3:6, that it is faith's capacity to grasp hold of Christ that is vital to its justifying nature: "to take hold of the Son and to believe in him with the heart as the gift of God causes God to reckon that faith, however imperfect it may be, as perfect righteousness" (*LW* 26:229, 234). Christ himself is the gift received by the believer. It is therefore clear that the imputation of Christ's righteousness to the believer is not defined over and against, or even in indifference to, union with Christ. Rather, imputation itself involves union with Christ. God imputes because the Christian believes, but the faith of the Christian is itself a divine gift in which Christ is present.[10]

Further, it is this presence of Christ in the faith of the believer that creates the possibility of living the life of Christ. Christians are able to engage in the apocalyptic struggle between opposing modes of existence, and to live as righteous, only because their lives have been invaded by Christ, and their selves have been crucified with Christ. It is through this that they have been made new creations.

---

9. *LW* 26:132. Ian D. K. Siggins, *Martin Luther's Doctrine of Christ* (New Haven: Yale University Press, 1970), 147, comments, "Luther loves to illustrate the character of faith by the figure of an empty container. Faith is merely a husk, but Christ is the kernel. It is a purse or coffer for the eternal treasure, an empty vessel, a poor little monstrance or pyx for gems of infinite worth."

10. Luther is explicit that Christ is more than the object of faith. See *LW* 26:129: "It takes hold of Christ in such a way that Christ is the object of faith, or rather not the object but, so to speak, the One who is present in faith itself."

Obedience results from justification and not vice versa. Works "should be done as fruits of righteousness, not in order to bring righteousness into being. Having been made righteous, we must do them; but it is not the other way around: that when we are unrighteous, we become righteous by doing them. The tree produces fruit; the fruit does not produce the tree" (*LW* 26:169). To describe the believer as simultaneously justified and a sinner is not for Luther a pessimistic estimation of the possibilities of the Christian life but instead a battle cry. It summons those liberated from the previous certainty of defeat to the struggle to live in union with Christ and therefore within Christ's victory over sin, death, and the devil.

10.4. Union with Christ: Receiving Christ's Righteousness

It is, of course, axiomatic for Luther that this victory is Christ's victory, and that believers receive it and live into it but contribute to it nothing from their own resources and works. In union with Christ, believers are not so much empowered to live another life but rather inserted into the life of a victorious other. Set free from all and any reliance on a self that is doomed to defeat, the Christian seeks not to cooperate with divine grace in order to come to merit justification but instead relies solely on the righteousness of Christ granted to those united with him by faith. This reliance on Christ alone is certainly partly a matter of freedom from anxiety about salvation. The Christian need not fear that continuing sins result in a loss of grace that calls justification into question. Such sins are blotted out by the righteousness of Christ.

Yet Luther's assertion of reliance on Christ alone does not simply serve the cause of personal serenity. For anyone who receives Christ's righteousness can join battle against the flesh with gusto, for ultimate victory is secure.[11] There is not only assurance of salvation but also assurance that the relationship between being justified and a sinner is asymmetrical: "righteousness is supreme and sin is a servant" (*LW* 27:74). For Luther, confident engagement in the struggle of the Christian life stems from this certainty that the Christ grasped hold of by faith is righteousness from God for every believer. To be united with Christ by faith is

---

11. There is thus a temporal aspect to "simultaneously justified and a sinner." On the one hand, sin will cling to the flesh of the Christian throughout earthly life, the conflict between the flesh and the Spirit ceasing only with death. On the other, God's act of justification determines the whole of existence such that the Christian lives now from the future on the basis of promise and hope. See Daphne Hampson, *Christian Contradictions: The Structures of Lutheran and Catholic Thought* (Cambridge: Cambridge University Press, 2001), 27; and Eberhard Jüngel, *Justification: The Heart of the Christian Faith* (Edinburgh: T&T Clark, 2001), 218–19.

to receive this infinite righteousness. It is thus clear that when Luther speaks of imputation, he is not speaking of a righteousness that is transferred from Christ to the believer apart from Christ's person but instead of a righteousness that is received by believers because, in being united with Christ, they are joined with one who personifies righteousness.

It is therefore a serious misunderstanding to think that Luther's rejection of works as in any sense a contributory cause of justification stands in contrast to a bare declaration of acquittal. Rather, it stands in contrast to his particular account of union with Christ. Luther rejects concepts of justification based in part on the merits of what a person becomes because he perceives any element of self-reliance, even in cooperation with grace, as standing in contrast to exclusive reliance on sharing in the person and deeds of Christ. Human beings do not need to live a new, improved version of their existing life but instead as new creations to live the life of Christ. The justification of the individual is therefore an apocalyptic event that participates in and relies upon God's larger apocalyptic intervention in Christ for the redemption of the world. God's act of justification for the individual Christian is rooted in God's wider action in the world. It depends on incarnation,[12] and it flows from the life, death, and resurrection of Jesus.

This can be seen particularly clearly in Luther's frequent assertions that between Christ and the believer, there is a "joyous exchange" in which, having taken upon himself the sins of the world, Christ gives to the believer his righteousness.[13] What is ours becomes his, while what is his becomes ours. In the *Commentary on Galatians* (1531/1535), this is expressed particularly clearly in Luther's lengthy comments on Gal 3:13, "Christ redeemed us from the curse of the law by becoming a curse for us." Luther rages against those, especially Jerome, who are nervous at the apparent impiety of the idea that Christ was cursed by God. Instead, Luther thinks it absolutely necessary to emphasize that, although innocent in his own person, Christ became "the greatest thief, murderer, adulterer, robber, desecrator, blasphemer etc., there has ever been anywhere in the world."[14] If he is not, then his

---

12. See George Yule, "Luther's Understanding of Justification by Grace Alone in Terms of Catholic Christology," in *Luther: Theologian for Catholics and Protestants*, ed. George Yule (Edinburgh: T&T Clark, 1985), 87–112.

13. The understanding that justification takes place through joyous exchange is vital to a proper appreciation of the exegetical basis of imputation. Luther reads all texts that contain the idea of exchange (e.g., Rom 8:3; Gal 3:13; Phil 2:5–11) as supporting the view that Christ's righteousness is given to believers. Luther takes the idea from the Fathers, especially Athanasius and Augustine, but focuses it particularly strongly (but not exclusively) on Christ's righteousness as it provides the answer to sin and is prominent in Paul's vocabulary.

14. *LW* 26:277. Unsurprisingly, Luther uses Gal 3:3 and 2 Cor 5:21 to expound the idea of

righteousness cannot become the righteousness of believers, and salvation is lost. As it is, having taken on himself the sins of the world, Christ is able to give to believers his righteousness. "By this fortunate exchange with us He took upon Himself our sinful person and granted us His innocent and victorious Person" (*LW* 26:284).

Luther links this exchange with Christ's emptying of himself (Phil 2:7), a text that he also used to express the same idea years previously in an important sermon entitled *Two Kinds of Righteousness* (preached late 1518/early 1519). Because of Christ's willingness to empty himself by taking upon himself all sins, believers "can with confidence boast in Christ and say: 'Mine are Christ's living, doing and speaking, his suffering and dying, mine as much as if I had lived, done, spoken, suffered and died as he did'" (*LW* 31:297). It is not only that Christ accomplishes something on behalf of believers but also that believers share in what Christ does. Luther inserts "the believer directly into the history of Christ."[15] We can see once again that the exchange is not an exchange of detachable qualities between those who have sin as a component of their identities and someone who has righteousness as a component of his identity. Rather, it is an exchange of persons made between those whose existence is currently constituted by enslavement to sin and the one who personifies righteousness. It is the same Christ, the incarnate Son of God, human and divine, who fought and conquered sin and death in his person, who exchanges his righteousness with the sinfulness of believers, who is present in the faith of believers, and whose life believers now live.

10.5. Union with Christ: Living an Alien Life

That believers are granted such a joyous exchange with the person of Christ allows Luther to hold together truths that would otherwise stand in tension. He insists that the righteousness received by believers is not their own but is instead that of Christ. It remains an alien righteousness even in relation to those who are justified. Yet its alien nature does not result in it being a fictional righteousness since, united with Christ, believers live an alien life. Galatians 2:19–20 is a crucial text for Luther, for it is here that he finds Paul himself placing both these truths together:

---

joyous exchange in his *Lectures on Deuteronomy* (1523–1525) when commenting on 27:26. See *LW* 9:215–16.

15. Marc Lienhard, *Luther: Witness to Jesus Christ; Stages and Themes of the Reformer's Christology* (Minneapolis: Augsburg, 1982), 273, referring to Karin Bornkamm, *Luthers Auslegungen des Galaterbriefs von 1519 bis 1531: Ein Vergleich* (Berlin: de Gruyter, 1963), 166–67.

I am not living as Paul now, for Paul is dead. Who then is living? "The Christian." Paul, living in himself, is utterly dead through the Law but living in Christ, or rather with Christ living in him, he lives an alien life. Christ is speaking, acting, and performing all actions in him; these belong not to the Paul-life, but to the Christ-life. . . . "By my own life I am not living, for if I were, the Law would have dominion over me and hold me captive. To keep it from holding me, I am dead to it by another Law. And this death acquires an alien life for me, namely, the life of Christ, which is not inborn in me but is granted to me in faith through Christ." (LW 26:170)

The Christian has Christ's righteousness through union with him, but that union does not work on the basis of a transformation of the self of the Christian. It works rather on the basis of the leaving behind and abandonment of that self. As one contemporary Lutheran theologian expresses it, "faith as self-forgetfulness is the most intensive form of certainty of God."[16] To speak of union with Christ understood in this way as involving a changed or renewed life is therefore potentially misleading. It is simply not radical enough to capture Luther's sense that union with Christ involves the re-creation of the person. If we are to speak of a restoration or healing of the self in this regard, then it can be only on the basis that the Christian has to come out of him- or herself in order to come to him- or herself.

In this insistence that faith "places us outside ourselves,"[17] Luther is repeating an idea that had long been central to his theology. For in 1520, in his famous tract *The Freedom of a Christian*, Luther had written that "a Christian lives not in himself, but in Christ and his neighbor. Otherwise, he is not a Christian" (LW 31:371). This soteriological necessity to live an alien life means that "there is no linear progress from being a sinner to being justified. It is not that that which is given in creation is transformed through grace. It is only through a discontinuity, through repentance and failure, that in response to the good news of the gospel the human being can come to gain a sense of himself through trusting not in himself but in God."[18]

16. Jüngel, *Justification*, 243.

17. See *LW* 26:387: "This is the reason why our theology is so certain: it snatches us away from ourselves and places us outside ourselves, so that we do not depend on our own strength, conscience, experience, person, or works but depend on that which is outside ourselves, that is, on the promise and truth of God, which cannot deceive." Luther is here commenting on the cry "Abba, Father" in Gal 4:6.

18. Hampson, *Christian Contradictions*, 101. For Luther, salvation does reinstate what creation was meant to be so that we relate to God in the manner first intended (hence my use of the term "re-creation" above). The radical discontinuity stems from the fact that through sin what was intended for creation was so grievously and entirely lost.

Luther knows well that this radical discontinuity between a person's own life and his or her life in Christ is open to an obvious objection. To the charge that Paul still appears as Paul with no apparent change, Luther affirms that to the casual, surface-level observer, Paul still indeed appears as Paul. He uses physical things such as food and clothing just like any other human being. However, this is only "a mask of life" (*LW* 26:170), for although Paul lives in the flesh, it is not on the basis of his own self. Before his conversion, Paul spoke blasphemy, but, after it, words of faith. Before, Paul spoke, but after, Christ speaks. The voice and tongue were the same in each case, but the words came from an entirely different source. Luther himself cannot teach, preach, write, pray, or give thanks except by using the physical instruments of the flesh, but "these activities do not come from the flesh and do not originate there; they are given and revealed divinely from heaven" (*LW* 26:171). This alien and spiritual life cannot be perceived by the unspiritual person, who does not recognize its true source. The unspiritual person remains ignorant of the fact that "this life is not the life of the flesh, although it is a life in the flesh; but it is the life of Christ, the Son of God, whom the Christian possesses by faith" (*LW* 26:172).

10.6. Union with Christ: Faith and Good Works

Perhaps unsurprisingly, Luther is confident that if believers live the alien life of Christ, good works will inevitably follow. Context is everything here. Whereas Luther never tires of asserting that justification is not by works of the law and that human works cannot merit anything before God, he also places considerable emphasis on the works that flow from justifying faith in which Christ is present. Both these emphases can be seen together in Luther's famous introduction to the argument of the epistle with which the *Commentary on Galatians* (1531/1535) begins. This Luther organizes around the distinction between active and passive righteousness, in which righteousness by faith is not the active righteousness that strives to do what lies within (*quod in se est*) but instead passive righteousness, "which we do not perform but receive, which we do not have but accept" (*LW* 26:6).

The active righteousness that does not justify, which Luther can also term civic or political righteousness, comprises every other kind of righteousness, including the Mosaic law. It is to be highly valued in its rightful sphere, but appalling consequences follow from any confusion between the two kinds of righteousness. In 1532, when commenting on Ps 51:16, a verse that expresses God's refusal to delight in animal sacrifices, Luther asserts that "political righteousness is a very delightful and good thing for its purpose, that there might be peace and mutual association among men. But if you want to be righteous before God because you are a good citizen, a chaste spouse, or an honest merchant, you make a most delightful thing into an abomination which God cannot stand."[19]

This is another apocalyptic dualism, with political or active righteousness a possibility for fallen human beings but passive righteousness possible only through faith in Christ. Nevertheless, this dualism is too often interpreted exclusively in relation to the activity or passivity involved with the conscience of the believer as its sole arena. Luther's focus is not on the contrast between activity or passivity per se as if to be active is a human disposition angering to God and to be passive a human disposition that secures God's favor. Rather, Luther also applies the dualism to the radical discontinuity between the believer's own life and life in Christ: "Christian righteousness applies to the new man, the righteousness of the Law applies to the old man, who is born of flesh and blood" (*LW* 26:7). He is also explicit that "we set forth two worlds, as it were, one of them heavenly and the other earthly. Into these we place these two kinds of righteousness, which are distinct and separated from each other" (*LW* 26:8).

That righteousness by faith exists in the context of these sharp contrasts between active and passive, old and new, earthly and heavenly means that when the believer is united with Christ by faith, he or she is empowered actively to live an alien life for the sake of the world: "When I have this righteousness within me, I descend from heaven like the rain that makes the earth fertile. That is, I come forth into another kingdom, and I perform good works whenever the opportunity arises" (*LW* 26:11). As Luther will express the same idea in his *Prefaces to the New Testament* (1522): "Faith, however, is a divine work in us which changes us and makes us to be born anew of God. . . . It kills the Old Adam, makes us entirely different people in heart, spirit, mind, and all our powers, and brings the Holy Spirit with it. Oh, faith is a living, busy, active, mighty thing, so that it is impossible for it not to be constantly doing what is good. Likewise, faith does not ask if good works are to be done, but before one can ask, faith has already done them and is constantly active" (*LW* 35:370).

It is therefore apparent that while righteousness is passive (nothing a human being can do will kill the Old Adam, but only an act of God), justifying faith in which Christ is present is inherently active (it is the act of God that makes us entirely different people). For Luther, faith and good works belong together, the works being the good fruit that every good tree will inevitably bear (Matt 7:17).

---

19. *LW* 12:400. On political or civic righteousness, see also *LW* 12:363–64; 17:63; 25:86, 410–11.

10.7. Union with Christ: Faith and Love

That justification by faith is for Luther an apocalyptic concept is vital to understanding the way in which he expresses the relationship between faith and love. The love of God and neighbor that pleases heaven is not a possibility for human beings apart from faith in Christ. The good works that express such love flow from justifying faith and not vice versa. Even when Luther uses the imagery of marriage to explain justification, he is clear that there is love before marriage only on the divine side of the relationship. For the believer, love results from being united with Christ. He comments on Gal 2:16 that the faith that unites a person with Christ the Savior "justifies without love and before love. . . . By faith we are in Him, and He is in us (John 6:56). The Bridegroom, Christ, must be alone with his bride in His private chamber, and all the family and household must be shunted away. But later on, when the Bridegroom opens the door and comes out, then let the servants return to take care of them and serve them food and drink. Then let works and love begin" (*LW* 26:137–38). Works and love are thus not the consummation of the believer's union with Christ but are instead a new possibility opened up only because in justifying faith that consummation has taken place. It is for this reason that Luther utterly rejects the widespread medieval interpretation of Gal 5:6 ("in Christ Jesus neither circumcision nor uncircumcision counts for anything; the only thing that counts is faith working through love") in terms of "faith formed by love" (see 4.1, 7.4). Luther finds it monstrous that his opponents teach that unformed faith (i.e., intellectual assent to the truth of the gospel) is both genuine faith (i.e., a gift of God) and yet not able to justify since it requires to be formed by love: "Who could stand for the teaching that faith, the gift of God that is infused in the heart by the Holy Spirit, can coexist with mortal sin. . . . [T]o believe this way about infused faith is to admit openly that they understand nothing about faith" (*LW* 27:28).

From Luther's perspective, an ineffective divine gift is a contradiction in terms. If faith is truly a divine gift, it will justify. Further, the basic sense of Paul's words indicates that genuine faith is inherently alive and active: "Paul does not make faith unformed here, as though it were a shapeless chaos without the power to be or to do anything; but he attributes the working itself to faith rather than to love. . . . He does not say 'Love is effective.' No, he says: 'Faith is effective.' He does not say: 'Love works.' No, he says: Faith works.' He makes love the tool through which faith works."[20]

20. *LW* 27:29. The middle and passive forms of the Greek participle in Gal 5:6 (*energoumenē*, "working") are identical. If the participle is passive in voice, Paul is saying that "faith is made

Luther thus considers it essential to hold that faith works or it is not faith. It is faith that justifies and that unites with Christ and leads to love, not love that justifies and unites with Christ and leads to faith. As Luther reads Paul, there is no place for human love that justifies. Luther's apocalyptic dualism here leads him sharply to distinguish faith and love in an attempt rightly to order their relationship, for confusion between the two can only obscure in deluded and dangerous ways the necessity of new creation. Nevertheless, the relationship between faith and love matters profoundly for Luther. While faith and love must be distinguished, it is equally important that they are not separated. For if faith justifies and unites with Christ and thereby makes a new creation, then love must follow. The cliché that faith alone justifies but that justifying faith is never alone is true to Luther. The believer who produces no works of love is not a believer.

10.8. Conclusion: United with the Victor

For Luther then, as for the other Reformers, faith is inherently active and alive, or it is not faith. Yet such faith does not justify because it leads to good works or is itself meritorious but because it looks away from the self of the believer and to Christ, receiving his alien righteousness. This is widely and correctly understood as Luther's teaching, but what is so often misunderstood is that for Luther the alien righteousness received is not a substance or commodity transferred from Christ to the believer. Faith indeed trusts in God's promises, but, as it does so, those who believe are united with Christ. The presence of Christ in faith means that although there is indeed an exchange—with Christ receiving the sins of believers and them receiving his righteousness—this exchange takes place within a union of persons. The gift of Christ's righteousness cannot be understood apart from the totality of Christ's person and work or the necessity for believers to live the alien life of Christ (Gal 2:19–20).

As Alister McGrath points out, it is because Luther perceives Christ as present in faith that he is "able to assert at one and the same time that the righteousness of believers is, and will remain extrinsic to them, while Christ is nonetheless really present within believers, effecting their renovation and regeneration."[21] Luther

---

effective through love." If middle, Paul speaks of "faith working through love." With the majority of translations (including the Latin Vulgate) and commentators in all eras, Luther takes the participle as middle. His exegetical point is that if this is correct, Paul's words do not easily speak of faith as something passive or unformed but as something active and working.

21. Alister McGrath, *Iustitia Dei: A History of the Christian Doctrine of Justification*, 3rd ed. (Cambridge: Cambridge University Press, 2005), 229.

therefore has no need to separate from each other the justification and renewal of believers any more than he needs to separate from each other different parts of Christ's person and work. Precisely because believers must live the alien life of Christ, their renewal can never be regarded as their accomplishment or as in any sense meritorious.

In relation to Luther, the common criticisms of Protestant accounts of justification with which this chapter began are therefore simply misconceived. To emphasize that the righteousness received in justification is and remains alien does not eliminate from justification the transformation of believers. Nor does an emphasis on the transformation of believers in justification make the righteousness they receive their own. The two are not in a competitive relationship, and so there is no wedge driven between declaring and making righteous, between justification as a once-and-for-all external act and regeneration as an internal lifelong process.

One of Luther's most distinctive contributions to understanding Paul's teaching about justification is thus his dual insistence on both alien righteousness and the necessity for believers to live an alien life. It is this double focus that enables Luther to attack righteousness by works while avoiding any hint that justification is merely fictional. It is also this double focus that enables him to avoid establishing a contractual view of justification. Faith does not justify because it is the appropriate response to God's grace, or because it believes in an abstract system or theory of justification, or because it is the right kind of religious disposition to fulfill the human side of a bargain between God and humanity. Instead, faith justifies because it grasps hold of Christ: "For Luther, 'faith in Christ' is Christocentric."[22] Paul's formula that justification is not by works of the law but through faith in Jesus Christ (Gal 2:16) serves to "confess Christ, who is present in faith, as the *one* in, by, and on the basis of whom God justifies the ungodly."[23]

Yet even as it answers many common objections to his Pauline exegesis and theology, the very strength of Luther's emphasis on union with Christ in justification potentially raises others. In what way does this union work? Beyond asserting that Christ is received through faith, Luther will often use marital imagery ("faith couples Christ and me more intimately than a husband is coupled to his wife") (*LW* 26:168), or compare it to the mystery of the divine presence in biblical contexts such as at Mount Sinai or in the Jerusalem temple, but he does not spell out

---

22. Jonathan A. Linebaugh, "The Christocentrism of Faith in Christ: Martin Luther's Reading of Galatians 2:16, 19–20," in *The Word of the Cross: Reading Paul* (Grand Rapids: Eerdmans, 2022), 200.

23. Linebaugh, "Christocentrism," 201.

what this means for the status of those in Christ. If they are understood simply to be merged with Christ, then is the distinction between God as Creator and believers as creatures in danger of being collapsed? But if they are understood merely to remain separate partners in a close relationship, does this do justice to the strength of either Luther's or Paul's imagery?

A way forward may be to think of a mutual indwelling that operates in a manner analogous to the relationship between the divine and human natures of Christ in classical Christology, which are not confused and remain distinct but do so in one person without division or separation.[24] Yet although such questions are important, Luther's own focus is not here on explaining the mystery of Christ's presence or on the need to maintain appropriate distinctions between Creator and creatures. Indeed, it seems likely that he would be perplexed by any suggestion that his understanding of justification runs the risk of unduly exalting believers.

For Luther's relentless insistence on the alien nature of all aspects of justification—the righteousness received by believers, the divine word that evokes the faith in which Christ is present, and the life that the believers now lead—highlights instead that human beings stand before God only as beggars who have no soteriological resources of their own to offer. Even as they make progress in faith, those who believe are not building their own righteousness as if it is a quality that can be increased over time. Rather, righteousness always remains a matter of living in someone external. Believers must struggle to appropriate Christ and his perpetually superabundant righteousness daily in faith. All progress they make in faith is therefore also a return to their baptism and to the beginning of their life in Christ.[25]

Luther thus does not recognize any tension between the alien nature of Christ's righteousness received by believers and Christ's presence in believers. On the basis of Paul's teaching, he thinks that the two simply belong together. The tension of which Luther is acutely aware is rather the apocalyptic contrast between the old self dead in sin and captive to the devil, and the believer as new creation. The old self must die through being crucified with Christ (Gal 2:19), and to say otherwise is from Luther's perspective to set aside the grace of God. Commenting on Gal 2:16 and its assertions that justification is by faith and not by works of the law, Luther

24. This suggestion is made by Olli-Pekka Vainio, *Justification and Participation in Christ: The Development of the Lutheran Doctrine of Justification from Luther to the Formula of Concord (1580)* (Leiden: Brill, 2008), 35.

25. On this distinctive view of sanctification and the radical differences between it and medieval accounts, see Miikka Ruokanen, *Trinitarian Grace in Martin Luther's* The Bondage of the Will (Oxford: Oxford University Press, 2021), 145–46.

says of the believer, "For to the extent that he is a Christian, he is above the Law and sin, because in his heart he has Christ, the Lord of the Law, as a ring has a gem. Therefore when the Law accuses and sin troubles, he looks to Christ; and when he has taken hold of Him by faith, he has present with him the Victor over the Law, sin, death, and the devil—the Victor whose rule over all these prevents them from harming him" (*LW* 26:134). In union with Christ through faith, by having Christ "as a ring has a gem," the justified believer shares in Christ's victory.

CHAPTER ELEVEN

Philip Melanchthon: Justification on Account of Christ

As Luther's closest colleague and friend, Philip Melanchthon played a crucial role in mediating Luther's ideas to subsequent generations. He did so in multiple ways, two of which are especially significant in relation to Pauline interpretation. First, it was Melanchthon and not Luther who produced commentaries on Romans, the letter that Luther himself famously described as "the chief part of the New Testament and the very purest gospel" (*LW* 35:365). This occurred primarily because once Melanchthon joined the faculty at Wittenberg in 1518, it was he who afterward lectured on Romans while Luther focused on Galatians.[1] Second, Melanchthon systematized Luther's key convictions in a widely influential textbook, *Loci Communes* ("The Commonplaces"), first published in 1521.[2] Melanchthon replaced the categories of the standard medieval textbook, Peter Lombard's *Sentences*, with ones based upon Paul's topics in Romans. Now there was an appropriately Pauline educational tool with which to shape the theology that future pastors would preach to their congregations.

11.1. Luther's Legacy: Melanchthon's Complex Role

Luther, who characteristically produced combative tracts for the times or expositions of Scripture rather than systematic theological statements, was overjoyed ("No better book has been written after the Holy Scriptures") (*LW* 54:440; *Table*

---

1. Melanchthon produced a commentary on Romans in 1532, with revised versions in 1540 and 1556. It is the 1540 commentary that appears in English as Philip Melanchthon, *Commentary on Romans*, trans. Fred Kramer (Saint Louis: Concordia, 1992).

2. Major editions of *Loci Communes* appeared in 1521, 1535, 1543 (all Latin), and 1555 (German).

Talk no. 5511). He recognized that Melanchthon had achieved something important that he was ill-equipped to do for himself. Yet despite his status as Luther's greatest supporter, Melanchthon, who survived Luther by just over fourteen years, is often portrayed as responsible for misdirecting Luther's legacy. For it was Melanchthon, and not Luther, who was principally responsible for highlighting the forensic nature of justification and interpreting it in legal terms. Given that union with Christ is central to Luther's own account of justification, it is tempting to acquit Luther of the charge of making justification a cold legal fiction that leaves believers essentially unchanged and instead convict Melanchthon.

In fact, this is an oversimplification. Melanchthon's account of justification amounts to a great deal more than simply the forensic metaphor, and the charge of a legal fiction is unfair. Yet Melanchthon does differ from Luther on crucial points and in ways that did have significant consequences for the future of Protestant theology. These differences emerge in how Melanchthon expresses the christological focus of justification and in how he expresses the relationship between justification and renewal. Luther and Melanchthon agree in insisting that the righteousness received by believers is not their own, but they diverge in what they say about how this alien righteousness is received. The two agree in eliminating meritorious works from justification but diverge about how best to avoid any danger of their reintroduction. To understand this pattern of significant differences that existed within a framework of fundamental agreements, it is necessary first to grasp Melanchthon's own contribution to understanding Paul's teaching about justification. Only then can Melanchthon's Pauline exegesis be carefully compared with that of Luther.

11.2. The Very Purest Gospel: Romans and Rhetoric

Before he published anything on Paul's letters, Melanchthon was already the author of a Greek grammar and of textbooks on rhetoric (the arts of discourse used by speakers to inform or persuade audiences) and dialectics (the resolution of disagreement through rational argument). Unsurprisingly he applied his humanist training and skill in the analysis of ancient texts to the interpretation of Romans. Melanchthon's analysis of the rhetoric of Romans begins with a correct definition of the main terms or topics (*loci*) used by Paul. His commentaries on the epistle do not immediately begin with exegesis of Rom 1 but first define key terms such as sin, justification, grace, faith, works of the law, and so on.

Melanchthon believed that this concern with the definition of terms mirrored Paul's own, with Rom 5:12–8:11 offering extended and careful definitions of terms such as sin, law, and grace vital to his earlier argument. Through understanding in this way how Paul's argument is organized, Melanchthon was able to identify the *scopus* (the main thing Paul had in mind in his argument), which was justification by faith apart from the works of the law. He was also able to identify the *status caussae* (the summary statement or proposition that sums up this main concern) of the letter. In Romans, the *status* is introduced in 1:16–17 where, speaking of the righteousness of God, Paul provides "a summary of the Gospel . . . when he mentions the righteousness of God, he embraces all the benefits of Christ." This summary is expounded at greater length in 3:21–26, where there is "the principal proposition which . . . contains the real and chief statement of the Gospel."[3]

This analysis of the rhetoric of Romans was not only crucial to understanding the argument of the letter. It in fact also provided a hermeneutical key to understanding Scripture. For it indicated that 1:16–17 and 3:21–26 are essential to truly understanding Romans in an interpretative context where this letter was acknowledged as the purest expression of the gospel within the New Testament canon. These texts offered a lens through which accurately to view Romans, while Romans offered a lens through which accurately to view the whole of Scripture. Further, Melanchthon's rhetorical analysis provided assurance that Romans was being interpreted according to Paul's own intentions. For Melanchthon's audience included many who shared his humanist education and therefore appreciated his skills of analysis of ancient rhetoric. This made Melanchthon a particularly convincing interpreter for many. As Timothy Wengert puts it, "he produced a commentary that to contemporary readers, who were also steeped in humanism's rhetorical techniques, would have sounded like the Apostle Paul's own voice commenting on the sixteenth century's most critical theological debates."[4]

11.3. Justification in Context: The Drama of Salvation

Melanchthon's rhetorical analysis of Romans thus places interpretation of Paul's letter and the understanding of the gospel and of all of Scripture into direct relationship with each other. If Rom 1:16–17 and 3:21–26 speak profoundly about forensic justification, then forensic justification must be central to the argument of Romans and therefore to the truth of the gospel. Yet the reverse also follows.

3. Melanchthon, *Commentary on Romans*, 80, 98.

4. Timothy Wengert, "Philip Melanchthon's 1522 Annotations on Romans and the Lutheran Origins of Rhetorical Criticism," in *Biblical Interpretation in the Era of the Reformation*, ed. Richard A. Muller and John Lee Thompson (Grand Rapids: Eerdmans, 1996), 118.

Forensic justification only makes sense if it stands at the center of the drama of salvation about which the whole of Scripture speaks. The parts and the whole are essential to each other. To abstract forensic justification from its place in the drama of salvation and to analyze Melanchthon's understanding of it apart from his perspective on this wider drama risks distorting his views. It is important to begin discussion of the content of Melanchthon's interpretation of Romans not with detailed discussion of Paul's use of the verb "justify" (*dikaioō*) but with the overall drama of salvation.

For Melanchthon, this drama begins with the human plight apart from Christ, which he understands in line with the common account shared widely by early Protestant interpreters (see chapter 6). In Melanchthon's view, philosophy and reason do reveal that a civil righteousness of disciplined and upright deeds is possible for fallen human beings. Yet this is not the perfect obedience required by the law of God, and it is the inability to meet this requirement that makes it impossible for sinful human beings to be justified by their deeds. To confuse civil righteousness with the righteousness that justifies before God is therefore a tragic mistake. This is the error made by the Reformers' Catholic opponents when they attempt to restrict the reference of Paul's phrase "works of the law" to ceremonies only and refuse to recognize that the apostle speaks also about moral works. They fail to see that human beings are utterly incapable of contributing to their own salvation through meritorious obedience.

It is this confusion to which Paul refers when he says in Rom 2:1 that those who judge others for the sins previously described in 1:18–32 do the same things. They confuse the civil righteousness of their outward deeds with justifying righteousness, failing to see "the uncleanness of the heart, namely these sins: doubt about God; lack of the fear of God, trust, and love. . . . They do not see these vices, much less the fact that they are sins."[5] It is noteworthy that in this list, Melanchthon focuses the sins of those who erroneously consider themselves righteous on their attitude toward God. For Melanchthon understands salvation through Christ principally as a restoration of relationship with God. From the very moment that human beings fell, God responded not only with judgment but also with gracious promises of salvation:

> When Adam had fallen and was accused, he could think nothing except what the Law showed—that he would perish because he had not obeyed God. But God comes forward, and although he subjects the human race to death of the body and other ills, he nevertheless sets forth a consolation: he promises liberation from sin and death, and the restoration of the human race. He says

5. Melanchthon, *Commentary on Romans*, 133.

that it would come to pass that the seed of the woman would crush the head of the serpent [Gen 3:15]. When this had been said, the Son of God moved the heart of Adam and poured new light and life into him.[6]

The law judges and condemns human failure to obey God's commandments, but the gospel promise of gratuitous forgiveness and new life dogs its footsteps. Already Adam, the father of humanity, was righteous through faith, and already in its opening narratives, Scripture is to be interpreted according to Luther's hermeneutic of law and gospel. The knowledge of sin brings conviction of judgment and results in terror, but Paul's purpose is not to leave his readers simply with a right understanding of their bondage. Instead, it is that they should transition from law to the comfort of the gospel, the hermeneutic of law and gospel itself becoming a lived experience: "on several occasions in his exposition of Romans, Melanchthon used and relied upon the examples of Adam and David (as Paul had used the example of Abraham in Romans 4), because they showed that justification by faith alone was not a matter of some 'cold, lifeless concept of the soul' but had to strike fear into a person's heart and provide true comfort."[7]

It is in the context of this transition from law to the comfort of the gospel that Melanchthon's insistence on the forensic nature of justification belongs. For Melanchthon is convinced that Paul's purpose in using a legal metaphor is to express this crucial transition in the relationship of sinners with God: "This word 'relational' (Latin: *relative*), which Melanchthon consistently used after 1531, is a more accurate description of his intention than the standard term, forensic. When Melanchthon compared justification to what happens *in foro* (in a court of law) to a guilty person who is pronounced not guilty, he did so to explain Paul's Hebraism and to explain the relational aspect of such righteousness-producing faith."[8]

The relational purpose of Paul's legal imagery is closely connected to Christ's role as mediator in his saving death. Paul's description of Christ's death as a redeeming sacrifice in Rom 3:24–25 prompts Melanchthon to comment that "the world does not see the greatness of the wrath of God against sin, and says that sin is an unimportant thing. But here let us learn that the wrath is so great that no sacrificial victim could placate God, save only the death of his Son."[9] In his

6. Melanchthon, *Commentary on Romans*, 23.

7. Timothy Wengert, *Defending Faith: Lutheran Responses to Andreas Osiander's Doctrine of Justification, 1551–1559* (Tübingen: Mohr Siebeck, 2012), 350.

8. Timothy Wengert, "The Rhetorical Paul: Philip Melanchthon's Interpretation of the Pauline Epistles," in *A Companion to Paul in the Reformation*, ed. R. Ward Holder (Leiden: Brill, 2009), 155.

9. Melanchthon, *Commentary on Romans*, 100.

crucifixion, Christ is the propitiator whose obedient sacrifice is effective, whereas all efforts to rely on works and what they merit are doomed to failure: "For we are righteous, that is, accepted by God, not on account of our perfection but through mercy on account of Christ, as long as we take hold of it and set it against the wrath of God."[10]

Melanchthon will sometimes say that the righteousness received by the believer is the righteousness of Christ, but his phrasing in this quotation that believers are justified "on account of [*propter*] Christ" (alternatively translated "because of/for the sake of Christ") is far more characteristic. He does not argue that Christ is present in faith and that consequently, united with him by faith, the believer receives Christ's righteousness. Nor does he characteristically argue that Christ's righteousness is in some sense transferred to the believer. Melanchthon seems content to say that Christ is and remains the mediator whose death pleads the believer's case before the Father.

It is Christ and his saving work on the cross who turns away divine judgment against sin and who continuously secures access to the Father for believers. Melanchthon again and again emphasizes this relational dynamic in his accounts of justification. It helps him to clarify exactly what he understands Paul to mean by faith as trust (*fiducia*), and to keep it distinct from the infusion of virtue-producing grace characteristic of medieval understandings of justification. When expounding Rom 3:25, Melanchthon notes that to say, "we are justified by faith," is correlative to saying, "we are pleasing to God through mercy," that is, they are alternative ways of expressing the same truth. Melanchthon then continues,

> Although I fully agree that faith and trust are qualities, they nevertheless become, like the names of the other desires, relational, as love behaves itself in a way relative to that which we love, fear to the object which is feared, and trust to its object on which it rests. . . . [I]t is necessary that mention be made of faith because it is necessary that there be some impulse by which we accept the gift and apply it to ourselves. . . . This impulse of faith in our minds is not an idle cogitation, but it wrestles with the terrors of sin and death.[11]

Faith thus has a strong cognitive dimension, for it is an impulse of the mind. Yet this cognitive element is not primarily a question of knowledge but of desire.

---

10. "Apology of the Augsburg Confession," in *The Book of Concord: The Confessions of the Evangelical Lutheran Church*, ed. Robert Kolb and Timothy J. Wengert (Minneapolis: Fortress, 2000), para. 227.

11. Melanchthon, *Commentary on Romans*, 29.

Melanchthon will go on to speak of the devil's attempts to break weak minds so that there is either contempt of God or despair. Yet he also emphasizes that faith "fights lest it lose God, lest it be torn away from God. . . . God is seen in his Word, and when the mind looks upon the Word, its faith is strengthened." Given life by its encounter with God's word, faith justifies "because it takes hold of the mercy [of God]."[12]

The *Apology of the Augsburg Confession* expresses things similarly when it says that "faith is the very righteousness by which we are reckoned righteous before God, not because it is a work that is worthy in and of itself, but because it receives the promise by which God has pledged that on account of Christ he desires to be gracious to those who believe in him."[13] Faith is so important from Melanchthon's perspective because, through Christ the mediator, it brings and keeps human beings in relationship with God. It is reliance upon this relationship secured by justification that he places in opposition to accounts of justification centered upon an infused righteousness. The alien righteousness upon which believers rely is the righteousness of Christ who intercedes for them before the Father with complete sufficiency.

11.4. Forensic Justification: Courtroom Imagery and Scipio Africanus

It is only within this relational context, with its enormous emphasis on Christ's role as mediator on behalf of sinners, that Melanchthon's explanation of the specifically forensic nature of justification can be fully understood. The legal nature of Paul's imagery is highlighted in the definition of justification Melanchthon provides in his Romans commentary of 1540, where it is explicitly coordinated with his relational perspective:

> According to the Hebrew usage of the term, to justify is to pronounce or to consider as just, as is said in Hebrew: "The Roman people justified Scipio when he was accused by the tribunes," that is, absolved him or pronounced him just. Thus we know for certain that in these disputations of Paul justification signifies the remission of sins and acceptance to eternal life, as the fourth chapter of Romans testifies in a sufficiently clear manner, where it defines justification as the forgiveness of sins. Therefore when we say we are justified by faith it is the same thing as saying that we are accounted just by God on account of

12. Melanchthon, *Commentary on Romans*, 30, 57.
13. "Apology of the Augsburg Confession," para. 86.

[*propter*] Christ when we believe. . . . It signifies the imputation of *iustitia*, or acceptance. And *iustus* is in this way understood relationally [*relative*] as acceptance to eternal life.[14]

The historical reference here is to the Roman general Scipio Africanus (236–183 BCE), victor over Hannibal in the Second Punic War at the battle of Zama in 202 BCE. When later accused in the mid-180s BCE of having taken a bribe from the Seleucid king Antiochus III, Scipio did not deign to defend himself against the charges but to popular acclaim on the anniversary of Zama simply reminded the court of his victory on behalf of Rome. He then left the court to go offer sacrifices of thanksgiving to the gods, followed by virtually all present, leaving the tribunes with no defendant and no trial.

It is odd that Melanchthon should write here as if the Roman people pronounced Scipio innocent in Hebrew. What he appears to mean, given that the accounts of Scipio's trial in our Latin and Greek sources do not actually speak of his acquittal as a justification, is that the Hebrew verb in the Old Testament equivalent to the Greek *dikaioō* ("justify") is a forensic term. If one were to speak about Scipio's acquittal in Hebrew, then one would speak of him as having been justified by the people. Melanchthon writes in a less confusing way in the *Loci Communes* (1535) and *Loci Communes* (1543), but, in those places, he also uses the example of Scipio to illustrate a Hebrew expression.[15]

The episode clearly appeals strongly to Melanchthon. This may partly be due to Scipio's idealized status within the humanist tradition. Petrarch had conceived Scipio as a "living symbol of what history and philosophy teach regarding what man should strive to be."[16] To use an individual outstanding in civic righteousness as a primary illustration of how sinners are justified before God would certainly seem to serve Melanchthon's theological purposes. More important are the parallels presented by the details of the episode to his relational understanding of justification. Scipio is pronounced righteous by the Roman people not because he disproves the charges against him but because they set against the charges the overwhelming virtue of his service to Rome, without which, had he not defeated

---

14. Melanchthon, *Commentary on Romans*, 25.

15. See *CR* 21:421 (*Loci Communes* [1535]), and Philip Melanchthon, *Loci Communes 1543*, trans J. A. O. Preus (Saint Louis: Concordia, 1992), 86.

16. Aldo Bernardo, *Petrarch, Scipio, and the "Africa": The Birth of Humanism's Dream* (Baltimore: Johns Hopkins University Press, 1962), 10. Also to be noted is Augustine's identification of Rome's ingratitude to Scipio with the tipping point in the decline of Rome's morals. See Augustine, *The City of God against the Pagans*, trans. R. W. Dyson (Cambridge: Cambridge University Press, 1998), 3.21 (129–31).

the Carthaginians, a Roman court in which to put him on trial would not even exist. Similarly, the believer does not disprove his or her sinfulness, but in God's court there is set against this charge the overwhelmingly greater work of Christ as a propitiating sacrifice. It is Christ's total obedience as mediator that grants complete righteousness to the believer.

11.5. Justification and Renewal: Keeping Them Together

From the beginning, there were critics who heard Melanchthon's account of justification as fictional because the legal metaphors do not appear directly to address the transformation of the believer.[17] Yet from Melanchthon's own perspective, his account was very far from constituting a kind of fiction. For Christ's sacrifice is the ever-present reality that is set against and overwhelms sin in the divine courtroom. As Wengert puts it, Melanchthon was "not simply talking about a mental construct, a fictive judicial 'as if,' but an actual turn of events before God's judgment seat. Thus, the actual sinner, oppressed by sin (that is, under the law), heard the judge speak a completely unexpected word of grace ... for Melanchthon everything changed because of this divine pronouncement of judgment (law) and forgiveness (gospel)."[18] To rely on the complete and perfect righteousness found in Christ's self-offering is to trust what is solid and certain in contrast to the lack of assurance available to those who grant a place in justification to the meritorious works of the believer.

Further, the divine declaration of acquittal that constitutes justification is an effective word, in which divine speech accomplishes what it pronounces. It is, as twentieth-century Melanchthon scholarship has often termed it, a "word-event" (*Wortgeschehen*) that is the gateway to new life.[19] The divine word of acquittal fulfills the divine word of promise on account of the offering of Christ, himself the Word of God, which is testified to in the Scriptures that are also the word of

17. As early as 1538, in his *Enchiridion christianae institutionis*, the Catholic scholar Johannes Gropper objected that those whom God justifies are not like acquitted prisoners but more like those truly convicted but subsequently restored. See the discussion in Brian Lugioyo, *Martin Bucer's Doctrine of Justification: Reformation Theology and Early Modern Irenicism* (Oxford: Oxford University Press, 2011), 103–33.

18. Wengert, *Defending Faith*, 341.

19. See especially Martin Greschat, *Melanchthon neben Luther: Studien zur Gestalt der Rechtfertigungslehre zwischen 1528 und 1537* (Wittenberg: Luther-Verlag, 1965), 83, who speaks of the "central significance" ("zentrale Bedeutung") that the "word-event" occupies in the theological thought of the Reformer.

God. As Melanchthon says when commenting on Rom 10:8 ("The Word is near, in your mouth"): "God is found nowhere outside of his Word, or without his Word; he wants to be known through it. By means of this instrument he wants to work."[20]

This bringing of life by the justifying word of God means that alongside justification, the believer also receives renewal through the gift of the Holy Spirit. Even as he introduces the example of Scipio to illustrate the forensic nature of the verb "to justify," Melanchthon insists that "one must know that in the forgiveness of sins there is given at the same time (*simul*) the Holy Spirit. . . . Thus the gift of the Holy Spirit is connected with justification, which begins not only one virtue—faith—but also others: fear and love of God, love of the truth, chastity, patience, justice toward the neighbor, as I shall say later about works."[21]

Commenting on Rom 5:15, Melanchthon will write that grace overcomes sin "doubly, by imputation and by its effect. It overcomes by imputation, because God accounts those who lay hold of grace to be righteous, although in fact they still have the remnants of sin. Thereafter, it also overcomes it in effect, because in them, although they are weak, there are new impulses which resist sin."[22] Melanchthon characteristically attributes this renewal and the capacity to produce good works to the work of the Holy Spirit in the believer. Such statements show that, far from ignoring renewal, Melanchthon is careful in his exegesis of Romans to provide an overall account of salvation that includes the ethical renewal of the believer. Justification is a forensic declaration, and renewal is a distinct phase consequent upon justification, but renewal is made prominent.

11.6. Justification and Renewal: Keeping Them Distinct

Such careful articulation by Melanchthon of the relationship between different aspects of salvation took several decades to achieve. In the 1520s, Melanchthon appears content to argue that the good works of renewal are not in any sense a cause of justification or a source of merit but nevertheless to speak as if such good works are in some sense included in what is meant by justification. In *Loci Communes* (1521), justification "is described as participation in Christ's righteousness while it is actualized in the new affects that are evoked by the Spirit and renewed according to the Law of God."[23] Faith is itself a gift evoked by the Holy Spirit, and

---

20. Melanchthon, *Commentary on Romans*, 198.
21. Melanchthon, *Commentary on Romans*, 25.
22. Melanchthon, *Commentary on Romans*, 136–37.
23. Olli-Pekka Vainio, *Justification and Participation in Christ: The Development of the Lu-*

"this faith in the good-will of God permeates the whole life, all works, all physical and spiritual trials." It is therefore quite clear that this faith is active and performs works. While it is plain that the works of faith are not meritorious, what is conspicuously not said is that such works of faith are to be sharply distinguished from justification. No clear boundary is delineated.

However, by the time of the *Commentary on Romans* (1532), Melanchthon was drawing a clear distinction between justification as acceptance and renewal by the Spirit: "Although it is necessary that the new movements will occur in those who are reconciled, justification does not, however, mean having new virtues. It is understood as a matter of relation (*relative*), which refers to God's will of those who are approved and accepted by God."[24] The traditional term "imputation" by which justification is described is therefore to be identified with acceptance by God in a way that excludes the renewal that brings new virtues. Imputation does not have an effective aspect: "Melanchthon henceforth holds exclusively to imputation, with which acceptation is equated."[25]

As Melanchthon will express it in the *Commentary on Romans* (1540), "We must include these things when we dispute about justification: remission of sins and imputation of righteousness—that is, acceptance—joined to which is the gift of the Holy Spirit and acceptance to life eternal."[26] Melanchthon insists that justification is always accompanied by renewal through the Holy Spirit, but he also insists that this renewal is not itself to be identified with, or included in, justification. Renewal by the Holy Spirit is still an essential part of how Melanchthon understands Paul's soteriology, but it is a different albeit closely related aspect of salvation from justification.

Later in Melanchthon's career, after Luther's death, he became involved in the Osiander controversy that gripped the Lutheran movement in the 1550s. Andreas Osiander (1498–1552), who had been a key figure in the adoption of the Reformation in Nuremberg in the 1520s, and who later became professor of theology at the new Königsberg University, claimed that Melanchthon and others were distorting Luther's teaching. Osiander wrote that "they teach [doctrines] colder than ice,

---

theran Doctrine of Justification from Luther to the Formula of Concord (1580) (Leiden: Brill, 2008), 63–93, provides an account that distinguishes three phases in Melanchthon's development of his views on justification.

24. *MSA* 5:39, 12–16. The translation is that of Vainio, *Justification and Participation in Christ*, 77.

25. Robert Stupperich, "Die Rechfertigungslehre bei Luther und Melanchthon 1530–1536," in *Luther and Melanchthon in the History and Theology of the Reformation*, ed. Vilmos Vajta (Philadelphia: Muhlenberg, 1961), 83: "Melanchthon hält sich nunmehr ausschließlich an die imputatio, mit der die acceptatio gleichgesetzt wird" (my English translation).

26. Melanchthon, *Commentary on Romans*, 100.

that we are accounted righteous only on account of the remission of sins, and not also on account of the righteousness of Christ dwelling in us by faith. God is not indeed so unjust as to regard him as righteous in whom there is really nothing of true righteousness."[27]

Thus, Osiander's basic complaint is that union with Christ in faith is being neglected in Melanchthon's account of justification. Yet Osiander's attempt to insist that imputation involves the presence of Christ in faith was compromised by problems in his own articulation of justification. He focuses the presence of Christ in faith only on his divine nature, separating it from his obedience and death on the cross. The crucifixion is the moment when Christ's sacrifice takes away divine wrath and brings forgiveness, but this simply serves to make possible the believer's subsequent union with Christ by faith. Unsurprisingly, this severing of Christ's person from his work received a universally negative reaction. Osiander was also unable successfully to clarify the relationship between the presence of Christ in faith and the good works performed by believers, and this led to the suspicion that he was allowing works once again to play a part in justification.[28]

Melanchthon vigorously pressed this point. In his *Commentary on Romans* (1556), he alleges that "Osiander understands the righteousness of God to be God dwelling in the re-born person and moving that one to do righteous things. So, by this approach [*res*] itself he teaches that a human being is righteous by renewal [*novitas*] and works."[29] For Melanchthon, if Osiander's teaching is accepted, then the comfort of the gospel promise is lost since the believer is left dependent for salvation upon the uncertainties of his or her own works. Melanchthon still wants to maintain that imputation is relational and is to be understood in terms of the forgiveness of sins and divine acceptance.

Yet Melanchthon is clearly sensitive to the charge that his theology neglects the truth that God dwells in the believer, and he is even more emphatic in his later works that he, too, embraces this. Without conceding the distinction between justification and renewal, Melanchthon will speak of the eschatological righteousness to which Paul refers in Gal 5:5 ("the hope of righteousness"), when

27. The translation is from Reinhold Seeberg, *Textbook of the History of Doctrines*, trans. Charles E. Hay (Philadelphia: Lutheran Publication Society, 1905), 370, quoting Osiander's *Disputatio de justificatione*, in his *Gesamtausgabe*, ed. Gerhard Müller and Gottfried Seebaß, 10 vols. (Gütersloh: Gütersloher Verlagshaus, 1975–1997).

28. There are those who regard Osiander as generally and unfairly misunderstood. See, for example, Anna Briskina, "An Orthodox View of Finnish Luther Research," *LQ* 22 (2008): 16–39. Yet even if this were proven to be true, Osiander as I have presented him is how he was understood by his contemporaries.

29. *CR* 15:855. The translation is that of Wengert, *Defending Faith*, 338.

in eternity "God himself is in the saved, and makes them like himself, so that they are entirely pure, without sin." This eschatological righteousness is anticipated in the life of the believer here and now: "The Holy Spirit is a living divine motion in us, producing in us that which is akin to God. . . . Thus there is a spark of new obedience in those who are converted to God; but the faith that *for the sake of the Lord Christ* we have forgiveness of sins, and are pleasing to God, must always precede, and this faith must be grounded on the *obedience of the Lord Christ*, God and man. When this comfort is in the heart, then we are the dwelling place of God and obedience is begun."[30]

In such statements, clearly anti-Osiandrian sentiments are leavened with recognition of the truth of divine indwelling. It is also in this context that Melanchthon will again speak not only of justification as "on account of/because of/for the sake of" Christ but also, as he had in *Loci Communes* (1521), as the imputation of the righteousness of Christ (*die Gerechtigkeit des herrn Christi*). Whether this means that the gift of the Holy Spirit is now for Melanchthon properly to be spoken of as part of justification is unclear. However, it does remain clear that the works of the believer do not belong within justification. He says of justification and sanctification (*Heiligung*) that "these two words are clear and distinct."[31] For Melanchthon, justification and renewal must not be divorced, and are received together, but they are not the same thing, and they also must be distinguished.

11.7. Conclusion: Relational Righteousness

At the heart of Melanchthon's perspective on justification in Paul's letters lies the conviction that the work of Christ changes the relationship between the believer and God. Justification is because of, or on account of, Christ, whose obedience unto death secures mercy for those who believe. Melanchthon's perspective is in this sense thoroughly christological, with enormous emphasis placed upon the role of Christ as mediator.[32] This insistence that justification is relational also demonstrates that the accusation that Melanchthon makes justification a cold

---

30. Melanchthon, *Melanchthon on Christian Doctrine*, 158–59, 162.

31. Melanchthon, *Melanchthon on Christian Doctrine*, 155–56, 161, 163.

32. This makes not entirely just Mark Seifrid's characterization of Melanchthon's account of justification as "anthropological" as opposed to "christological." Melanchthon may neglect union with Christ, but Christ is central to his account of justification in other ways. See Mark Seifrid, "The Text of Romans and the Theology of Melanchthon: The Preceptor of the Germans and the Apostle to the Gentiles," in *Reformation Readings of Paul: Explorations in History and Exegesis*, ed. Michael Allen and Jonathan A. Linebaugh (Downers Grove, IL: InterVarsity Press, 2015), 107–20.

legal fiction is in important respects unfair. There is no dispassionate forensic transaction but instead a transition from the terrors of the conscience experienced by sinners to the comfort supplied by the promises of the gospel. If there is a danger here, it is not Osiander's fear of a doctrine colder than ice but instead that there might be created the expectation of an experience of terror over sin and judgment as an essential emotional prelude to a breakthrough to true faith and assurance of salvation.

Melanchthon also ought not to be accused of an unhealthy separation of justification as a once-and-for-all event, which happens externally to the believer, from renewal as a lifelong process within the believer. If this became a problem in later Protestantism, it is a development that in Melanchthon's own day still lay in the future. He is clear that, although justification and renewal are distinct, the two always belong together in the experience of the believer. He is also clear that renewal is to be principally attributed to divine indwelling in the life of the believer.

Yet Melanchthon's emphasis here is nearly always on the work of the Holy Spirit within the believer. In his *Commentary on Romans* (1540), Melanchthon says much about this but little about union with Christ. He does not make a direct response to Paul's participatory vocabulary. The contrast with Luther is striking, for whom union with Christ is central to justification itself. Given the very significant influence exercised by Luther and Melanchthon over subsequent Protestant Pauline interpretation, it is important to clarify the nature of this difference and to understand its significance.

CHAPTER TWELVE

Luther and Melanchthon on Justification: Continuity or Contrast?

The conclusion that Melanchthon departed from Luther in his account of justification in such an important matter as union with Christ is a controversial one. Could Luther's closest colleague really have done so without this leading to public disagreement? And, given that there was no such public disagreement, would not sixteenth-century readers have assumed that in all essential respects, Melanchthon's opinions reflected those of Luther? Is it not more plausible that although the Finnish school may be right that union with Christ is important in Luther's theology, they are wrong that he treats it as part of justification? May not Luther in fact have understood justification within a similar relational framework to that proposed by Melanchthon?

12.1. Comparing Luther and Melanchthon: The Terms of the Debate

Such suggestions are consistent with the Lutheran tradition. The Formula of Concord (1577) is a key confessional document that found resolutions to multiple doctrinal controversies threatening to tear apart Lutheranism in the decades after Luther's death. It defines justification in a way that would certainly have been congenial to Melanchthon. It insists "that neither renewal, sanctification, virtues, nor good works are to be viewed or presented *tanquam forma aut pars aut causa iustificationis* (that is, as our righteousness before God or as a part or a cause of our righteousness). They are also not to be mixed into the article of justification under any other pretense, pretext, or terminology. Instead, the righteousness of faith consists alone in the forgiveness of sins by sheer grace, because of Christ's merit alone."[1]

---

1. "The Solid Declaration, Article III: Righteousness," in *The Book of Concord: The Confessions*

Here there certainly remain significant moral consequences of justification. God's word is powerfully creative, and the believer is a new creation. Transformation is affirmed, but renewal is not to be identified with forensic justification itself (renewal is not only excluded as a cause of justification but also as a part of justification in any sense). On this view, to do so would be to merge what Luther intended to remain inseparable but clearly distinct. The formula insists that salvation involves the indwelling of God in the believer but also that "this indwelling of God is not the righteousness of faith, which St Paul treats. . . . Rather, this indwelling is a result of the righteousness of faith which precedes it."[2]

Yet despite the Lutheran tradition's rejection of any clear differentiation between Luther and Melanchthon on justification, there have always been dissenting views who have asserted that Lutheranism has not followed Luther at this point. We have already seen the flawed protest of Osiander that belongs to the period after Luther's death, but, even in Luther's own lifetime, there were those who perceived differences between his teaching about justification and that of Melanchthon. In 1536, Conrad Cordatus, preacher at Niemegk, made a formal complaint about what he regarded as departures from Luther's teaching contained in a lecture given by Caspar Cruciger, a student of Melanchthon. As Cruciger based his lecture on Melanchthon's notes, the accusation was essentially also leveled against Melanchthon.[3]

To resolve the issue of whether there are significant differences between Luther and Melanchthon concerning justification therefore requires careful exploration of this episode. First, however, it also requires careful attention to their exegesis. For Luther and Melanchthon were above all biblical interpreters who grounded their theology in their exegesis. Their goal was fidelity to Scripture. If there are indeed significant differences between them in understanding justification, these should emerge first and foremost as they interpret texts. What results emerge if their comments on the same texts in the Pauline Letters are placed side by side? The division of exegetical labor between the two, with Luther focusing on Galatians and Melanchthon on Romans (see 11.1), makes this surprisingly difficult to do. Yet, if disparate sources are gathered, there are some texts where comparison is possible, and the results are instructive.

---

of the Evangelical Lutheran Church, ed. Robert Kolb and Timothy J. Wengert (Minneapolis: Fortress, 2000), para. 39.

2. "Solid Declaration, Article III," para. 54.

3. For a clear chronological account of the complex series of letters and meetings generated by this dispute, see Timothy J. Wengert, *Law and Gospel: Philip Melanchthon's Debate with John Agricola of Eisleben over Poenitentia* (Grand Rapids: Baker, 1997), 206–10.

12.2. Exegesis: The Righteousness of God (Rom 1:17; 3:5, 21–25; 2 Cor 5:21)

There is extensive agreement between Luther and Melanchthon in how they interpret Paul's important phrase "the righteousness of God." In their comments on Rom 1:17, both understand Paul to be speaking of the righteousness given by God to those who believe (an objective genitive construction in the Greek). The apostle is not here speaking of the righteousness of God's own character (a subjective genitive construction in the Greek).[4] Further, both agree that the righteousness granted to those who believe is not an initial gratuitous gift of grace with which they must cooperate by means of meritorious good works in order to gain God and eternal life. The righteousness given to those who confidently trust in divine promises is complete and full in Christ.[5]

They are also very close together in their comments on Rom 3:25–26, where Paul states that God provided Christ as an atoning sacrifice in order to demonstrate his righteousness and that he justifies the person who has faith in Jesus. Twice Melanchthon says that Paul's references here to God's righteousness denote a divine declaration that God is the one who justifies: "God would declare that he himself is the one who justifies."[6] As Luther similarly expresses it, "God, through the remission of sins which we have committed in the past, shows that He is the justifier of all." Further, both argue that God's justifying activity demonstrates something about his character. There is a reference here to the righteousness by which God is righteous in God's self, a righteousness that is exhibited in the justification of sinners. Luther is the more explicit on this point, saying that "the remission of sins proves that He is righteous *and* that He is able to justify" (*LW* 25:249), but Melanchthon, too, will say that "God reveals his righteousness, that is, that he himself is the one who will justify in the way He promised in the promises."[7] God's own righteousness is displayed in God's fidelity to God's promises.

Yet despite these strong agreements, differences emerge in their interpretation of a text where Paul uses the phrase "the righteousness of God" alongside the idea of being in Christ. At 2 Cor 5:21 Paul says about what God has done through Christ that "for our sake he made him to be sin who knew no sin, so that in him we might become the righteousness of God." In Melanchthon's view, for believers

---

4. See *LW* 25:151 and Melanchthon, *Commentary on Romans*, trans. Fred Kramer (Saint Louis: Concordia, 1992), 70.

5. See *LW* 26:270 and Melanchthon, *Commentary on Romans*, 71, where they comment on Paul's quotation from Hab 2:4, "The righteous shall live by faith."

6. Melanchthon, *Commentary on Romans*, 101.

7. Melanchthon, *Commentary on Romans*, 101.

to become the righteousness of God in Christ is for them to be accepted by God through imputation:

> But the righteousness about which the Gospel specifically speaks signifies relationally, the imputation of righteousness, that is, gratuitous acceptance to eternal life, although joined to it is the gift of the Holy Spirit. So when you hear the word *justified*, you should think about the Hebrew phrase which signifies "to be accounted or pronounced righteous," or that the accused person is absolved. And *righteous* signifies "accepted by God to eternal life." 2 Cor. 5[:21]: "He made him to be sin for us who knew no sin, so that in him we might become the righteousness of God," that is, Christ was made guilty for us so that we might become accepted because of him. This is the simple grammatical and true explanation of the words.[8]

It is striking that the concept of becoming the righteousness of God in Christ does not prompt Melanchthon to think at all in terms of union with Christ. Melanchthon, of course, does here discuss divine indwelling in the believer, for he emphasizes the gift of the Holy Spirit. Yet he is very clear that this is not included in justification but is instead joined to it. As important as the gift of the Holy Spirit is, it is not this to which the phrase "the righteousness of God" refers. The phrase itself is interpreted entirely within the framework of justification understood in relational terms, with believers pronounced righteous on account of Christ's sacrificial death.

That Luther reads the same verse in a significantly different way can be seen in the postscript he added to a letter that Melanchthon wrote to Johannes Brenz (1499–1570) in May 1531, in which he corrects Brenz's view of justification. Melanchthon stresses the danger of the idea that faith is the foundation and root (*radix*) of good works and that a person is justified on the basis of fulfilling the law through the agency of the Holy Spirit. Melanchthon says that "we are justified by faith alone, not because it is the root, as you write, but because it apprehends Christ, on account of which we are accepted,"[9] and that this acceptance is "not on account of the gift of the Holy Spirit in us."[10] In contrast, Luther writes,

---

8. Melanchthon, *Commentary on Romans*, 56.

9. *MBWT* 5:109, 15–17 (no. 1151): "sola fide sumus iusti, non quia sit radix, ut tu scribis, sed quia apprehendit Christum, propter quem sumus accepti" (my translation). Brenz was an early Lutheran theologian and biblical commentator, who spearheaded the Reformation in Württemberg.

10. *MBWT* 5:111, 41–42 (no. 1151): "non propter dona Spiritus sancti in nobis" (my translation).

And I am accustomed, my Brenz, for the sake of understanding it better, to think of it in these terms: as if there is no quality in my heart that might be called "faith" or "love," but in that place I put Jesus Christ and say, "This is my righteousness; he is the quality and (as they say) formal righteousness," so that I may in this way set myself free and disentangle myself from considering the law and works—even from considering that objective Christ, who is understood as teacher or giver. But I want him to be the gift and teaching in himself, so that I may have all things in him. Thus Christ says, "I am the way, the truth, and the life;" he does not say I give you the way, truth, and life, as if Christ stood outside of me and worked such things in me. He ought to be, dwell, live, speak in me, not through me or into me etc. 2 Cor 6[:16], so that we would be the righteousness of God in him, not in love or the gifts that follow.[11]

Luther clearly here wishes to support Melanchthon in denying that qualities worked by the Holy Spirit as a consequence of faith are justifying. But it is equally clear that Luther identifies becoming "the righteousness of God in him" with Christ being, dwelling, living, and speaking in the believer. The analogy with John 14:6 in which Luther explicitly denies that Christ stands outside of him is particularly telling, as is the fact that Christ himself is specifically named as the divine gift. Luther's postscript simply does not express the idea of becoming the righteousness of God in Christ in the same terms as Melanchthon's description of it as being accepted by God on account of Christ's sacrifice. Luther finds union with Christ central to Paul's meaning in 2 Cor 5:21, whereas Melanchthon does not.

Indeed, Luther's manner of expression demands the presence of Christ in faith for his teaching to remain coherent. For if it is denied that faith is a quality or virtue in the heart, and if it is said that Christ himself is the quality, then, if one wishes to continue to speak of justification by faith (and Luther certainly does wish to do so), Christ must be present in justifying faith. Luther here expresses very similar ideas about justification to those we found in his exegesis of Gal 2:20, where he distinguishes the righteousness by which Christ lives in the believer from the righteousness that is in the believer's own person.[12] United with Christ by faith, the believer lives not his or her own life but that of Christ, such that while the believer genuinely has righteousness, it can never properly be termed his or her own or used as a claim of merit.

---

11. *WA Br* 6:98–101 (no. 1818) = *MBWT* 5:104–13 (no. 1151). The translation is that of Timothy J. Wengert, "Melanchthon and Luther/Luther and Melanchthon," in *Philip Melanchthon, Speaker of the Reformation: Wittenberg's Other Reformer* (Burlington, VT: Ashgate Variorum, 2010), 69.

12. We should note the chronological proximity of this letter in May 1531 to Luther's lectures on Gal 2, delivered between July 24 and August 21, 1531.

12.3. Exegesis: Joyous Exchange (Gal 3:13; 2 Cor 5:21; Rom 8:3, 13)

Luther's comments on 2 Cor 5:21 are also significant because it is one of a number of texts that he interprets using the motif of "joyous exchange," in which Christ becomes what we are (sinners) in order that we might become what he is (righteous). When commenting on Gal 3:13, where it is stated that "Christ became a curse for us," Luther draws 2 Cor 5:21 into the discussion:

> Thus he calls Him "sin" in 2 Cor 5:21 when he says: "For our sake God made him to be sin who knew no sin." Although these statements could correctly be expounded by saying that Christ became a "curse," that is, a sacrifice for the curse, or "sin," that is, a sacrifice for sin; nevertheless, it is more pleasing if the precise meaning of the terms is preserved for the sake of greater emphasis [*si servetur propria significato vocum, propter maiorem Emphasin*]. For when a sinner really comes to knowledge of himself, he feels himself to be a sinner not only concretely or adjectivally but abstractly and substantively. That is, he seems to himself to be not only miserable but misery itself; not only a sinner, and an accursed one, but sin and the curse itself. Thus in Latin, when we want a strong way to say that someone is a criminal, we call him a "crime." It is something awful to bear sin, the wrath of God, the curse, and death. Therefore a man who feels these things in earnest really becomes sin, death, and the curse itself. (*LW* 26:288)

Thus, while Luther can accept the explanation of Christ being made sin as Christ being made a sacrifice for sin, it also matters to him to insist that significance be accorded to Paul's choice of nouns in Gal 3:13 and 2 Cor 5:21 ("curse" [*katara*], "sin" [*hamartia*]), and their literal sense ("precise meaning"). He can then explain atonement in terms of a duel within the person of Christ in which sin and death are annihilated as they are confronted by divine righteousness and life. In contrast, when commenting on Rom 8:3, where Paul says that God condemned sin in the flesh by sending his Son in the likeness of sinful flesh, Melanchthon brings together the same texts without making the same points:

> He says that Christ was made sin, or the sacrifice for sin. For here in "on account of sin," the word sin after the Hebraic manner signifies the sacrificial victim for sin, that is, the penalty or satisfaction for sin, or as the Latins say, the propitiatory sacrifice, and the Greeks κάθαρμα [*katharma*] (that which is thrown away in cleansing). It means the same thing as in the words *curse* and *anathema*, which signify things destined for satisfaction, for placating the wrath of God. Thus Isaiah [53:10] says of Christ: "Because he will make his

soul sin," that is, a sacrifice for sin. For this reason Paul so often inculcates, as in 2 Cor 5[:21]: "Him who did not know sin he made sin for us," that is, he was made the sacrificial victim who should bear the punishment of sin and make satisfaction for our sins. And to the Galatians [3:13] he says likewise that Christ was made a curse, that is, a propitiatory sacrifice, bearing the curse and wrath of God against sin.[13]

Melanchthon is happy to regard Paul's nouns as figures of speech indicating that Christ was a sacrificial victim, but to Luther it is necessary to insist that Christ was not simply a sacrifice for sin but actually became sin and a curse. The primary reason for this difference is *not* contradictory theologies of atonement. Gustav Aulén famously used passages from Luther such as the one quoted above in order to set Luther's teaching on atonement against Latin theological traditions in which the fundamental concepts are satisfaction and merit.[14] Yet there is no evidence that Luther would have perceived the conflict. In response to other texts, he has no difficulty in expressing atonement in terms similar to Melanchthon: "It was not possible to overcome God's wrath, judgment, conscience, hell, death, and all evil things, and indeed to gain all benefits, unless God's righteousness received satisfaction, sin was given its due reward, and death was overcome by justice. Accordingly, St Paul generally refers to the suffering and blood of Christ when he proclaims the grace of God in him, in order to indicate that all the benefits that are given to us through Christ, are granted only because of his ineffable merit and the price he paid."[15]

The significance of the difference is rather that a particular nexus of texts (Gal 3:13; 2 Cor 5:21; Rom 8:3, 13) prompts a different exegetical response from Luther than they do from Melanchthon. Luther finds in them the motif of exchange, and so, when discussing these texts, he expresses both atonement and justification in terms compatible with that motif, whereas Melanchthon does not. Agreement elsewhere shows that this is not in Luther and Melanchthon's own context a doctrinal contradiction, but neither will it do to underplay the difference. Luther simply and importantly finds in Paul a wider range of ways of expressing these key aspects of the gospel than does Melanchthon. Luther comments on Gal 3:14 that "through the curse, sin, and death of Christ we are blessed, that is, justified and

---

13. Melanchthon, *Commentary on Romans*, 165.

14. Gustav Aulén, *Christus Victor: An Historical Study of the Three Main Types of the Idea of the Atonement* (London: SPCK, 1931), 117–38.

15. *LW* 52:280. In relation to later debates about atonement, it is perhaps worth noting, however, that Luther does not here speak directly of the satisfying of divine wrath but of the satisfying of divine righteousness.

made alive. So long as sin, death, and the curse remain in us, sin damns us, death kills us, and the curse curses us; but when these things are transferred to Christ, what is ours becomes His and what is His becomes ours. Let us learn, therefore, in every temptation to transfer sin, death, the curse, and all the evils that oppress us from ourselves to Christ, and, on the other hand, to transfer righteousness, life, and blessing from Him to us."[16]

This exchange cannot be interpreted as a transfer of qualities from Christ to believers apart from a union of persons. For Luther has already expounded Gal 2:20 in terms of such a union, saying that "Christ is fixed and cemented to me and abides in me. The life that I now live, he lives in me. In this way, therefore, Christ and I are one" (*LW* 26:167). Luther means rather that righteousness, life, and blessing are received by believers because they are united with Christ by faith. Luther must insist that Christ literally became sin and a curse if the reality of Christ's righteousness in the persons of believers, received in union with Christ, is to be matched by, and grounded upon, the preceding reality of the sins of the world in the person of the Savior. Once such a pattern of exchange is found in Paul's texts, it is impossible to expound justification solely within Melanchthon's relational paradigm.

12.4. Exegesis: Grace and Gift (Rom 5:15)

A similar difference appears in Luther and Melanchthon's interpretations of Rom 5:15, where Paul speaks of "the grace of God and the free gift in the grace of the one man Jesus Christ."[17] Both agree that Paul uses the word "grace" (*charis/gratia*) to speak not of infused grace but of divine favor. However, they understand the term "gift" (*dōrea/donum*) in quite different ways. Melanchthon identifies the gift with the Holy Spirit given as a consequence of grace. In his *Commentary on Romans* (1540), Melanchthon aligns the distinction between gift and grace with different persons of the Trinity: "Grace signifies gratuitous acceptance because of Christ, that is, gratuitous remission of sins, and gratuitous imputation of righteousness because of Christ. The gift through grace signifies the giving of the Holy

---

16. *LW* 26:292. This quotation is from a sermon on Matt 2:11 in the *Church Postil* (1521–1522).

17. On this verse, see Rolf Schäfer, "Melanchthon's Interpretation of Romans 5.15: His Departure from the Augustinian Concept of Grace Compared to Luther's," in *Philip Melanchthon (1497–1560) and the Commentary*, ed. Timothy J. Wengert and M. Patrick Graham (Sheffield: Sheffield Academic, 1997), 79–104; and Simo Peura, "Christ as Favor and Gift: The Challenge of Luther's Understanding of Justification," in *Union with Christ: The New Finnish Interpretation of Luther*, ed. Carl E. Braaten and Robert W. Jenson (Grand Rapids: Eerdmans, 1998), 42–69.

Spirit and eternal life. . . . [T]he conscience declares that we are righteous, that is, accepted, because of Christ. It does not look to our own worthiness, but to the Word or promise, and according to that it speaks about the will of God toward us, and thus apprehends Christ, the mediator. When this happens the Holy Spirit is given and new impulses come into being in us."[18]

The gift is therefore distinguished from imputed righteousness and is identified with the consequent renewal of the believer wrought by the Holy Spirit. Things are quite different with Luther, who identifies "the gift in the grace of one man" with faith in Christ. This identification, with which Luther begins his treatment of the text in *Against Latomus* (1521), is crucial to understanding what follows, in which grace and gift are portrayed as mutually conditioning, that is, gift is understood as a consequence of grace and grace as a consequence of gift. Grace has conceptual priority in the sense that the gift "is given to us through the grace of Christ, because he alone among all men is beloved and accepted and has a kind and gentle God so that he might merit for us this gift and even this grace" (*LW* 32:228). The divine intention to act graciously in Christ for sinners comes before all things, and so "the grace of God is not contingent upon a gift of righteousness already received."[19]

Yet gift can also be spoken of as having priority for the believer, for justifying faith is gift, and it is only through such faith that the believer enters into divine favor. Thus, it is true that "everything is forgiven through grace, but as yet not everything is healed through the gift," but it is also true that "a person neither pleases, nor has grace, except on account of the gift which labors in this way to cleanse from sin." Luther plainly does *not* mean that justification is to be understood as granted partly on the basis of the works of the believer: "For what sin is there where God is favorable and wills not to know any sin, and where he wholly accepts and sanctifies the whole man? However, as you see, this must not be attributed to our purity, but solely to the grace of a favorable God" (*LW* 32:229). What he means rather is that since he holds Christ to be present in the gift of justifying faith, there is a sense in which the gift is a prerequisite for grace (the gift of faith results in the believer being accepted into God's favor) just as there is also a different sense in which grace is a prerequisite for the gift.

Luther therefore simply cannot make parallel exegetical moves to Melanch-

18. Melanchthon, *Commentary on Romans*, 137–38.

19. Mark Seifrid, "The Text of Romans and the Theology of Melanchthon: The Preceptor of the Germans and the Apostle to the Gentiles," in *Reformation Readings of Paul: Explorations in History and Exegesis*, ed. Michael Allen and Jonathan A. Linebaugh (Downers Grove, IL: InterVarsity Press, 2015), 114. A similar logical primacy of grace over gift in Luther's theology is asserted by Risto Saarinen, "Finnish Luther Studies: A Story and a Program," in *Luther and the Gift* (Tübingen: Mohr Siebeck, 2017), 200–201.

thon and identify Christ and justification primarily with grace, and the gift primarily with the Holy Spirit and with the renewal that is consequent upon justification. Luther instead associates Christ and the Spirit as gift, writing in his *Preface to Romans* that grace is God's favor, "by which he is disposed to pour Christ and the Holy Spirit with his gifts into us."[20] Even in his later years, Luther maintains this interpretation of Paul's statements. In July 1542, at the licentiate examination of Heinrich Schmedenstede, Luther comments that "Paul embraces two parts in justification, according to Romans 5[:15–17], grace and the free gift" (*LW* 34:320). Thus, while Melanchthon and Luther share a strong sense that Paul teaches the union of the believer with God, they understand this union in quite different ways. Melanchthon identifies it primarily with the work of the Holy Spirit consequent upon justification, whereas Luther identifies it primarily with the presence of Christ in faith and as an intrinsic part of justification.

12.5. Justification and Good Works: The Dialogue at Pastor Bugenhagen's House

That Luther understands the presence of Christ in faith as intrinsic to justification has consequences for his understanding of the relationship between justification and the works of believers (see 10.8). Although he insists again and again that works do not justify, he feels no more need to separate them from each other than he does to separate different aspects of the person and work of Christ. This sets his position apart from that of Melanchthon, for whom righteousness by works is best avoided by keeping the works of believers separate from justification. This difference emerges clearly in a dialogue that took place in late 1536 at the home of Johann Bugenhagen (1485–1558),[21] held in an attempt to resolve the difficulties caused by the complaint of Cordatus against Cruciger (see 12.1).

Cordatus perceived Cruciger, and behind him his teacher Melanchthon, as promoting justification by works because Cruciger held that contrition in the person justified is necessary as an indispensable cause (*causa sine qua non*) of justification. This seemed in tension with Luther's insistence, especially against Erasmus in *The Bondage of the Will* (1525), that contrition is a divine gift. In fact,

---

20. *WA DB* 7.9: 10–14. Peura, "Christ as Favor and Gift," 43n3, provides this translation and critiques *LW* 35:369 where the sentence is erroneously translated in such a way as to separate Christ and the Holy Spirit: "by which he is disposed to give us Christ and to pour into us the Holy Spirit with his gifts."

21. Bugenhagen was pastor at Saint Mary's Church in Wittenberg, combining this from 1533 with a chair in theology. He had considerable organizational gifts and was a key figure in facilitating reform across northern Germany and Scandinavia.

this was an area where Melanchthon had developed distinctive views. He worried that Luther's rigorous insistence on the bondage of the unregenerate human will might deter people from even trying to obey or to believe. From Melanchthon's perspective, afflicted sinners had to know that the gospel promise is universal and that they could struggle against the weakness of the will if they were sustained by the word and the work of the Spirit.

In *Loci Communes* (1535), Melanchthon had written that in justification, "three causes are conjoined: the Word, the Holy Spirit and the will, not really as a passive thing [*otiosam*], but fighting its weakness."[22] In *Loci Communes* (1543), he was later to write that the third cause of good works is "the human will which assents to and does not contend against the Word of God."[23] It is not quite clear in these texts what kind of "cause" the human will is being said to be, with different possible senses of the term leaving it uncertain how extensive is the active role Melanchthon ascribes to the will.[24] Similarly, much depended upon the exact sense in which Cruciger used the phrase *causa sine qua non*, and both Luther and Bugenhagen were publicly to present the dispute merely as one over the definition of words.

Yet the recorded details of the dialogue at Bugenhagen's house suggest a more substantial if still amicable disagreement. Accused of opening the door to justification by works by allowing that the contrition of the sinner can be termed a cause of justification, Melanchthon does not focus on defending his own view. Instead, he questions Luther's own way of formulating justification, implying that Luther's failure to adopt an exclusively relational view of justification courts exactly the same danger. By refusing to exclude works from justification, Luther risks falling back into a position like that of Augustine, where the believer must cooperate through good works with an initial gratuitous gift of grace and love in order to gain God and eternal life.

Melanchthon points out to Luther, "You grant a twofold righteousness, and also that both are necessary in the sight of God, namely, the righteousness of faith and that other, of a good conscience, in which faith supplies what is lacking in regard to

22. CR 21:376. The translation is that of Timothy J. Wengert, *Human Freedom, Christian Righteousness: Philip Melanchthon's Exegetical Dispute with Erasmus of Rotterdam* (Oxford: Oxford University Press, 1998), 143–44.

23. Philip Melanchthon, *Loci Communes 1543*, trans J. A. O. Preus (Saint Louis: Concordia, 1992), 43.

24. Robert Kolb, *Bound Choice, Election, and Wittenberg Theological Method* (Grand Rapids: Eerdmans, 2005), 93, points out that in Aristotelian analysis, "the material 'cause' or element described or defined the object upon which the effective element—the actual cause responsible for the object—worked to produce the phenomenon." The degree to which Melanchthon is ascribing an active role to the human will could therefore still be limited.

the Law. What else is this than saying that a person is not justified by faith alone?" He will press Luther repeatedly on this issue: "It seems that one is righteous not by God's mercy alone. For you teach yourself that the righteousness of works is necessary, and that, in the sight of God. And Paul is acceptable both as a believer and as a doer; if he were not a doer, he would not be acceptable. Hence, our own righteousness is, at least, a kind of partial cause [*aliqua partialis causa*]."[25]

For his part, Luther refuses to identify Augustine so closely with the errors of his own opponents. He sees Augustine as closer to the evangelical position than does Melanchthon. Luther also refuses to give any ground on the main points that Melanchthon raises. On the one hand, he will not accept that justification includes good works as a cause: "I hold that a righteous person becomes, is, and remains righteous, or a righteous person, simply by mercy alone. For this righteousness is perfect; it is set up against God's wrath, death, and sin, and swallows up all these, and renders a person absolutely [*simpliciter*] holy and innocent, just as if, in reality, there were no sin in him" ("Cordatus' Controversy," 198).

Yet on the other hand, neither will Luther accept that to uphold this truth requires an exclusively relational account of justification in which the renewal manifested in good works is consequent upon justification rather than constitutive of it. He will not answer Melanchthon's question about works as a partial cause of justification using the same terminology. Instead, Luther admits and defines his belief that the righteousness of works is necessary:

> It is necessary, however, not by a legal necessity, or one of compulsion, but by a gratuitous necessity, or one of consequence, or an unalterable condition. As the sun shines by necessity, if it is a sun, and yet does not shine by demand, but by its nature and its unalterable will, so to speak, because it was created for the purpose that it should shine so a person created righteous performs new works by an unalterable necessity, not by legal compulsion. For to the righteous no law is given. Further, we are created, says Paul, unto good works. . . . [I]t is impossible to be a believer and not a doer. ("Cordatus' Controversy," 199)

Luther returns to this point of the nature of the believer again and again: "believers are new creatures, new trees; accordingly, the aforementioned demands of the law do not apply to them, *e.g. faith must do good works*, just as it is not proper to say: *the sun must shine, a good tree must produce good fruit, 3 + 7 must equal 10*. For the sun shines *de facto*, a good tree is fruitful *de facto*, 3 + 7 equal 10 *de facto*" ("Cordatus' Controversy," 202). Because faith works or it is not faith, so works cannot be

---

25. The only English translation of this dialogue is Anonymous, "Cordatus' Controversy with Melanchthon," *ThQ* 11 (1907): 193–207. Page references are given in parentheses in the text.

excluded from discussion of justification by faith, for "faith is a work of promise, or a gift of the Holy Spirit, and . . . it is . . . necessary, in order that the Law be fulfilled, but it is not obtained by the Law and its works" ("Cordatus' Controversy," 201).

Melanchthon was apparently unconvinced by the necessity of unalterable condition. In *Loci Communes* (1543), he discusses the reasons why good works must be performed. Various kinds of necessity are identified, but gratuitous necessity is not included, and, first and foremost, he places what he terms the necessity of command: "For although it is one thing to speak of compulsion, yet there does remain in force the eternal ordering of the immutable God that the creature shall render obedience to the will of God. This immutable ordering is the necessity of command and the necessity of debt, as Paul says in Rom 8:6, 'We are under obligation to God, not to the flesh.'"[26]

There thus emerges from the discussion at Bugenhagen's house two different senses of the relationship between justification by faith and the good works performed by believers, and also of how this is to be articulated without lapsing into works-righteousness. For Melanchthon, it is essential that works are done if faith is to be retained "because the Holy Spirit is driven out and grieved when we permit sins against conscience."[27] Therefore, faith can never be without works, but he does not speak like Luther as if to be active in works is constitutive of faith. For Melanchthon, it is only if justification on account of Christ and renewal by the Holy Spirit are distinguished that the danger of righteousness by works can be avoided. In contrast, Luther sees the same danger as posed more seriously by separating the gratuitous necessity of good works from justification: "It is, therefore, an unhappy distinction to divide a person (as far as he is a believer) into beginning, middle, and end. Accordingly, a person's works shine because they are rays of his faith, and are accepted because of his faith, not vice versa. Otherwise, in the matter of justification, the works which follow faith would be more excellent, and thus, faith would be justifying faith only in the beginning, afterwards it would step aside and cease and would leave the distinction (of justifying a person) to works, and become void and defunct" ("Cordatus' Controversy," 200).

12.6. Conclusion: Difference without Contradiction

It is apparent that when our sources allow Luther and Melanchthon's views about justification to be compared directly, differences between them emerge. They

26. Melanchthon, *Loci Communes 1543*, 103.
27. Melanchthon, *Loci Communes 1543*, 103.

understand important christological dimensions of justification differently from each other. Luther emphasizes the presence of Christ in faith and employs the motif of joyous exchange between the sinner and the incarnate Christ to help explain what Paul means by justification. This leads him to include the works of believers within justification even as he insists that such works are not in any sense the basis of justification. In contrast, Melanchthon asserts that justification means acceptance on account of Christ's sacrificial death. The renewal of the believer expressed in works is consequent upon justification rather than part of it.

As the dialogue at Bugenhagen's house demonstrates, Luther and Melanchthon themselves seem to have been aware of these differences. Yet they also clearly did not regard themselves as standing in contradiction to each other. The historian Hans Scheible asks of Luther, "Why did he not jump all over Melanchthon as he did his Roman Catholic opponents, the prince of humanists, Erasmus, or even his own student John Agricola?" Scheible's answer to his own question is that Luther displays "the ability to put up with the individuality of a colleague with whom he felt in basic agreement. The added conviction that he needed him may have assisted Luther in being able to do this."[28]

Here it is helpful to recall that the differences between Luther and Melanchthon concerning justification existed in the context of extensive agreement between them about fundamental theological issues. They agreed about the nature of sin and grace and therefore were united in rejecting the idea that faith is a quality or virtue by which a person cooperates in his or her own justification. They agreed that the righteousness received by the believer is an alien righteousness and that acceptance by God is based not on any aspects of a person's deeds but is grounded in God. They agreed that this righteousness is received by faith alone when the believer trusts in the divine promises communicated in Scripture. They agreed that the alien nature of this righteousness is vital in granting to the believer assurance of salvation since, despite the continued presence of sin in the believer's life, a final eschatological word has been pronounced in justification. They agreed that union with the divine is a vital aspect of soteriology. They agreed that although faith plays no instrumental role in justification, it is even so never without works.

Given such extensive agreements, especially in a situation of extreme conflict with a common enemy like the early Reformation, it is unsurprising that they did not interpret their remaining differences as contradictions. Yet, as the necessity for the Formula of Concord to define the position of Lutheranism on justification

---

28. Heinz Scheible, "Luther and Melanchthon," *LQ* 4 (1990): 317–39 (esp. 335, 337–38). Johannes Agricola (1494–1566) was a student and supporter whose views about the law led to a breach in relations with Luther and Melanchthon in the Antinomian Controversy.

and the good works of believers illustrates, such differences may become more significant subsequently as statements made in one time and place are interpreted according to the demands and concerns of later contexts. When Luther and Melanchthon's differences concerning justification are viewed as an episode in Pauline reception history, it is both striking and significant that Luther interprets what Paul says about justification in terms of union with Christ, whereas Melanchthon's *Commentary on Romans* (1540) does not. Melanchthon instead offers an interpretation of the letter that, as distinct from his frequent discussion of the work of the Spirit within the believer, offers no direct response to Paul's vocabulary of participation in Christ.[29]

29. It could be argued that Melanchthon's relational account of justification itself provides an explanation of union with Christ: he takes Paul's vocabulary of being "in Christ" to signify justification on account of Christ's saving death. However, Melanchthon nowhere seems to equate the two in this way or to argue for an equivalence between his relational language and Paul's participatory vocabulary.

CHAPTER THIRTEEN

John Calvin: The Double Grace of Union with Christ

John Calvin was twenty-six years younger than Martin Luther, and even twelve years younger than Luther's younger colleague Melanchthon. By the time Calvin published his first work of Pauline interpretation, his *Commentary on Romans* (1540), their most important works of Pauline exegesis were readily available to him. Although Calvin rarely indicates when he is responding to perspectives expressed in the work of others, the structure of Calvin's soteriology suggests that he engaged closely with Luther and Melanchthon's Pauline exegesis.[1] Like Luther, but unlike Melanchthon, Calvin integrates union with Christ and his understanding of justification by faith. Like Melanchthon, but unlike Luther, Calvin nevertheless distinguishes clearly between justification and sanctification and makes extensive use of forensic imagery to describe the former. Like both Luther and Melanchthon, Calvin strives to clarify the relationship between justification and the good works of the believer. Unlike either, Calvin wants not only appropriately to value such works but also to stand in continuity with the medieval tradition by regarding them as a lifelong pathway along which believers progress and so grow in sanctity. Calvin totally rejects any place for notions of human merit in salvation and yet also provides a strong account of reciprocal human response to divine initiative.

13.1. Calvin's Context: Interpreting Paul after Luther and Melanchthon

This pattern of similarities and differences suggests that Calvin sought to bring together what he valued as the best features of the work of each of the Wittenberg

---

1. Bruce Gordon, *Calvin* (New Haven: Yale University Press, 2009), 109, suggests that "although it cannot be proved directly, it is highly likely that he wrote his commentary with Melanchthon's works open in front of him."

interpreters and to resolve what he perceived as their difficulties or inadequacies. He wants to preserve the basic insights into Paul's message that fueled Luther's breach with Rome but to do so while offering his own distinctive soteriological synthesis that incorporates the widest possible range of Pauline texts and ideas. The integrative theme that stands at the heart of Calvin's synthesis is union with Christ. It is only when Calvin's interpretation of Paul's statements about union with Christ is carefully explored that the overall shape of his synthesis comes clearly into focus. It is also only then that the role Calvin ascribes to human reciprocity in salvation can be accurately understood. The rest of this chapter will focus on union with Christ, while the following chapter will consider the way in which Calvin affirms human works performed in response to the grace of God without compromising his conviction that justification is by faith.

13.2. Union with Christ: Forensic Justification

At the very outset of book 3 of the *Institutes* ("The Way in Which We Receive the Grace of Christ"), Calvin makes an explicit statement that apart from union with Christ, there is no salvation: "First, we must understand that as long as Christ remains outside of us, and we are separated from him, all that he has suffered and done for us for the salvation of the human race remains useless and of no value to us . . . all that he possesses is nothing to us until we grow into one body with him" (*Institutes* 3.1.1 [537]). Union with Christ is essential if human beings are to receive the benefits available through his saving work. Calvin is also extremely clear about the agency through which that union is achieved: "The Holy Spirit is the bond by which Christ effectually unites us to himself" (*Institutes* 3.1.1 [538]). Human faith is vital, but such faith "is the principal work of the Holy Spirit" (*Institutes* 3.1.4 [541]).

Calvin makes this point exegetically in his discussion of 1 Cor 6:11, where Paul says that the Corinthians were washed, sanctified, and justified "in the name of the Lord Jesus Christ and in the Spirit of our God." Everything is obtained from Christ, "but Christ Himself, with all His blessings, is communicated to us by the Spirit. For we receive Christ by faith; and it is by faith that his benefits [*gratiae*] are applied to us. The author of faith is the Spirit."[2] Whatever aspects of salvation Calvin identifies will involve union with Christ, and whatever aspects of salvation Calvin identifies will be realized through the agency of the Spirit. It is this agency and not infused habits of grace that provides the bond between God and

2. *Comm. 1 Cor. 6:11*, *CNTC* 9:127. This commentary was first published in 1546.

redeemed humanity. In this way, Calvin anchors "human participation only in God himself, beginning with the self-gift of God to us in the person of the Spirit."[3] In contrast to medieval interpreters, for whom the rootedness of the Christian in divine grace makes possible meritorious works, Calvin's understanding of union with Christ leaves no space for human merit in salvation. Merit and the appropriate dependency upon God represented by union with Christ stand in sharp opposition to each other.

The nature of union with Christ itself Calvin understands in a twofold way. He identifies twin principal saving benefits received in union with Christ by the agency of the Spirit, a *duplex gratia* or double grace. The first of these is justification, and the second is regeneration or sanctification.[4] It is at this point that potential for considerable confusion arises, for Calvin clearly defines justification in forensic terms even as he insists that it is part of union with Christ. This conflicts with the marked tendency in modern interpretation of Paul to treat the forensic and the participatory as contrasting twin tracks in Paul's thought, with justification belonging to the former and union with Christ to the latter.[5] On such a view, it is regeneration or sanctification alone that is the focus of Paul's concern with union with Christ. And if sanctification is the principal focus of union with Christ, then to place justification alongside it may risk making sanctification part of the basis of justification and so compromise the Reformation rejection of righteousness by works.[6]

This difficulty in appreciating Calvin's interpretation of Paul arises in part because Calvin simply does not share the frequent later assumption that forensic justification is less participatory than sanctification. However, this does not mean that Calvin has overlooked a potential flaw in his exegesis successfully identified by later interpreters. For him, any danger of making sanctification part of the basis of justification is obviated by Paul's teaching about the nature of saving grace. In his comments on Rom 5:15 ("the grace of God and the free gift in the grace of the one man, Jesus Christ, abounded for the many"), Calvin insists that the grace of which Paul speaks is a divine disposition and is God's unmerited love for us. Grace

3. Julie Canlis, *Calvin's Ladder: A Spiritual Theology of Ascent and Ascension* (Grand Rapids: Eerdmans, 2010), 98.

4. For a concise overview of Calvin's concept of the *duplex gratia*, see Paul Helm, *Calvin at the Centre* (Oxford: Oxford University Press, 2010), 196–226.

5. The identification of these two tracks dates back to 1853 and the work of R. A. Lipsius. See Albert Schweitzer, *Paul and His Interpreters* (London: Black, 1912; German original 1911), 19.

6. See Bruce L. McCormack, "What's at Stake in Current Debates over Justification? The Crisis of Protestantism in the West," in *Justification: What's at Stake in the Current Debates?*, ed. Mark Husbands and Daniel J. Treier (Downers Grove, IL: InterVarsity Press, 2004), 81–117.

is not infused but remains external to the believer. Instead of grace itself, it is the "effect of grace that is in us." This gift in the grace of Christ is "the fruit of this mercy which has come to us, viz. the reconciliation by which we have obtained life and salvation. It is also righteousness, newness of life, and every other similar blessing" (*Comm. Rom.* 5:15, *CNTC* 8:115). This logical prioritizing of grace, along with the denial that it is an infused quality, removes all danger of merit and allows Calvin without anxiety to associate not only newness of life with the "gift in the grace" but also reconciliation and righteousness.

Thus, justifying faith and sanctifying regeneration can both be rooted in union with Christ without implying that the former results from the latter because both depend on grace. Indeed, Calvin bases his rejection of the concept of infused grace on the contrast between it and union with Christ, who is made by the Father "the fountain out of whose fullness all may draw" (*Comm. Rom.* 5:15, *CNTC* 8:115). Justification is a work of God for us received always and only in union with Christ. Nevertheless, there is an order to the relationship between justification and sanctification in Calvin's soteriology: "the Spirit grants the faith to receive Christ for justification and for sanctification, but, analogous to God's performative utterance in creation, it is the forensic verdict ('Let there be!') that evokes the inner renewal that yields the fruit of the Spirit ('Let the earth bring forth . . .')."[7]

Far from rooting justification in sanctification, this careful ordering of the relationship makes sanctification logically dependent (although not chronologically subsequent: see 13.5) upon justification.[8] Yet both justification and sanctification are equally grounded in union with Christ. Justification cannot be logically prior to union with Christ itself since the gift of faith that unites those who receive it with Christ is logically prior both to the divine declaration of righteousness and to sanctifying regeneration. For Calvin, forensic justification is no less of a participatory concept than sanctification and is understood as an aspect of union with Christ.[9]

This christological account of forensic justification is crucial to Calvin's discernment of the structure of Romans. In his summary of the argument of the

---

7. Michael S. Horton, "Calvin's Theology of Union with Christ and the Double Grace: Modern Reception and Contemporary Possibilities," in *Calvin's Theology and Its Reception: Disputes, Developments, and New Possibilities*, ed. J. Todd Billings and I. John Hesselink (Louisville: Westminster John Knox, 2012), 91.

8. Nico Vorster, *The Brightest Mirror of God's Works: John Calvin's Theological Anthropology*, PrTMS 236 (Eugene, OR: Pickwick, 2019), 78–79, argues that justification is the first grace, in the logical sense that sanctification flows from it but not in a chronological sense since it cannot exist separately from sanctification.

9. See Alister McGrath, *Iustitia Dei: A History of the Christian Doctrine of Justification*, 3rd ed. (Cambridge: Cambridge University Press, 2005), 253–57.

epistle (*CNTC* 8:5–11), Calvin identifies justification as its main subject, arguing that this is dealt with in Rom 1–5 and that Paul turns to discuss sanctification at the start of chapter 6. It is perilously easy for twenty-first-century interpreters, accustomed to identifying only sanctification with Paul's participatory motifs, to read into Calvin's summary an assertion that union with Christ is discussed primarily from chapter 6 onward. In fact, union with Christ is prominent at crucial points in Calvin's exegesis of chapters 1–5 also.

A particularly clear example of forensic justification understood in terms of union with Christ occurs in relation to Rom 3:22 where Paul speaks of the revelation of "the righteousness of God through faith in Jesus Christ for all who believe." Calvin takes this righteousness to be that which is found in Christ and is received by faith. However, Paul terms it the righteousness of God, making it clear for Calvin that God is its author and that it flows from God. Its first cause is therefore "the tribunal of God" (*Comm. Rom.* 3:22, *CNTC* 8:73). Since before that court only perfect obedience to God's law is reckoned as righteousness, no human being possesses righteousness in him- or herself. Only Christ can render human beings just through the granting to them of his righteousness.

However, Calvin will go on to explain further and clarify what he means by this forensic account of justification in explicitly christological terms: "When, therefore, we are justified, the efficient cause is the mercy of God, Christ is the substance [*materia*] of our justification, and the Word, with faith, the instrument. Faith is therefore said to justify, because it is the instrument by which we receive Christ, in whom righteousness is communicated to us. When we are made partakers of Christ [*facti sumus Christi participes*], we are not only ourselves righteous, but our works also are counted righteous in the sight of God, because any imperfections in them are obliterated by the blood of Christ" (*Comm. Rom.* 3:22, *CNTC* 8:73).

For all the emphasis here on the instrumental role of faith, Calvin does not say that it is the instrument by which righteousness is received. Instead, he says that it is the instrument by which *Christ* is received, and that righteousness is communicated in him. And while Calvin is quite clear that it is the righteousness of Christ that justifies, by saying that Christ is the substance of justification, he refuses to sever righteousness as a benefit of Christ from Christ's person. It is only in union with Christ that anyone can receive his righteousness. The point is further hammered home in Calvin's comment on Rom 3:24 where Paul describes justification as being by God's grace as a gift: "The meaning is that since there is nothing left for men in themselves but to perish, having been smitten by the just judgment of God, they are therefore freely justified by His mercy, for Christ comes to the aid of their wretchedness, and communicates Himself to believers, so that they find in Him alone all those things of which they are in want" (*Comm. Rom.* 3:24, *CNTC* 8:74). Faith justifies because it grasps hold of Christ and unites the believer with his person.

13.3. Union with Christ: Faith and Life

Once Calvin has established the christological basis of justification in his exegesis of Rom 3, he can go on to give full weight to Abraham's human faith in Paul's argument in Rom 4 without any risk of making justification a human accomplishment. Calvin expounds Abraham's faith in terms of saving faith that trusts firmly in God's promises and that rescues human beings from the despair of their encounter with a divine law they cannot fulfill. This emphasis is especially clear in Calvin's comments on Rom 4:14, where Paul says that if it is those who are of the law who are the heirs of Abraham's inheritance, then "faith is null and the promise is void": "The apostle tells us that faith perishes if our soul does not rest securely in the goodness of God. Faith is therefore not the mere acknowledgement of God or of His truth, nor is it even the simple persuasion that there is a God, and that His Word is truth, but it is the sure knowledge of divine mercy which is conceived from the Gospel, and brings peace of conscience in the presence of God and repose" (*Comm. Rom.* 4:14, *CNTC* 8:93).

That this peace of conscience in God's presence is anchored christologically becomes clear when Calvin follows Paul back into direct discussion of Christ's saving work in Rom 4:24-25.[10] Precisely because he has earlier defined forensic justification in terms of union with Christ, Calvin experiences little difficulty with Paul's thought that Christ was "raised for our justification" (4:25). He resists any notion that this phrase refers to "newness of life," that is, sanctification, and insists that Paul is speaking of imputed justification but comments of Christ that "He is said to have been raised for our justification, because He fully restored life to us by His resurrection" (*Comm. Rom.* 4:25, *CNTC* 8:103).

In what sense this full restoration of life stems from imputed justification can be seen clearly in Calvin's comments on other texts in Romans that relate righteousness and life. When dealing with Paul's quotation in 1:17 of Hab 2:4, "the righ-

---

10. Mark A. Garcia, *Life in Christ: Union with Christ and Twofold Grace in Calvin's Theology* (Eugene, OR: Wipf & Stock, 2008), 131-33, argues that Calvin here correlates the death of Christ with justification and the resurrection of Christ with sanctification. Yet Calvin discusses not the two parts of salvation but the two parts of the cause of salvation (*salutis causam*), that is, Christ's death and Christ's resurrection. Throughout his comments on 4:24-25, Calvin discusses justification. See *Comm. Rom.* 4:24-25, *CNTC* 8:101-3.

teous shall live by faith," Calvin says that the ungodly may have the illusion of life, but destruction awaits, and "the faith of the righteous alone brings everlasting life." He also argues that "the verb in the future tense designates the undivided perpetuity of the life of which he is speaking, as though he had said, 'It shall not continue for a moment, but shall endure forever'" (*Comm. Rom.* 1:17, *CNTC* 8:28–29). Thus, the life granted by imputed justification in 4:25 is eternal life received through God's forgiveness of sins. This becomes even clearer at Rom 5:18 where Christ's righteous act "leads to justification and life for all." Calvin says, "In my judgment *justification of life* means absolution, which restores life to us, or is 'life-giving.' Our hope of salvation is God's being propitious toward us, and we cannot be accepted by him unless we are righteous. Life therefore has its origin in justification."[11] It is the risen Christ who was "exalted into the kingdom of life, so that he might freely give his people righteousness and life" (*Comm. Rom.* 4:25, *CNTC* 8:103).

Calvin's convictions about how God rescues human beings through justification are therefore clear. Sin brings death, and death is the human destiny apart from Christ, because divine judgment will ultimately fall upon all who are not righteous. Acceptance by God depends upon being righteous and therefore so too does life. Works cannot lead to this righteousness and life, which can be received only in Christ and only by means of faith, because Christ is the one who has defeated sin and death. The risen Christ "having been received into the glory of heaven, reconciled God to us by his intercession" (*Comm. Rom.* 4:25, *CNTC* 8:102). Thus, precisely because Paul's texts do not allow him to, Calvin does not understand justification exclusively in relation to the cross. Yet this does not modify his conviction that justification is centrally concerned with reconciliation and forgiveness of sins. Instead, Calvin positively and directly relates these saving benefits of Christ to the gift of eternal life. Righteousness is not an independent commodity available to believers as a result of Christ's sacrificial death but instead a personal attribute of the Christ who died and rose again, which can be received only in union with him.

Many of the different elements of this pattern of thought can be seen in Calvin's exegesis of Rom 5:17 where Paul says that through Christ the free gift of righteousness will "exercise dominion in life." Calvin comments, "We are not accounted righteous because we have righteousness within us, but because we possess Christ Himself with all his blessings, given to us by His Father's bounty. The gift of righteousness therefore does not signify a quality with which God endows us, for this is a misinterpretation, but is the free imputation of righteousness. The apostle is

---

11. *Comm. Rom.* 5:18, *CNTC* 8:118. Calvin's "justification of life" and the NRSV's "justification and life" reflect different ways of understanding Paul's genitive Greek construction.

expounding his interpretation of the word *grace.* . . . In order, however, that we may participate in the grace of Christ, we must be ingrafted into Him by faith . . . we attain fellowship [*consortium*] with Him by faith" (*Comm. Rom.* 5:17, *CNTC* 8:117).

In this quotation, it is striking that Calvin has no hesitation in using the noun "imputation" in the context of union with Christ. Indeed, the application of the atonement to believers makes sense for Calvin only in this context of union. When Paul discusses life in relation to justification, for Calvin it is always life in an eternal, eschatological sense and not life in the sense of renewal or fullness of life here and now. It is, however, nonetheless life in union with Christ.

13.4. Union with Christ: Sanctification

The fear that participatory righteousness in Christ as Calvin describes it runs the risk of rooting justification in regeneration is not the only possible concern about this concept. It is also possible to hold the opposite concern that in denying that participatory righteousness in Christ is an infused quality, Calvin proposes a fictional righteousness. Believers are reckoned righteous before God, but there is no corresponding transformation in their lives. Calvin addresses this by insisting on the inseparability of justification and sanctification. The faith that justifies is trust (*fiducia*) in God's promises, but for Calvin faith is nevertheless not to be narrowly construed as relevant only to justification. He holds an expansive understanding of faith as "a firm and certain knowledge of God's benevolence toward us, founded upon the truth of the freely given promise in Christ, both revealed to our minds and sealed upon our hearts through the Holy Spirit" (*Institutes* 3.2.7 [551]).

Such a definition of faith as a kind of knowledge of God's benevolence is certainly not intended to contrast with faith as trust since this knowledge is itself founded upon a divine promise. Trust is characteristic of faith as knowledge, but the fact that faith is a kind of knowledge and is not solely restricted to trust makes clear its wider relevance. For God's benevolence extends beyond justification to the life of faith. Faith in God's salvation is to be accompanied by faith in God's providence. Not only God's redeeming activity is known through faith but also God's activity as Creator. Faith is relevant not only to justification but also to sanctification.[12]

Even more significantly, Calvin bases the inseparability of justification and sanctification on the unity of Christ's person. At Rom 6:1, where Paul raises and

12. See Barbara Pitkin, *What Pure Eyes Could See: Calvin's Doctrine of Faith in Its Exegetical Context* (Oxford: Oxford University Press, 1999), 9–40.

dismisses the suggestion that we should sin in order that grace might abound, Calvin asserts that "throughout this chapter the apostle maintains that those who imagine that Christ bestows free justification upon us without imparting newness of life shamefully rend Christ asunder" (*Comm. Rom.* 6:1, *CNTC* 8:121). Justification and sanctification are distinct, and Calvin believes that Paul here transitions from discussing justification to discussing sanctification, but one cannot be received without the other since together they are the principal benefits of union with Christ: "we are justified for this very purpose, that we may afterwards worship God in purity of life" (*Comm. Rom.* 6:2, *CNTC* 8:122).

Unsurprisingly, Calvin will therefore insist that dying and rising with Christ in baptism in Rom 6:2–4 is not a washing alone and that newness of life is not simply an imitation of Christ. Paul is speaking again of union with Christ, and the thought that union with Christ in a death like his will lead to a future sharing in a resurrection like his (Rom 6:5) prompts Calvin to explain this progression from death to life by borrowing from later in the letter Paul's own horticultural imagery of ingrafting (Rom 11:17–24). Ingrafting signifies "the secret union [*arcanam coniunctionem*] by which we grow together with Him, in such a way that He revives us by His Spirit, and transfers His power to us. Therefore, as the graft has the same life or death as the tree into which it is ingrafted, so it is reasonable that we should be as much partakers of the life as of the death of Christ" (*Comm. Rom.* 6:5, *CNTC* 8:123–24).

However, there is also a difference between this secret union and the details of Paul's horticultural imagery. The reality of the union in fact extends beyond the imagery used to describe it: "In the grafting of trees the graft draws its nourishment from the root, but retains its own natural quality in the fruit which is eaten. In spiritual ingrafting, however, we not only derive the strength and sap of the life which flows from Christ, but we also pass from our own nature into His. The apostle desired to point quite simply to the efficacy of the death of Christ, which manifested itself in putting to death our flesh, and also the efficacy of His resurrection in renewing within us the better nature of the Spirit" (*Comm. Rom.* 6:5, *CNTC* 8:124).

In the final sentence of this quotation, Calvin identifies what he takes to be Paul's two main emphases in discussing sanctification, first the putting to death of the flesh, or its mortification, and second, the granting of the better nature of the Spirit, or vivification.[13] The first of these, mortification, involves the putting to death of the self that existed before faith since "man, when left to his own nature

13. For discussion of the twofold nature of sanctification in Rom 6, see Garcia, *Life in Christ*, 125–33.

is a mass of sin" (*Comm. Rom.* 6:6, *CNTC* 8:125). Everything must change through the rooting out of sinful desires, and Calvin conceives this as a possibility now open that was previously closed. Paul's comment in 6:7 that "whoever has died is justified from sin"[14] is interpreted as implying this possibility: *"Justified* means freed or reclaimed from bondage. Just as the prisoner who is absolved by the sentence of the judge is freed from the bond of his accusation, so death, by releasing us from this life, sets us free from all its responsibilities" (*Comm. Rom.* 6:7, *CNTC* 8:125). Having been released from their previous lives, those who have been justified can be effective in battling against sin, although this struggle will endure for the whole of a person's earthly life. Calvin expresses Paul's meaning in the following paraphrase: "If you are a Christian, you must show in yourself a sign of your communion in the death of Christ [*communionis cum morte Christi*], and the fruit of this is that your flesh will be crucified together with all its desires. Do not assume, however, that this communion is not a real one if you find traces of the flesh still existing in you. But you are continually to study to increase your communion in the death of Christ, until you arrive at the goal" (*Comm. Rom.* 6:7, *CNTC* 8:126).

However, this emphasis on the crucifying of sinful desires is not the whole of mortification for Calvin. Mortification also involves sharing in Christ's sufferings. Prompted by Paul's statement that those justified by God are also glorified, Calvin discusses this suffering in his comments on Rom 8:29: "the afflictions of believers, which cause their present humiliation, are intended solely that they may obtain the glory of the kingdom of heaven and reach the glory of the resurrection of Christ, with whom they are now glorified" (*Comm. Rom.* 8:29, *CNTC* 8:182). Calvin explores this theme at much greater length in his *Commentary on 2 Corinthians*, where Paul's description in 4:11 of always being given up to death for Jesus's sake is labeled as "external mortification" in contrast to the "internal mortification" of putting to death the desires of the flesh described in Rom 6. This "external mortification" means that "the elect have participation in the Son of God so that all their miseries that are in their own nature curses are made helpful for their salvation" (*Comm. 2 Cor.* 4:10, *CNTC* 10:60). Although he does not say so directly, Paul's reports of continual harassment and exposure to danger presumably evoked for Calvin and his sixteenth-century readers the persecution, exile, and martyrdoms experienced by early Protestant communities. Sanctification is for Calvin not only an internal struggle with sin but also a bearing of the cross in the public arena by declaring the evangelical faith and faithfully accepting the consequences. As

---

14. This is my own translation. Most English translations erroneously employ the phrases "set free from sin" or "liberated from sin." While justification results in freedom, the Greek verb used by Paul is "justify" (*dikaioō*) not "set free" (*eleutheroō*).

such it is not simply an imitation of Christ, but an aspect of union with him, a reflection of the pattern of his death and resurrection.[15]

The second aspect of sanctification, which is vivification, is to share in Christ's resurrection. In one respect, this has a fundamentally eschatological orientation since believers await bodily resurrection beyond this life and experience in greater measure here and now the mortification of sharing in Christ's death. Yet since believers are in Christ and the risen Christ is in glory in heaven, then, when Paul speaks of the glorification of believers in Rom 8:30 in the past tense, Calvin says that "although glorification has as yet been exhibited only in our Head, yet, because we now perceive in Him the inheritance of eternal life, His glory brings to us such assurance of our own glory, that our hope may justly be compared to a present possession" (*Comm. Rom.* 8:30, *CNTC* 8:182). The present troubles of believers deform this glory before the world, "yet before God and the angels it always shines in perfection" (*Comm. Rom.* 8:30, *CNTC* 8:182).

In another respect, vivification is the positive counterpart of mortification. It is the good works of believers enabled by the Holy Spirit. Here the liberation of the consciences of believers is vital. Calvin says in relation to Paul's instruction to present the body as a living sacrifice (Rom 12:1) that "a godly mind is not formed to obey God by precepts or sanctions so much as by a serious meditation upon the divine goodness towards itself" (*Comm. Rom* 12:1, *CNTC* 8:263). The law will still provide guidance for living, but the assurance of salvation in Christ means that the law's accusation against the conscience is gone. The Spirit has been given "to bring our minds to a state of tranquility, and to stir us up to call on God with confidence and freedom" (*Comm. Rom.* 8:15, *CNTC* 8:167–68). We can say, "Abba Father" (Rom 8:15), because the Spirit of adoption has replaced a covenant of law with a covenant of grace.

Love of neighbor is the fulfilling of the law (Rom 13:8), "for true love to men flows only from the love of God, and is the evidence and effect of this love" (*Comm. Rom.* 13:8, *CNTC* 8:285). When describing the fruit of the Spirit (Gal 5:22–23) in his *Commentary on Galatians* (1548), Calvin comments that "all virtues, all good and well regulated affections, proceed from the Spirit, that is, from the grace of God, and the renewed nature which we have from Christ. . . . In the sight of God nothing is pure but what proceeds from the fountain of all purity" (*Comm. Gal.* 5:22, *CNTC* 11:105). For Calvin the whole of the believer's life is a daily journey toward sanctification through the power of the Spirit in union with Christ.

---

15. Garcia, *Life in Christ*, 140–43, helpfully terms this patterning of the believer's experience after that of Christ as a "replication principle."

13.5. Union with Christ: 1 Corinthians 1:30

Calvin's equal emphasis on both forensic justification and sanctification as aspects of union with Christ raises the issue of how the relationship between these two main elements of salvation functions. In his comments on Rom 8:2, Calvin says that sanctification and justification are "at the same time" (*Comm. Rom.* 8:2, *CNTC* 8:157), thus removing any temptation to read them as chronological stages in an *ordo salutis* (order of salvation). We have also already seen Calvin argue in his exposition of Rom 6:1 that to separate justification and sanctification is to rend Christ asunder (see 13.4), thus suggesting that explanations of the relationship will focus on the person of Christ. Yet this is not further developed, and neither of these statements were part of the first 1540 edition of Calvin's *Commentary on Romans*.[16] They were revisions made for the later 1556 edition. For readers of the first edition, it was clear only that sanctification cannot be conceived apart from justification, since the latter grants the cloak of Christ's righteousness that provides believers, who still sometimes lose their struggle with vestigial sin, with the assurance that the incomplete nature of their sanctification in this life does not result in their rejection by God.

Calvin's main exegetical resource for providing an explanation of how the relationship between justification and sanctification works in fact lies outside Romans. It is 1 Cor 1:30, where Paul says that Christ Jesus "became for us wisdom from God, and righteousness and sanctification and redemption." This text became Calvin's favorite means of explaining the relationship between justification and sanctification in union with Christ. He uses it for the first time in the first major revision of the *Institutes* (Latin 1539; French translation 1541),[17] and the explanation warrants quotation in full:

> For from where does it come that we are justified by faith? It is because by faith we grasp Christ's righteousness which alone reconciles us to God. Now we cannot grasp this righteousness without also having sanctification. For when it is said that Christ is given to us for redemption, wisdom, and righteousness, it is likewise added that he is given to us for sanctification [1 Cor 1:30]. From that it follows that Christ does not justify anyone whom he does not at the same time sanctify. For these benefits are joined together by a perpetual tie; when He illumines us with His wisdom, He ransoms us; when He ransoms us, He justifies us; when

16. There were also revisions made earlier for the edition of 1551.

17. The *Institutes* were first published in 1536. The standard English translation by Battles is of the 1559 edition.

He justifies us, He sanctifies us. But because it is now only a question of righteousness and sanctification, let us stop with these two. So although they must be distinguished, nevertheless Christ contains both inseparably. Do we want to receive righteousness in Christ? We must first possess Christ. Now we cannot possess Him without being participants in his sanctification, since He cannot be torn in pieces. Since, I say, the Lord Jesus never gives anyone the enjoyment of His benefits except in giving Himself, He gives both of them together and never one without the other. From that it is clear how true the sentence is: that we are not justified without works, although it is not by works, since participation in Christ, in which our righteousness consists, contains our sanctification no less.[18]

Here Calvin focuses intensely on the person of Christ and its unity. Since Christ is a living person, his saving benefits cannot be detached from his person and can be received only in union with him. For the same reason, these saving benefits cannot be separated from each other. They are received together in him or not at all. This line of argument makes it extremely plain that in his frequent use elsewhere of the noun "imputation" (*imputatio*), Calvin simply cannot mean that righteousness is first given to the believer as a preliminary forensic step that then makes union with Christ possible. He does not mean that righteousness is given to the believer as a quality abstracted from Christ's person, initially passed on to the believer independent of any other of Christ's properties.

Instead, Paul's forensic imagery functions for Calvin within the wider context of participation in Christ, and Calvin states that it is necessary first to possess Christ in order to receive his righteousness. His logical order of reasoning is therefore different from some later popular Protestant concepts of imputation in which forensic justification is the gateway to union with Christ.[19] The divine verdict that constitutes justification is indeed for Calvin essential to union with Christ, but it is so as one of the principal components of that union and not as its prelude. Calvin will carefully maintain the distinction between justification and sanctification. Justification is a forensic declaration and not an infusion of righteousness. It is in that sense a work of God for us and not a work of God in us. Yet Calvin is equally

18. John Calvin, *Institutes of the Christian Religion: 1541 French Edition*, trans. Elsie A. McKee (Grand Rapids: Eerdmans, 2009), 356. This is an English translation of the 1541 French translation of the 1539 Latin version. However, the French translation was undertaken by Calvin himself.

19. Calvin can sometimes speak as though justification is logically prior to union. See *Institutes* 3.11.21: "Thus, him whom he receives into union with himself the Lord is said to justify, because he cannot receive him into grace nor join him to himself unless he turns him from a sinner into a righteous man." It is not that Calvin must speak in one order or the other, but rather that he can do either because justification and sanctification are simultaneously received.

keen to maintain that it is received only as part of the wider union with Christ discussed in 1 Cor 1:30 and similar texts.

Further aspects of the integrative function served by 1 Cor 1:30 in Calvin's soteriology can be found in his later *Commentary on 1 Corinthians* (1546). Here he repeats and personalizes his statement in the *Institutes* that justification and sanctification are inseparable since Christ cannot be torn into pieces: "if anyone tries to separate them he is, in a sense, tearing Christ to pieces."[20] He also responds directly to the accusation that the preaching of justification by faith alone leaves people with no motivation for good works. A person cannot be justified in Christ "unless at the same time he lays hold of Him for sanctification; in other words he must be born anew by His Spirit to blamelessness and purity of life" (*Comm. 1 Cor.* 1:30, *CNTC* 9:46). If there can be no justification without sanctification, then there can also be no faith without works even though justification is not by works. Finally, and most importantly, the meaning of faith is itself explored more deeply and broadly, not only as justifying faith but for the whole of the Christian life: "Faith lays hold of regeneration just as much as forgiveness of sins in Christ. . . . [S]ince there is scarcely another passage in Scripture which gives a clearer description of all the offices of Christ, it can also give us the best understanding of the force and nature of faith. For, since Christ is the proper object of faith, everyone who knows what benefits Christ gives to us, knows what faith is" (*Comm. 1 Cor.* 1:30, *CNTC* 9:46–47).

Thus, faith belongs not only in the discussion of justification but also in that of sanctification. Yet although the same faith lays hold of both, and receives them from the same person of Christ, they remain distinct from each other just as the attributes of a single person are distinct. In a later sermon on Gal 2:20, preached in 1557–1558, Calvin asserts that the work of the Spirit in sanctification and the remission of sins in justification "are inseparably joined together, just as the brightness of the sun cannot be separated from its heat." Nevertheless, although the sun is hot and shines at the same time, "the brilliance of the sun is not the same as its heat."[21]

13.6. Union with Christ: The Spirit and Christ's Humanity

Calvin's careful articulation of the relationship between justification and sanctification in union with Christ was to become of great importance in his response to

---

20. *Comm. 1 Cor.* 1:30, *CNTC* 9:46. Garcia, *Life in Christ*, 228–41, provides an extended discussion of Calvin's use of this metaphor.

21. John Calvin, *Sermons on the Epistle to the Galatians*, trans. Kathy Childress (Edinburgh: Banner of Truth, 1997), 198–99 (sermon 13).

the Osiander controversy (see 11.6) in the 1550s. Finding himself under suspicion from Lutheran quarters as standing dangerously close to Andreas Osiander, Calvin is determined in the 1559 *Institutes* emphatically to distinguish his teaching on union with Christ from Osiander's concept of "essential righteousness." In contrast to Osiander's emphasis on the specific presence of the divine nature of Christ in the believer, Calvin strives to reassert the significance for justification of Christ's incarnate obedience unto death.

Here 1 Cor 1:30 is again a significant text, for it had also been important to Osiander. Anxious to avoid making justification a legal fiction, Osiander had used the verse to deny the propriety of a sharp distinction between justification and sanctification. He and Calvin agree that Paul's text treats both justification and sanctification as aspects of union with Christ and therefore indicates their simultaneity. However, Calvin will not have it that simultaneity implies a lack of clear distinction: "Scripture, even though it joins them, still lists them separately.... For Paul's statement is not redundant: that Christ was given to us for our righteousness and sanctification [1 Cor 1:30]" (*Institutes* 3.11.6 [732]).

Further, Calvin insists that the granting of the righteousness of Christ to the believer in justification is conceivable only on the basis of Christ's incarnate role as mediator. Calvin asserts that "we are justified in Christ, in so far as he was made an atoning sacrifice for us, something that does not comport with his divine nature [*quod a divina eius natura abhorret*]" (*Institutes* 3.11.9 [736]). How, he asks, can it be said at 1 Cor 1:30 that Christ was *made* righteousness for us according to his divine nature when he already shared divine righteousness with the Father and the Spirit? Paul's statement is "surely peculiar to the person of the Mediator, which, even though it contains in it the divine nature, still has its own proper designation by which the Mediator is distinguished from the Father and the Spirit" (*Institutes* 3.11.8 [734]).

Christ carried out his saving acts according to his human nature, taking on the form of a servant and justifying believers through his obedience to the cross. Calvin says, "From this we conclude that in his flesh, righteousness has been manifested to us" (*Institutes* 3.11.9 [735]). Calvin is not here simply pitting an emphasis on Christ's human nature as vital to justification against Osiander's insistence on Christ's divine nature as essential to justification. Calvin is quite clear that Christ's divinity is essential to his saving work, and elsewhere Calvin will defend the doctrine of the communication of properties between Christ's divine and human natures as essential to his mediation between God and humanity.[22] Nev-

---

22. Calvin does so directly in a dispute with Francesco Stancaro (1501–1574), professor of Hebrew at Königsberg, who held that Christ's divinity played no part in his role as mediator. See

ertheless, Christ's human nature is especially vital to justification on Calvin's view since believers "are not simply united to a divine nature that is righteous because it is divine or even united to a second Adam who lived a righteous life and hypothetically could have died a natural death. Rather, the righteousness of Jesus Christ is the righteousness of the cross—the mystery of the cross connected to the 'wondrous exchange' language which is so closely related to imputation—in which the sin of sinners is imputed upon Christ, and the righteousness of Christ is imputed to sinners."[23]

From Calvin's perspective, Osiander also overlooks a crucial pneumatological point: "Now it is easy for us to resolve all his difficulties. For we hold ourselves to be united with Christ by the secret power of his Spirit" (*Institutes* 3.11.5 [730]). It is this role for the Spirit as the bond of the believer's union with Christ that defines the nature of that union. Calvin agrees with Osiander that "we are one with Christ" (*Institutes* 3.11.5 [730]). He even agrees that if appropriately defined, "the righteousness of which Christ makes us partakers with himself is the eternal righteousness of the eternal God" (*Institutes* 3.11.9 [736]). Yet this is completely different for Calvin from what he regards as Osiander's insistence that "Christ's essence is mixed with our own" or that there is "a mixture of substances by which God—transfusing himself into us, as it were—makes us part of himself" (*Institutes* 3.11.5 [730–31]). Calvin rejects the vocabulary of substance in favor of the bond of the Spirit, and this allows Calvin to maintain a strong doctrine of union with Christ without compromising what he regards as a proper distinction between Creator and creature. The believer and Christ are one, but this does not involve sameness. Instead, their unity is the "bringing together of two 'unlikes' in a relationship of mutual indwelling."[24]

Here Calvin draws a distinction between mutual indwelling and a sharing of substance or of essence that he had not previously made with consistency. For, while insisting on the role of the Spirit in union with Christ, he had previously spoken directly of the sharing of Christ's substance.[25] There is no doubt that, when attacking Osiander, polemical necessity forces Calvin to reconsider his vocabu-

---

Joseph Tylanda, "Christ the Mediator: Calvin versus Stancaro," in *Articles on Calvin and Calvinism*, ed. Richard C. Gamble, 14 vols. (New York: Garland, 1992), 5:161–72.

23. J. Todd Billings, "Union with Christ and the Double Grace: Calvin's Theology and Its Early Reception," in Billings and Hesselink, *Calvin's Theology and Its Reception*, 61.

24. Canlis, *Calvin's Ladder*, 142. Vorster, *Brightest Mirror*, 59–99, argues that Calvin's construal of the relationship between justification and sanctification is grounded in his understanding of the relationship between the two natures of Christ.

25. See, for example, *Comm. Eph.* 5:30, *CNTC* 11:208: "we grow into one body by the communication of his substance."

lary. Yet this reconsideration helps him to distinguish even more clearly his own understanding of participation in Christ from those that understood it as enabled by infused grace.[26] It also allows him to emphasize union with Christ in a manner entirely consistent with the alien nature of the righteousness of Christ received by the believer. As Julie Canlis expresses it, Calvin is "extrospective" rather than "introspective," for "while Osiander was preoccupied with whether the individual subject was really righteous, Calvin no longer looked to the bounds of the person to define truth about the person. The new 'Reformation ontology' did not begin with the human being as a substance prior to all community, but it began with the truth of the person-in-Christ."[27]

This beginning with the truth of the person in Christ is crucial for understanding how Calvin conceives the works of the believer performed in response to God's gracious saving initiative in Christ. For part of the gracious character of this initiative is its participatory and mediated nature in which, in the person of Christ, the saving work itself is already human as well as divine. Philip Butin articulates the part played by the Spirit in orchestrating this human and divine dynamic: "The Holy Spirit is the Spirit of Christ, who is the epitome of humanity and the authentic embodiment of the divine image. This Spirit actualized and empowered the incarnate Christ to fulfill genuine humanity. This same Spirit unites believers by faith to that same Christ; authenticating in turn their humanity; not over against God, but rather by incorporation into the divine life."[28]

This takes us back to the opening statements of book 3 of the 1559 *Institutes* with which we began our discussion of union with Christ in Calvin's Pauline exegesis (see 13.2). The Trinitarian context of the union between divinity and humanity received by faith is asserted using a medley of Pauline quotations:

> To share with us what he has received from the Father, he had to become ours and to dwell within us. For this reason, he is called "our Head" [Eph 4:15], and "the first-born among many brethren" [Rom 8:29]. We also, in turn, are said to be "engrafted into him" [Rom 11:17], and to "put on Christ" [Gal 3:27]; for as I have said, all that he possesses is nothing to us until we grow into one body with him. It is true that we obtain this by faith. Yet since we see that not

---

26. François Wendel, *Calvin: Origins and Development of His Religious Thought* (Grand Rapids: Baker, 1997), 236, suggests that Calvin "did not perceive the danger, or at least imprudence of certain formulations until he had read some of Osiander's writings which appeared in 1550 or 1551."

27. Canlis, *Calvin's Ladder*, 146. Canlis (139–47) provides extensive commentary on the dispute with Osiander.

28. Philip W. Butin, *Revelation, Redemption, and Response: Calvin's Trinitarian Understanding of the Divine-Human Relationship* (Oxford: Oxford University Press, 1995), 93.

all indiscriminately embrace that communion with Christ which is offered through the gospel, reason itself teaches us to climb higher and to examine into the secret energy of the Spirit, by which we come to enjoy Christ and all his benefits. (*Institutes* 3.1.1 [537])

Christ, the second person of the Trinity, does not benefit humanity while remaining apart from humanity but only by becoming ours, and, dwelling within us, he shares what he has received from the Father. The dynamic of this sharing is the Spirit who "empowers, enables, and authenticates faithful human response to the grace that God the Father offers humanity, through the renewal of the divine image in Christ."[29] In responding in faith to the saving divine initiative, believers are reciprocating God's actions for them but can do so only when united with Christ, because it is only in Christ that authentic humanity is to be found. For Calvin, there can be no separate human response to an exclusively divine initiative, because in the incarnate Christ, this divine initiative, and indeed the divine nature, is expressed in perfect humanity. The divine saving work is already itself, in the person of Christ, a human response.

13.7. Conclusion: Union with Christ and Calvin's Soteriology

Calvin's careful interpretation of Paul's statements about union with Christ shapes his soteriology in important ways. What we have discovered can be summarized as follows:

1. Faith unites believers with Christ. It is in Christ—as twin aspects of union with him—that believers receive the double grace of justification and sanctification, which as saving benefits of his undivided person can be received only together.
2. Justification is a forensic concept, but it is not for that reason any less a participatory one than sanctification and renewal. Calvin hears Paul speak of union with Christ in Rom 1–5 when discussing justification as clearly as he does in Rom 6–8 when discussing sanctification. This does not base sanctification on justification, since the gracious favor of God shown to human beings in Christ is prior to either (Rom 5:15).
3. Sanctification involves both mortification and vivification. The former is the putting to death of the self that existed before faith through sharing in Christ's death. The latter is the sharing by believers in Christ's resurrection, something

29. Butin, *Revelation, Redemption, and Response*, 93.

that will ultimately mean their own bodily resurrection but that here and now is expressed in their good works. That the whole of the Christian life is conceived as a journey into ever greater sanctification demonstrates that the righteousness received by faith is not a legal fiction.

4. Calvin interprets 1 Cor 1:30 as an enumeration of the saving benefits of Christ's person—wisdom, righteousness, sanctification, redemption—and therefore also as a confirmation of the central importance to salvation of union with Christ.

5. The bond that unites believers with Christ is the Holy Spirit. That this is so enables Calvin to emphasize union with Christ while ensuring that believers' participation in Christ remains appropriately creaturely. It also highlights the dependence on the incarnation of the union with Christ enjoyed by believers. As the embodiment of authentic humanity, Christ's own responsiveness to the Father was itself empowered by the Spirit and provides the basis for believers' response to God in union with him.

CHAPTER FOURTEEN

John Calvin: Human Response in Union with Christ

I n recent decades, Calvin has been vigorously criticized for his allegedly inadequate account of the way in which he characterizes the relationship between divine and human agency in salvation. Yet his critics are far from agreed about the nature of his error. Calvin is said to emphasize the good works of believers so heavily that he jeopardizes the principle of justification by faith alone.[1] Or, at an opposite extreme, Calvin's rejection of an infused habit of justice is held to undermine his commitment to union with Christ and to leave human beings unable to reciprocate the divine gift.[2] Or, somewhere in between these two perspectives, Calvin is regarded as hopelessly inconsistent, refusing to make a proper choice between an emphasis on divine initiative or human reciprocity.[3]

14.1. Calvin's Critics: The Issue of Reciprocity

Since their criticisms conflict with each other, Calvin's detractors clearly cannot all be correct, and the incompatibility of their perspectives suggests there are under-

1. Steven Ozment, *The Age of Reform 1250–1550: An Intellectual and Religious History of Late Medieval and Reformation Europe* (New Haven: Yale University Press, 1980), 372–80.

2. John Milbank, "Alternative Protestantisms," in *Radical Orthodoxy and the Reformed Tradition: Creation, Covenant, and Participation*, ed. James K. Smith and James H. Olthuis (Grand Rapids: Baker, 2005), 32–33.

3. Douglas A. Campbell, *The Deliverance of God: An Apocalyptic Rereading of Justification in Paul* (Grand Rapids: Eerdmans, 2009), 276. To these could be added Natalie Zemon Davis, *The Gift in Sixteenth-Century France* (Madison: University of Wisconsin Press, 2000), who argues that Calvin's emphasis on the gratuity of God's gift led to the sweeping away of a host of traditional practices predicated on reciprocal gift-giving and resulted in great uncertainty about when and how legitimately to receive. For discussion of this issue, see Stephen J. Chester, *Reading Paul with the Reformers: Reconciling Old and New Perspectives* (Grand Rapids: Eerdmans, 2017), 306–12.

lying issues prompting such confusion. One such issue is that Calvin's comments about divine initiative and human reciprocity in salvation are being read in isolation from their proper context in union with Christ. As we saw when exploring the theme of the Spirit and Christ's humanity (see 13.6), for Calvin authentic human response to divine initiative is possible only in union with the incarnate Christ who died and rose again. Human reciprocation of the gift of salvation participates in the responsiveness of the Son to the Father through the power of the Spirit. Therefore, the only way to receive and respond to any of the benefits of Christ's saving work is in union with him. Whatever Calvin says about the works of believers, even when he does not directly mention union with Christ, can accurately be understood only within that context.

They can also be understood only in relation to the life of the church as the people of God and to the status of believers as God's children. For union with Christ possesses for Calvin a profound ecclesial dimension expressed primarily in his use of familial imagery, especially that of adoption, to interpret Paul. In justification, those who believe become children of God in Christ Jesus (Gal 3:26). Here the paradigmatic figure is the patriarch Abraham, who provides the pattern of faith now found among those who believe in Jesus. Abraham matters not only because he is justified by faith and not by works, although Calvin, of course, emphasizes this strongly, but also because of the nature of his faith as confidence in God's desire to be his father: "And so, when Abraham heard, 'Thy seed shall be as the sand which is upon the seashore,' he did not confine himself to that word, but included in it the grace of adoption as a part in the whole. And in the same way, every other promise was received by him as a testimony of God's fatherly kindness, from which he could apprehend the trust of salvation."[4]

As it was for Abraham, so Calvin considers it still to be for those who believe in Jesus: "By this word 'faith' Paul means being assured of the grace and fatherly love of our God through his promises, having our eyes fixed on Jesus Christ, through whom we have free access to the Father."[5] God adopts in Christ those who share

---

4. *Comm. Gal.* 3:6, *CNTC* 11:51. Calvin develops the theme of Abraham as father of those who believe far more in later works that he does in his *Commentary on Romans*, his first work on Paul. See Stephen J. Chester, "Faith and Family: Calvin, the Figure of Abraham, and the New Perspective on Paul," in *Reformatorische Paulusauslegungen*, ed. Stefan Krauter and Manuel Nägele (Tübingen: Mohr Siebeck, 2023), 479–502.

5. John Calvin, *Sermons on the Epistle to the Galatians*, trans. K. Childress (Edinburgh: Banner of Truth, 1997), 246 (sermon 16). Calvin is here preaching on Gal 3:3–6. God's desire to adopt human beings and to be their father is for Calvin also the driving force behind God's covenant-making. See John Calvin, *Sermons on Genesis: Chapters 11–20*, trans. Rob Roy McGregor (Edinburgh: Banner of Truth, 2012), 461 (sermon 74).

the faith of Abraham, and those adopted in this way participate in Christ's filial relationship with the Father. This ongoing participation makes it clear that the significance of adoption cannot be restricted to justification. Like faith, adoption is also relevant to sanctification, and adoption appears strongly in Calvin's comments on texts where he hears Paul discussing sanctification.

When commenting on Paul's statement that "all who are led by the Spirit of God are children of God" (Rom 8:14), Calvin notes that although the Spirit sustains life in general and all human life in particular, "by Spirit Paul here means sanctification" (*Comm. Rom.* 8:14, *CNTC* 8:167). This is how Calvin defines the context of Paul's discussion of the spirit of adoption received by believers. By this spirit, they cry "Abba, Father!" and their spirits and the Holy Spirit jointly give testimony that they are God's children (Rom 8:15–16). Thus, adoption is for Calvin "a prominent biblical and theological image used to speak about the double grace of union with Christ."[6] Given this prominence of adoption as a general description of union with Christ, it is unsurprising that Calvin conceptualizes the human response to the gift of Christ within the framework of a familial relationship. It is the response of truly beloved children to their loving parent.

14.2. Obeying without Meriting: Divine and Human Agency

That union with Christ, and adoption as an image by which to describe it, forms the essential context of Calvin's understanding of human reciprocity emerges strongly when he discusses the relationship between faith and works. For it is his positioning of reciprocity in relation to these more fundamental themes in his soteriology that allows Calvin to avoid some of the dilemmas that Paul's statements about faith and works might otherwise pose. Calvin can reject all notions of merit while insisting that Paul teaches that performing good works is essential for believers and recognizing that Paul does sometimes speak of a reward for good works. The importance of the image of adoption in achieving this is seen clearly when Calvin discusses works in relation to the themes of assurance and reward (see 14.4), but that of union with Christ more generally becomes plain as Calvin discusses works in relation to questions of divine and human agency.

When commenting on Phil 2:12b–13, Calvin takes the text to demonstrate that any notion of meritorious human cooperation with divine grace is completely misguided. Paul's instruction to "work out your own salvation with fear and trem-

---

6. J. Todd Billings, "Union with Christ and the Double Grace: Calvin's Theology and Its Early Reception," in *Calvin's Theology and Its Reception*, ed. J. Todd Billings and I. John Hesselink (Louisville: Westminster John Knox, 2012), 67.

bling" is accompanied by the explanation that "it is God who is at work in you, enabling you both to will and to work for his good pleasure." This reference to God enabling the very possibility of Paul's readers willing to do good prompts Calvin to comment that "this is the true artillery for destroying all haughtiness; this is the sword for killing all pride, when we hear that we are utterly nothing, and can do nothing, except through the grace of God alone" (*Comm. Phil.* 2:13, *CNTC* 11:253–54). It is a terrible error to assign to the human free will a separate power by which it can cooperate with the initial divine gift of grace.

The unwary reader might take this argument to imply that for Calvin the working involved in salvation is human in appearance only and is, in reality, exclusively divine. Yet in *On the Bondage and the Liberation of the Will* (1543), Calvin offers a fuller explanation of his views on Phil 2:13 that demonstrates different intentions. The human will stands in bondage to sin, but this bondage does not consist in external constraints that compel sinful choices. Instead, it consists in the perennial inclination of the human will to evil. Human beings are not forced to sin but necessarily always choose to do so. As Calvin explains, "For we do not say that man is dragged unwillingly into sinning, but that because his will is corrupt he is held captive under the yoke of sin and therefore of necessity wills in an evil way. For where there is bondage, there is necessity. But it makes a great difference whether the bondage is voluntary or coerced. We locate the necessity to sin precisely in corruption of the will, from which it follows that it is self-determined."[7]

On this view of unredeemed humanity, sin is simultaneously entirely unavoidable and entirely our own choice. Our problem is precisely that we inevitably will what is wrong. Unsurprisingly, Calvin also goes on to argue that believers' good works are genuinely their own since they can be performed only if believers will to do so. Yet, at the same time, these good works are also entirely due to the work of the Spirit, who is responsible for the existence of a renewed will. Calvin says of God that so "he may have willing servants who follow of their own accord he creates a new heart in them and renews a right spirit in their inner nature." All this, Calvin argues, "is comprehended by Paul in a single statement when he teaches that there is one God who effects in us both to will and to do according to his good pleasure."[8] To use a contemporary image, human beings obey only because of a heart transplant performed by the divine surgeon.

---

7. John Calvin, *On the Bondage and the Liberation of the Will: A Defense of the Orthodox Doctrine of Human Choice against Pighius*, ed. Anthony N. S. Lane, trans. G. I. Davies (Grand Rapids: Baker, 1996), 69. In this work, Calvin identifies his own position on the human will with that of Augustine.

8. Calvin, *Bondage and Liberation of the Will*, 175, 193.

Twenty-first-century readers, accustomed to defining freedom in relation to concepts such as autonomy and independence, may understandably feel that such externally determined freedom to will the good does not constitute true freedom. Calvin would surely respond that as creatures made according to divine purpose, human beings are free only when able to fulfill that purpose. He asserts that the soteriology of his opponents erroneously divides responsibility for good works between God and believers, conceiving of a human free will "which can turn by its own movement, and have a peculiar and separate capacity, by which it can co-operate with the grace of God."[9] Calvin instead insists that believers' good works are wholly due to God and, precisely as such, are also simultaneously wholly and truly their own. Such good works are "enclosed, intended, and enabled within the divine act of salvation."[10]

This insistence on the compatibility of divine and human agency also finds expression in Calvin's comments on Eph 2:10 where it is said that believers were "created in Christ Jesus for good works, which God prepared beforehand to be our way of life."[11] This statement rules out any contribution by believers to their own salvation since the good works they do result from a prior divine decision and creation is by its nature something to which creatures do not contribute: "We are created is as much as to say that we were nothing at all before."[12] Yet while any pretensions to merit are therefore absurd, having arisen out of nothing also enables believers to apply themselves to good works, for "the whole man is formed by His hand to become good. It is not the mere power of choosing aright, or some indefinable preparation, or assistance, but the right will itself, which is His workmanship" (*Comm. Eph.* 2:10, *CNTC* 11:146). Only once in possession of this renewed will can believers walk in a way of life characterized by good works.

It is therefore plain once again that, as befits Calvin's defining of soteriology in terms of union with Christ, he believes that it is only from within this union, justified and sanctified through Christ, that believers can act to reciprocate God. They do so from within God's own saving initiative. This makes redundant all notions of merit but also means that, once this is acknowledged, the positive value of good works is impossible to exaggerate. They will be characteristic of all true children

9. *Comm. Phil.* 2:13, *CNTC* 11:254. For commentary, see J. Todd Billings, *Calvin, Participation, and the Gift: The Activity of Believers in Union with Christ* (Oxford: Oxford University Press, 2007), 40–48.

10. Francis Watson, "New Directions in Pauline Theology," *EC* 1 (2010): 13.

11. See Stephen J. Chester, "'Works Themselves Are a Part of Grace': John Calvin's Interpretation of Ephesians 2:8–10," in *The New Perspective on Grace: Paul and the Gospel after Paul and the Gift*, ed. Edward Adams et al. (Grand Rapids: Eerdmans, 2023), 236–50.

12. John Calvin, *Sermons on the Epistle to the Ephesians* (Edinburgh: Banner of Truth, 1973), 164 (sermon 11).

of God, for in union with Christ, believers must grow through obedience. While in this life believers remain imperfect, their sins covered by Christ's righteousness, if faith is genuine, there will be progress in holiness. They will come to conform in greater measure to the gift they have been given. Yet the fact that genuine faith will have this result does not eliminate the agency of believers. Their good works are not simply organic, with good trees automatically producing good fruit. Instead, their good works are believers' own since the exercise of their human wills is essential to their production.

Calvin's view is therefore that believers owe God and must take the debt seriously, but, at the same time, they must also acknowledge that everything they possess with which they might offer something back to God has been given to them by God. In preaching on Eph 2:8–10, he expresses this position using the image of a guest who pays his host with the host's own resources:

> There is the kind of host who is not only pleased to be charitable to a man, but who, carrying further his superabundance, after he has found him both bed and board, will say to him, "Take here something with which to pay; in order that it may not seem to you that my charitable dealing has made you contemptible, I will receive payment for it at your hand; but yet it shall come from my own purse." Now shall he to whom such generosity has been displayed go and say that he has paid his host well? But with what money? Even with the same money that was put into his hand. Thus the case stands with those who put forward their good works to say that God has not saved them freely, but that they themselves were a help towards it.[13]

Calvin's imagery here is strikingly unrealistic in terms of social practice, but it makes his theological points with admirable clarity. It is fitting and appropriate that the guest should pay the host, but, since the resources to do so come from the host himself, this payment can never be construed as meritorious. Just as the guest cannot claim to have paid the host well, neither can human beings claim to have contributed toward their own salvation through their works. For the works themselves have been given freely by God. Working belongs alongside believing in the divine economy of salvation, and works are an essential expression of faith. Yet the works involved can never merit anything before God or be positioned as a return to God that itself helps to secure a further gift or blessing from God.

In arguing that Calvin places too much or too little soteriological emphasis upon human works, or is inconsistent about them, his contemporary critics there-

---

13. Calvin, *Sermons on Ephesians*, 166 (sermon 11).

fore miss his point entirely. It is the soteriological location of human works, not the degree of their importance, which is the vital issue for Calvin. It is impossible to expend too much effort warning that such works cannot justify anyone, but equally impossible to expend too much zeal in performing them or in urging others also to do so.

14.3. Unmerited Rewards: Obedience and Adoption

As he emphasizes the importance of good works performed in union with Christ, Calvin is able to give full weight to texts in which Paul stresses the obligation of believers to grow in obedience and to those that discuss rewards. It might be expected to be difficult to do this without reintroducing notions of merit, or calling into question believers' assurance of salvation, but, if Calvin's pattern of thought is traced, it becomes clear how his emphasis on adoption helps him to avoid doing so.

When at 2 Cor 7:1 Paul says that he and his readers should "cleanse ourselves . . . making holiness perfect in the fear of God," Calvin comments, "It is of the very nature of God's promises that they summon us to sanctification, just as if God had inserted an implied condition" (*Comm. 2 Cor.* 7:1, *CNTC* 10:93). At Phil 3:10, where Paul expresses the wish to share in Christ's sufferings in order to attain the resurrection from the dead, Calvin says bluntly, "Let everyone, therefore, who has become through faith a partaker of all Christ's benefits, acknowledge that a condition is presented to him—that his whole life be conformed to His death" (*Comm. Phil.* 3:10, *CNTC* 11:276). The exegetical examples could be multiplied, but the point remains the same: good works are a requirement for salvation, and the Christian life is once again, as in the medieval tradition, a journey toward a fuller holiness.

Of course, it is true for Calvin that here God gives what God commands. The renewed will that enables good works is the work of the Holy Spirit, and, since this is so, the works involved are not meritorious. Yet because the human will is not bypassed, but is instead renewed in this way, these works are also fully those of believers. The exercise of the wills of believers is essential to them. The only explanation there could be for blatant disregard for holiness is that a person is not genuinely a believer and has not truly been justified and renewed. Thus, although the good works of believers are not meritorious and are not a cause of justification, they are essential to salvation. Nor, as the quotations above show, are they simply organic, with good trees automatically producing good fruit. Calvin takes their nature as a condition of salvation with the utmost seriousness, even if it is a condition that the true believer will satisfy.[14]

This has consequences for the nature of covenant as an important theological category in Calvin's thought. If we ask whether Calvin conceives of the covenant as unilateral or bilateral, the answer is both. As Calvin himself puts it, "in all covenants of his mercy the Lord requires of his servants in return uprightness and sanctity of life. . . . [N]onetheless the covenant is at the outset drawn up as a free agreement, and perpetually remains such" (*Institutes* 3.17.5 [808]). From one perspective it is unilateral in that there is no aspect of covenant that is not in its entirety the work of God, yet from another it is bilateral since in justification Christ's sinless humanity is vital, and in sanctification so too are the works of the believer.[15]

A more fruitful way of approaching the category of covenant is to ask about the other imagery with which Calvin associates it. How does he characterize what it means for God's attitude toward believers? Here the significance of adoption comes into sharp focus, with Calvin emphasizing that God's stance toward believers' works is that of a loving father rather than that of a strict judge.[16] The very first title given to the Holy Spirit in the *Institutes* is "the spirit of adoption because he is the witness to us of the free benevolence of God with which God the Father has embraced us in his beloved only-begotten Son to become a Father to us" (*Institutes* 3.1.3 [540]). And, as we have already seen, the conviction of God's desire to have sinners become his children in Christ is central to Calvin's concept of faith (see 14.2).

That it is central mitigates any possible challenge to the assurance of salvation enjoyed by believers posed by Calvin's emphasis on good works as a condition of salvation. The foundation of assurance for Calvin is the saving work of Christ, his righteousness covering over the sinfulness that remains even in the good works of believers who are serious about holiness. Yet Calvin is willing to allow that the experience of the Christian life has a part to play in confirming this assurance, speaking of "the grace of good works, which shows that the Spirit of adoption has

---

14. See Kevin P. Emmert, *John Calvin and the Righteousness of Works* (Göttingen: Vandenhoeck & Ruprecht, 2021).

15. On covenant in Calvin, see Peter Lillback, *The Binding of God: Calvin's Role in the Development of Covenant Theology* (Grand Rapids: Baker, 2001). On the relationship between the category of covenant and union with Christ, see Pierrick Hildebrand, "Calvin and the Covenant: The Reception of Zurich Theology," in *The Oxford Handbook of Calvin and Calvinism*, ed. Bruce Gordon and Carl Trueman (Oxford: Oxford University Press, 2021), 68–69.

16. See Lillback, *Binding of God*, 196n10, for an extensive list of relevant texts.

been given to us [cf. Rom 8:15]" (*Institutes* 3.14.18 [785]). Given this confirmatory role for good works, one might expect the question to arise of exactly how serious is serious enough when it comes to holiness. How much is needed to confirm that the Spirit has been given and that the believer numbers among the elect?[17]

In fact, this question does not seem to arise for Calvin, who is always willing to emphasize that the evangelicals enjoy assurance, whereas their Catholic opponents do not. Calvin's conviction of God's paternal benevolence toward believers is the fundamental reason for this absence of anxiety: "the fatherly indulgence of God ... forgives His people the infirmity of the flesh and the sins under which they still labour. Our confidence in this forbearance of God, Paul teaches us, is made certain by the Spirit of adoption, who would not bid us be bold in prayer without sealing to us free pardon" (*Comm. Rom.* 8:15, *CNTC* 8:168).

Similarly, confidence in God's fatherly affection helps Calvin to meet the exegetical challenge posed by texts where Paul speaks of or implies rewards for believers (e.g., 1 Cor 3:14; Gal 6:8–9). Do such texts demonstrate that good works must in some sense be meritorious? Even if God is always rewarding God's own gifts, does the granting of a reward not necessarily involve an assessment of the merits of the use made of these gifts by believers? It is his emphasis on adoption that enables Calvin to deny that rewards imply merit while still acknowledging the significance of rewards. How adoption achieves this is illustrated by a striking piece of imagery contained in a sermon on Gal 2:17–20 preached by Calvin in 1557/1558:

> Picture a child who is seeking to obey his father: when his father asks him to do something, he will accept what the child does, even though the child may not understand what he is doing. The child may even break something in the process, and yet the father will not fret about the broken object when he sees his child's affection and willingness to obey. But if a man hires a servant, he will expect him to perform his task perfectly. Why? Because he is going to receive wages, and, therefore, he cannot afford to ruin what has been committed to his hands. If the task is not done well, the master will not be content with it. Our Lord, speaking of the days of gospel grace, says that he will accept our service, just as a father accepts the obedience of his child, even if all that is done is of

17. Randall C. Zachmann, *The Assurance of Faith: Conscience in the Theology of Martin Luther and John Calvin* (Louisville: Westminster John Knox, 2005), argues that this is a point of instability in Calvin's theology, which made possible subsequent crises of assurance for later generations in the Reformed tradition. This may be correct, but it is still necessary to ask why there is no evidence that Calvin himself experienced this difficulty.

no value. That is to say, he does not accept it because it is perfect, for it is not, but he bears with us out of his abundant mercy. He shows himself to be so bountiful and kind to us by accepting what we do as if it were fully pleasing to him, although there is no inherent merit or worth in our works at all. Thus, we can have the freedom and the courage to serve God; we can know that God will bless all that we do for him because whatever is wrong with our offerings is washed away in the blood of the Lord Jesus Christ.[18]

Believers are to have confidence that the very attempt to be obedient will be favorably received by God. They are also to know that if God rewards what has been done, it will be because the attempt has been made and not because of the intrinsic worth of what has been achieved. The works performed are not accepted as fully pleasing because of the qualities they possess but because the believer is loved as a child of God. In medieval soteriologies that emphasized God's reward for individuals who do *quod in se est* (what lies within them), God already graciously accorded human works a value in the economy of salvation beyond their inherent worth. Yet in such soteriologies, God still operated in a judicial mode. Even if works were assigned a value greater than their actual worth, their value was still measured by relative achievement. But in Calvin's view, God has moved out of a judicial mode and into a fatherly one, and their justification by God has moved believers into the world of family relationships: "the children of God are not liable to accusation because God justifies" (*Comm. Rom.* 8:33, *CNTC* 8:184).

It is therefore unsurprising to find Calvin elsewhere interpreting promises of reward using familial language. He insists that all merits are Christ's own and that all rewards are an inheritance. Calvin appeals to Col 3:24 where slaves are encouraged to obey their earthly masters and to expect a reward from God if they do so, but the promised reward consists "of the inheritance" (*Institutes* 3.18.2 [822]). And although Calvin does not say so in his sermon on Gal 2:17–20, the image of a father valuing his child's attempt at obedience far beyond any achievement involved is noteworthy in another way. It asserts a real distance between God and humanity in that even our best attempts at goodness appear in God's sight like the faltering efforts of a young child. Yet at the same time, it leaves room for human reciprocity. The distance involved does not mean that the relationship runs only in one direction. In the child's affection and willingness to obey, the father receives exactly what he most desires. Calvin says in the *Institutes*, "God's children are pleasing and lovable to him, since he sees in them the marks and features of his own countenance. For we have elsewhere taught that regeneration is a renewal

---

18. Calvin, *Sermons on Galatians*, 202 (sermon 13).

of the divine image in us" (*Institutes* 3.17.5 [807]). Merit is irrelevant in relation to regeneration simply because it is not the basis of a healthy relationship between parent and child.[19]

14.4. Reciprocity: The Context of God's Family

The place of human response to the divine gift in Calvin's soteriology has been considerably clarified by viewing it in the context of union with Christ and the use of the image of adoption to describe that union. Each of the conflicting criticisms leveled against him in recent evaluations of the place of human response in his soteriology rests upon misunderstanding.

It is simply wrong to suppose that Calvin eliminates from his soteriology the human reciprocation of the divine gift in good works. Far from harboring any general skepticism about the appropriateness of such a response, Calvin emphasizes it. As his treatment of the theme of rewards demonstrates, Calvin's problem with medieval soteriologies is not that they wrongly try to give something back to God but that, in meritorious deeds, they offer the wrong things. To measure the human response to God using merit is an error not because there is something inherently wrong about measuring obligations but because only perfect obedience beyond the means of human beings could possibly satisfy the debt owed. God instead graciously makes believers God's own children through adopting them in union with Christ, and, within this union, giving and receiving follows a specific logic. It is not the logic that pertains to human gift-giving and reciprocation in general but instead more specifically to that which takes place between parents and children.

Nor at the opposite extreme does Calvin come dangerously close to reintroducing salvation by works through the strength of his emphasis on the good works of believers. As his treatment of the theme of assurance demonstrates, Calvin consistently asserts that God responds to the imperfect attempts of believers to be obedient with fatherly affection. God does so because the continued sin of believers has been dealt with in justification: "God will not admit any accusation against us, because He has absolved us from all blame. The devil, to be sure, accuses all the godly; and the law of God itself and their own conscience also reprove them.

---

19. See Brian Gerrish, *Grace and Gratitude: The Eucharistic Theology of John Calvin* (Minneapolis: Fortress, 1993), 90: "The theme of adoption, the new birth, the transition from 'children of wrath' to 'children of grace,' takes us to the heart of the Reformers' protest against the prevailing gospel of the day."

But none of these have any influence on the judge who justifies them" (*Comm. Rom.* 8:33, *CNTC* 8:185).

Finally, that Calvin rests this strong assurance of salvation specifically upon justification also helps to eliminate the possibility that he simply treats the theme of reciprocity in an inconsistent way. For while the works of believers are excluded from any part in justification, which is a forensic declaration of forgiveness founded on the saving work of Christ, such works are central in sanctification. Believers are to grow in Christ so that they are conformed to the gift they have received. Works occupy a defined place in the structure of Calvin's soteriology, and their exclusion from one part of the double grace of union with Christ does not necessitate or imply their exclusion from the other. Calvin's rhetoric against justification by works does not conflict with his assertion of their importance in sanctification.

If Calvin's treatment of divine initiative and human response in salvation is in fact coherent and clear, why do his critics fail to appreciate this? At least in part, the problem arises from their very decision to approach Calvin's soteriology with divine initiative and human response as a framing theme. For Calvin does not structure his soteriology using this theme.[20] As Calvin's insistence that the works of believers are at the same time genuinely their own and wholly the work of the Spirit demonstrates, he has no interest in defining human response in contrast to the gift that produces it. Calvin's focus is instead on what happens when divine and human agencies become one in Christ by the power of the Spirit. Union with Christ is central to his soteriology and is often expressed in terms of God's adoption of those in Christ. The theme of reciprocity finds its proper place only within this relationship of union, and remains important, but does so in the same way that patterns of giving and receiving are important in the relationship between parents and children.

Such patterns express the closeness and affection of this familial relationship, and a narrow focus upon the obligation of children to reciprocate their parents, or upon such reciprocal giving by children as the basis of a parent's love, could only be an indicator of its ill health. The radical edge of Calvin's soteriology lies not in any reconfiguration of the content of the appropriate human response to the gift of salvation, which remains works of love. It is found rather in his relocation of this human response away from notions of meritorious cooperation with divine grace. Calvin instead argues that this human response takes place always

20. See Billings, *Calvin, Participation, and the Gift*, 190: "The concept of 'gift' which tends toward the two options of being 'unilateral' or 'bilateral,' 'passively' or 'actively' received, is simply not adequate to express the biblical and theological complexity of Calvin's thought."

and only from within union with Christ, in whom believers are adopted as the children of God.

14.5. Conclusion: Calvin's Soteriology in Comparison with Luther and Melanchthon

It is thus somewhat ironic that Calvin's critics have so often perceived his teaching about divine initiative and human response as one-sided or lacking balance. In fact, Calvin's approach to this issue positions his teaching about it within a careful soteriological synthesis, organized around union with Christ. This synthesis is intended to reflect Scripture's teaching and the central place of the Pauline Letters within the canon. As such, it does not resonate powerfully with some Pauline texts and themes only to leave others largely out of account. Everything must be included. In line with his presuppositions about the nature of Scripture, Calvin expects the biblical texts to present a unified vision and strives for unity in his own interpretation of these texts. What results is comprehensive, subtle, and delicate.

If there is a characteristic vulnerability in Calvin's soteriology, it is that any upsetting of its precise balance can lead to the distortion of the whole. For example, if Calvin's careful rooting of justification and sanctification in union with Christ's person is neglected, then they can be turned into successive chronological stages in an *ordo salutis* ("order of salvation") with the accompanying risk that justification is then reduced to a legal fiction (since the renewal of believers is not merely distinguishable from justification but becomes a completely separate, subsequent stage). And if the strength of Calvin's emphasis on adoption and God's fatherly attitude toward believers is diluted, and sanctification as well as justification is treated in largely legal terms, then there is the immediate danger of introspective anxiety over election. It ceases to be a source of assurance and becomes instead one of anxiety, with believers worrying over how much they must do to satisfy divine requirements and so demonstrate their election.

Such distortions represent fundamental misinterpretations of Calvin's intentions, but their prevalence in some subsequent contexts, among admirers no less than critics, illustrates the necessity and challenge of seeing Calvin's soteriological synthesis in the round. If we are to reach any worthwhile evaluation of his work as a Pauline interpreter, it must be based upon accurate understanding. One way in which to gain a rounded picture of Calvin's work is to compare it with the Pauline interpretation of his Wittenberg predecessors. At the beginning of the previous chapter, I suggested that Calvin likely engaged closely with Luther and Melanchthon's Pauline exegesis (see 13.1). As he constructs his own soteriological synthesis,

Calvin attempts to bring together the best features of the Pauline interpretation of each of them, and other sixteenth-century interpreters of Paul, and to remedy perceived problems.

That he does so means that Calvin is indebted to Luther in relation to many of his most fundamental commitments. This indebtedness to Luther begins with Calvin's portrayal of the human plight apart from Christ. Here Luther's apocalyptic dualism is fully maintained. The discontinuity between the fallen self apart from Christ and the self in Christ renewed through faith by the power of the Spirit is profound. There is nothing in the former that can lead to or prepare for the latter, and conversion is a work of God alone.[21] Unsurprisingly, Calvin also shares Luther's emphasis on the alien nature of the righteousness received by the believer. And just as Luther treats alien righteousness in relation to union with Christ, so too does Calvin. It never occurs to Calvin to interpret justification by faith in isolation from Christology, or to present justification as in opposition to union with Christ. Nor does it ever occur to Calvin to detach the faith of the believer from the story of Jesus Christ. Calvin's sense of the importance of the righteousness of Christ in his human nature (see 13.6), which is demonstrated by his earthly obedience, is too strong to permit this. These criticisms, often made of later Protestant interpretations of Paul and erroneously projected back onto the Reformers, simply do not apply.

Further, Calvin continues Luther's protest against merit, sharing his profound sense of the complete sufficiency of the grace of God for salvation. Despite significant differences concerning the canonical and hermeneutical significance of the law (see 6.4), Calvin maintains Luther's insistence that in key Pauline texts the law's soteriological function is to reveal to human beings their own unrighteousness and incapacity to obey God. In this way, their need for Christ is demonstrated. Calvin is also at one with Luther in his interpretation of Paul's insistence that justification is "not by the works of the law." He hears it not merely as a rejection of any role for works performed prior to faith in causing justification but also as a rejection of any such role for the works of the baptized (see 7.2).

Yet for all this dependence on Luther, Calvin also incorporates into his soteriological synthesis some of Melanchthon's most characteristic themes. Melanch-

---

21. Calvin does not wholly share Luther's concern with the hiddenness of God and in contrast emphasizes that creation is a manifestation of divine glory. Yet creation serves only to reveal God to those able to view it through the spectacles of Scripture. See I. John Hesselink, "The Revelation of God in Creation and Scripture," in Billings and Hesselink, *Calvin's Theology*, 3–24. On the hiddenness of God as a theme in Luther's thought, see Steven Paulson, "Luther's Doctrine of God," in *The Oxford Handbook of Martin Luther's Theology*, ed. Robert Kolb, Irene Dingel, and L'ubomír Batka (Oxford: Oxford University Press, 2014), 187–200.

thon's emphasis on justification's forensic nature is strongly reflected. Calvin also shares Melanchthon's sense that the obedience offered to God by the believer does not simply arise spontaneously as the consequence of justification. It retains the character of an obligation. It is striking that Calvin gives these emphases considerable weight but that this is not done at the expense of Luther's emphasis on union with Christ. Rather than making justification by faith the central category in his theology into which everything else must fit, Calvin instead pairs it with sanctification as twin aspects of union with Christ. This positioning of union with Christ as the central soteriological category seems closer exegetically to the Pauline texts, where participatory language is ubiquitous but the vocabulary of justification, for all its undoubted significance, is not.

The establishment of sanctification as a distinct focus, distinguishable from justification even if never separable from it, also offers some exegetical advantages. For example, Paul does sometimes phrase imperatives in strongly conditional terms, and Calvin treats them fully as obligations in a manner that reflects Paul's language. Calvin does not deny Luther's important observation that good trees will organically bear good fruit, but he does decisively move beyond it. Alongside the insistence that they are not meritorious, human good works are given a positive value as a source of divine pleasure by Calvin in a way that makes it difficult to fall into the error of regarding the very attempt to obey God as a corrupt attempt to establish one's own righteousness.[22]

The potential weaknesses in Calvin's synthesis are very much the flip side of these strengths. The formula that the twin saving benefits of justification are distinct but inseparable in Christ masks a sharp distinction between them. While both benefits are received at the same time, justification represents an exclusively forensic movement, while renewal is allocated entirely to sanctification. That Paul uses the vocabulary of righteousness in relation to both justification and renewal at least raises the question of how stable this sharp distinction is in exegetical terms. Justification and sanctification are closely entwined in his texts.

This issue does not arise with Luther, who makes scarcely any division between justification and sanctification. His pairing of alien righteousness with the necessity for the believer to live an alien life produces a distinctive nonlinear vision of the Christian life. Christ is appropriated daily by faith, and any progress in faith is also a return to baptism and to the beginning of the Christian life. Righteousness always remains a matter of living in someone external. With Calvin by contrast,

---

22. This impacts the manner of Calvin's portrayal of Judaism as a religion of works-righteousness. Rather than constituting a form of idolatry, the attempt to be justified by works errs simply in attempting something impossible to achieve.

human life lived in union with Christ is a *via* or pathway for the transformation of the believer. Calvin's view is more linear, and while he will emphasize in various ways that the righteousness received in justification is and remains alien, he will not emphasize this in relation to sanctification. Even as he empties good works of merit, Calvin does make progress in them central to his vision of the Christian life and does assert a continued role for the law in shaping and guiding this progress. Whether this constitutes an interpretative gain and a proper holding together of divine gift and demand in Paul, or a backward step and a blunting of the radical edge of Pauline theology, is itself a matter of interpretation.

Yet what is undeniable is that Calvin's very attempt to construct a soteriological synthesis stands in contrast with most modern Pauline interpretation. Here the typical procedure is to identify the component parts of Paul's theology and order them hierarchically according to importance. Like Luther, Calvin does not play off against each other justification by faith and participation in Christ as if one must be emphasized at the expense of the other.[23] Instead, union with Christ functions as an integrating center in Calvin's soteriology that serves to highlight the significance of justification rather than diminishing it. In their different ways, both Calvin and Luther integrate these twin emphases in Pauline theology, but they do not do so by finding a means to hold together what would more naturally belong apart. Instead, for each of them, the plight of fallen humanity requires an alien righteousness that can be found only in the person of Christ and so can be received only when united with him by faith. If they have worthwhile resources to offer for Pauline interpretation today, such resources lie in these convictions.

23. The assumption that one of these two tracks must be primary in importance and the other only secondary was resisted by Käsemann (see 2.6), but he has been little heeded. See Stephen J. Chester, *Conversion at Corinth: Perspectives on Conversion in Paul's Theology and the Corinthian Church* (London: T&T Clark, 2003), 205–10.

PART FOUR

Reading Paul with the Reformers Today

CHAPTER FIFTEEN

Paul and the Reformers:
Moving beyond the New Perspective on Paul

At the conclusion of the last chapter, I suggested that a crucial aspect of what the Reformers' Pauline exegesis still has to offer to contemporary interpreters concerns their integration of justification by faith and union with Christ (see 14.5). They capture something essential to Paul when they emphasize both that salvation requires an alien righteousness that is not the believer's own and that this alien righteousness can be received only when united with the person of Christ by faith. However, contemporary Pauline theology does not provide a stable, stationary horizon against which to measure this claim. The New Perspective on Paul (NPP) is now more than forty years old and has inevitably itself been reexamined in light of subsequent research, with yet newer perspectives emerging that move beyond the interpretative framework established by the NPP. Before exploring the resources that the Reformers' exegesis can offer for interpreting Paul today in detail, it is necessary to understand the relationship between their work and new developments in Pauline theology.

15.1. The Reformers and New Developments in Pauline Theology

By the early 2000s, the NPP had already divided into various streams, principal among them those that emphasized either the apocalyptic Paul or the covenantal Paul (see 8.2 and 8.3). Over subsequent years, there have been two major new developments that have moved discussion of Pauline theology significantly beyond the framework established by the NPP into a new phase. One is the appearance of John Barclay's 2015 volume *Paul and the Gift*, which proposes a different perspective on the role of grace in Paul's theology and its relationship to the role of grace in other Second Temple Jewish sources. Paul is typical in emphasizing divine grace but unusual in stressing its incongruous nature. We have already seen the implications of Barclay's emphasis on the incongruity of grace for understanding what Paul means by "works of the law" (see 9.3), but it also necessary to explore the significance of his argument for appropriation of the Reformers' Pauline exegesis more generally.

The other major new development is not the work of an individual scholar but the emergence of a movement, now often referred to using the slogan "Paul within Judaism." Here the NPP is deemed inadequate because although Paul's gospel is no longer contrasted with Jewish works-righteousness, the NPP replaces works-righteousness with an ethnocentric identification of righteousness with Jewish identity. The "Paul within Judaism" movement (also sometimes referred to as the "radical new perspective") argues that in fact Paul has no critique of Judaism, that everything Paul says about the law in his letters is directed specifically against attempts to persuade gentile followers of Jesus to observe the law, and that Paul himself regarded observance as obligatory for all Jewish followers of Jesus. As with Barclay, an assessment of the implications of "Paul within Judaism" for the appropriation of resources drawn from the Reformers' Pauline exegesis is necessary.

15.2. The Reformers and "Paul within Judaism"

That Paul continued to see himself as Jewish throughout his career as an apostle of Christ, that he still believed in the election of Israel, and that he remained committed to the truth of the Scriptures of Israel are commonplaces almost universally affirmed by contemporary scholarship. Alongside such commonplaces is often held the view that Paul regarded the era of obligatory law observance as now over, even for himself and other Jewish followers of Jesus. Paul claims that he died to the law (Gal 2:19), and that in his work of mission he became as one under the law in order to reach Jews even though he was not under the law (1 Cor 9:20). Further, Paul's treatment of issues related to legal observance suggests a personal perspective in which Jewish believers who felt bound to observe all the commandments were weak in faith (Rom 14:1), and wrong in understanding (Rom 14:14), but nevertheless to be welcomed by all without judgment as fellow servants of Christ (Rom 14:3–4). Paul positions observance or nonobservance of the law by Jewish believers as something in and of itself neutral that is to be determined by the requirements of mission and fellowship among believers.

Although differing among themselves on many points of detail, interpreters within the "Paul within Judaism" movement reject this whole line of reasoning.

They push beyond commonplace perspectives on Paul's continuing Jewishness, insisting not only that Paul continues to see himself as Jewish but that he does so in a thoroughly conventional way. Only a Jewish Paul whose faith in Jesus as Messiah leaves his commitment to law observance unaltered is acceptable. In arguing for this position, "Paul within Judaism" scholars seek to provide credible alternative interpretations of those texts used to argue that law observance has become something neutral for Paul.[1] Yet they also often attempt broader arguments. For Paul certainly nowhere explicitly states that observance is obligatory for Jewish believers, and the disputed texts exist within the framework of Paul's wider treatment of the law. In order to establish Paul's commitment to obligatory law observance by Jewish believers, "Paul within Judaism" scholars often propose new understandings of this wider treatment of the law that they perceive to align with such a commitment.

None of these new proposals concerning Paul's broader attitude toward the law are endorsed by all scholars who identify with the "Paul within Judaism" movement, but prominent among the claims made are that Paul's experience on the Damascus Road should not be termed a conversion, and that Paul's remarks about the law have been falsely universalized by Christian interpreters. He intended them to apply only to the question of how gentiles were to become part of the people of God through Christ. The history of Christian interpretation of Paul, in which it is assumed that his letters contain a universal message of salvation relevant to all, is in fact a history of misinterpretation.

At this point there is, of course, a general incompatibly between the Reformers' interpretation of Paul's message and the claims of the "Paul within Judaism" movement. To deny the status of convert to someone like Paul, who was a persecutor of the church but then became an advocate of faith in Jesus as Messiah, would make little sense to the Reformers for whom faith in Jesus and justification by means of it stood at the heart of Paul's gospel. And their whole rebellion against medieval soteriology concerned the content of Paul's message of salvation, not to whom it applies. The universal nature of that message is simply assumed on all sides in sixteenth-century debates. If the broader claims of the "Paul within Judaism" movement are correct, then there is little point in attempting to interpret Paul in critical dialogue with Reformation perspectives since they can only mislead.

However, the evidence contained in Paul's letters weighs heavily against the broader claims made in "Paul within Judaism" scholarship.[2] As regards his conversion, Paul's attitude toward those who share his own former rejection of Jesus as

---

1. For examples of this literature, see notes 4, 5, and 6 below.

2. For a thorough but concise assessment, see Stephen Westerholm, "The First Readers of

Messiah is instructive. He says nothing that suggests they can or should cease to be Jewish, but he does regard those Jews who have not become Christ followers as having gone astray. Those who do not believe have stumbled (1 Cor 1:23; Rom 9:32–33), have sought to establish their own righteousness (Rom 10:3), and are like broken-off branches (Rom 11:20). Paul can even say that not all Israelites currently belong to Israel (Rom 9:6) and that he is anguished concerning their situation (Rom 9:3).

Although God will not abandon his people—the calling of God given to Israel is irrevocable (Rom 11:29), a hardening has come upon Israel only until the full number of the gentiles has come in (Rom 11:25), and God's ultimate purpose is mercy (Rom 11:31–32)—those who do not accept Jesus as Messiah are currently out of step with God's redemptive plan. Paul has reconfigured Jewish identity so that its primary defining issue is not legal observance but faith in Jesus as Messiah. It is to this faith that he regards those who currently do not share it as standing in need of conversion. They do so no less than gentiles, something that Paul is explicit about in Rom 10:5–21 where he identifies the message of the righteousness of faith as addressed to Jew and Greek alike (Rom 10:12–13).

In relation to the universality of the law, Paul is clear that through the speaking of the law, the whole world is held accountable for sin, and also clear that no person (literally "no flesh," *pasa sarx*) will be justified by doing the works of the law (Rom 3:19–20; Gal 2:16). As Gal 3:11 states completely unambiguously, by law "no one" (*oudeis*) is justified before God. Instead, it is faith in Jesus that justifies both the circumcised and the uncircumcised (Rom 3:30). Paul also makes it clear that he himself hopes to attain to resurrection from the dead by being found in Christ with the righteousness that comes through faith and not that which is from the law (Phil 3:7–11). Finally, in a context in which he is contrasting the saving work of Jesus for all with the death-bearing disobedience of Adam that impacts all (Rom 5:17–19), Paul stresses that justification results in eternal life (Rom 5:21).

Thus, although the occasions for Paul's letters concern the incorporation of the gentiles into God's people, and although the churches to which he writes are primarily gentile, his message is universal: "When Paul speaks to *gentiles* (as the primary, implied audience in Galatians and Romans), he must also speak *about* Jews, because the salvation of the whole world is founded on God's mercy to Israel."[3] What Paul says of the law concerns Jews as well as gentiles, and his teaching about the purpose of the law relates to the salvation of all. The law brings knowledge of sin (Rom 3:20), it increases trespass (Rom 5:20), it was given because

---

Romans and the 'Paul within Judaism' School," in *Romans: Text, Readers, and the History of Interpretation* (Grand Rapids: Eerdmans, 2022), 43–75.

3. John M. G. Barclay, *Paul and the Power of Grace* (Grand Rapids: Eerdmans, 2020), 146.

of transgressions (Gal 3:19), and it imprisoned and confined those to whom it was given until faith came (Gal 3:22–25). The Reformers' understanding that the central purpose of the law is the universal soteriological one of revealing human beings' true position as sinners before God resonates with Paul's statements about it. In relation to the general arguments made by "Paul within Judaism" scholarship about Paul's attitude toward the law, the precritical Reformers have more to offer those seeking the historical Paul.

Yet even if Paul does proclaim a universal message of salvation relevant to all, and even if the significance of his statements about the law made in the context of that message cannot be restricted to gentiles, does this necessarily mean that he did not hold that Jewish believers were obliged to be observant? Certainly, Paul cannot have thought that observance of the law had any directly soteriological function for Jewish believers. Paul states that the promise that he would inherit the world did not come to Abraham or his descendants through the law but through the righteousness of faith (Rom 4:13). And Paul also positions his insistence that a person is justified by faith and not by works of the law as something that Jewish believers in Jesus should know and recognize (Gal 2:15–16). However, while these statements are abundantly plain concerning righteousness and salvation, they do not in and of themselves eliminate the possibility that Paul held that Jewish believers were obliged to be observant *for other reasons.*

If such a distinction is made between how Paul perceives the law in relation to its soteriological function and what he holds about the law in relation to ecclesiological practice,[4] then the debate is thrown back onto those texts where he makes statements about the law that directly bear implications for the observance of the law by Jewish believers. Here "Paul within Judaism" scholarship rejects all previous interpretations of texts inconsistent with obligatory observance by Jewish believers. For example, Paul's insistence in Rom 14:14, 20 that all food is clean is taken to mean only that Jewish believers need not avoid foods that fall into gray areas. All food is clean in the sense that nothing is inherently impure by its own nature but instead only because it has been placed in that category by divine commandment. Paul is arguing that Jewish believers need not avoid foods other than those specifically prohibited. He is not suggesting that they can eat foods that are so prohibited.[5]

---

4. For an attempt to argue a "Paul within Judaism" perspective on the basis of a consistent distinction between soteriological and ecclesiological categories, see J. Brian Tucker, *Reading Romans after Supersessionism: The Continuation of Jewish Covenantal Identity* (Eugene, OR: Wipf & Stock, 2018).

5. See David J. Rudolph, "Paul and the Food Laws: A Reassessment of Romans 14:14, 20," in

Alongside such attempts to clear obstacles in the way of establishing the view that Paul upheld obligatory law observance by Jewish believers, efforts are also made to provide a positive textual basis for it. For example, Paul's insistence at 1 Cor 7:17–24 that believers should remain in the condition in which they were called, and his prohibition of the surgical removal of the marks of circumcision (1 Cor 7:18), is taken to imply that Jewish believers must remain observant.[6]

These arguments in favor of a consistently law-observant Paul naturally reflect contemporary concerns and perspectives. We may be confident that the Reformers did not share any of them and would not have found persuasive the exegesis upon which they depend. However, the Reformers do seem to hold that Paul is not simply forbidding all legal practice by Jewish believers following the coming of the Messiah. Luther is clear that circumcision and other aspects of law observance were obligatory for Jews before Christ's coming but that now circumcision is "a matter of indifference and permissible, just as is everything else concerning days, food, clothing, places, sacrifices etc" (*LW* 27:335). Both circumcision and uncircumcision "are of no value for salvation, and both may be accepted without qualms of conscience" (*LW* 28:41). It appears that Luther thinks that Jewish believers who regard law observance as obligatory for them are mistaken but not sinful.

Calvin is even more explicit about this and goes one step further. He interprets Rom 14 as prompted by issues related to Jewish and gentile believers eating together. Those who eat only vegetables (Rom 14:2), and who distinguish between days (Rom 14:5), are Jewish believers seeking to maintain legal observance. Calvin feels that they are wrong to do so, not hesitating to define their position as superstitious. Yet he also argues that others are not to despise them, and that God is not offended by their restraint. The reason is that "the life of a Christian is properly ordered only when it has the will of God as its object. . . . [I]t is quite wrong to attempt anything which we consider is displeasing to Him, indeed which we are not convinced will please Him" (*Comm. Rom.* 14:7, *CNTC* 8:293–94). Despite his lack of sympathy for their perspective, Calvin considers that it would be dangerous for Jewish believers to abandon observance of the law unless or until their convictions allow them to do so.

Luther and Calvin are thus representatives of the tradition of interpretation that treats observance or nonobservance of the law by Jewish believers as neutral. Their standpoint will be resisted by "Paul within Judaism" scholars for whom

---

Paul the Jew: Rereading the Apostle as a Figure of Second Temple Judaism, ed. Gabrielle Boccaccini and Carlos A. Segovia (Minneapolis: Fortress, 2016), 151–82.

6. See David J. Rudolph, *A Jew to the Jews: Jewish Contours of Pauline Flexibility in 1 Cor 9:19–23*, WUNT 2/304 (Tübingen: Mohr Siebeck, 2011), 75–88.

anything less than obligatory law observance constitutes an abrogation of Jewish identity. This is a significant disagreement, but, for all its importance, it does not by itself in any more general way hinder critical appropriation of the Reformers' Pauline exegesis. That the Reformers do not regard law observance by Jewish believers as prohibited potentially limits the scope of the disagreement even if not its intensity.

An advocate of "Paul within Judaism" who distinguishes consistently between the law in relation to its soteriological function and the law in ecclesiological practice could hold that law observance is obligatory for Jewish believers while adopting interpretations held by the Reformers in relation to many other issues. It is only when the position that Paul regards law observance as obligatory for Jewish believers is supported by arguments that restrict the scope of his message of salvation, denying that Paul was a convert and taking his statements about the law as relevant only to gentiles, that general incompatibility ensues.[7]

15.3. The Reformers and "Paul and the Gift"

John Barclay's starting point for interpreting Paul is very different from that of the "Paul within Judaism" movement. Although just as deeply engaged with Paul's Second Temple context, and with the social life of ancient communities of faith, Barclay does not begin with questions of social identity. Instead, he explores Paul's handling of the theme of grace and compares it to perspectives on grace in other Second Temple texts. What emerges is an apostle who can be understood only as a Jewish figure but also as a distinctive one whose convictions about Jesus have reconfigured his Judaism.

Barclay portrays grace as ubiquitous within Second Temple Judaism, but, whereas other Jewish authors often understand divine grace as directed toward those best equipped to make good use of it, Paul stresses its incongruity. The gift of Christ goes to the unworthy, and there are no criteria whatsoever by which any individual or group can qualify for grace. It is this absolutizing or perfecting of the incongruity of grace that is characteristically Pauline and not an emphasis on its noncircularity. Paul does not conceive the gift of Christ as one that expects no re-

---

7. My point is not that the argument that Paul regarded law observance as obligatory for Jewish believers is convincing (I am not persuaded that Paul's arguments permit a tidy separation between soteriology and the ecclesiological function of the law) but only that on the neutral view itself Paul teaches that this erroneous conviction about legal observance is nevertheless to be respected. For a recent restatement of the neutral position, see John M. G. Barclay, *Paul and the Gift* (Grand Rapids: Eerdmans, 2015), 508–16.

turn from its recipients. In line with ancient social practice, the gift is understood strongly to obligate its recipients to their divine benefactor. The intention of the gift is frustrated if concrete obedience in deeds does not follow.

As Barclay himself recognizes, this argument is one that places his work in a complex relationship with the NPP and older perspectives: "This book may be interpreted *either* as a recontextualization of the Augustinian-Lutheran tradition, returning the dynamic of the incongruity of grace to its original mission environment where it accompanied the formation of new communities, *or* as a reconfiguration of the 'new perspective,' placing its best exegetical and theological insights within the frame of Paul's theology of grace."[8]

On the one hand, the ubiquity of grace within Judaism means that there can be no return to its portrayal as a religion of works-righteousness. The fundamental insight of the NPP that Judaism is a religion of grace is affirmed. Paul is not combating a principle of works-righteousness. Rather, he is insisting that there is no form of human symbolic capital (whether acquired by birth, from status, or through practice) that conditions divine grace. His concern is with subverting criteria of worth in general, not with combating attempts to earn salvation in particular. Those who simply wish to repristinate the Reformers' exegesis for twenty-first-century contexts will therefore be disappointed by Barclay's book. It allows for no wholesale return to Reformation perspectives.

Yet if the incongruity of grace suggests that Paul's concerns are much broader than combating works-righteousness, it also suggests that the focus of the NPP on ethnocentrism is too narrow. It, too, hears Paul attacking a single criterion of worth when in fact he is rejecting them all. Further, to place the incongruity of grace at the center of Paul's theology loudly echoes Reformation concerns. For gratuitous mercy stands at the very heart of what the Reformers understand grace to be (see 7.3), and this understanding of the nature of grace fuels their assault upon the part played by merit in medieval soteriology. As Barclay's own careful engagement with Luther and Calvin demonstrates,[9] even as his work closes the door on any uncritical appropriation of their exegesis, it also rehabilitates the Reformers as critical dialogue partners with whom to think about the Pauline texts.

Barclay does identify Luther's legacy as the source of the erroneous view that grace expects no return. This is a later extension of Luther's view that the believer's response of gratitude for the gift of Christ should not be motivated by the desire for a benefit or a reward. Luther is so concerned to reject instrumental reciprocity (i.e., to reject any possible contribution by works to salvation in a causal sense)

---

8. Barclay, *Paul and the Gift*, 420.
9. Barclay, *Paul and the Gift*, 97–116 (Luther), 116–30 (Calvin).

that he establishes a trajectory of thought in which gifts that expect no return whatsoever will become the ideal. Luther's own thought does have a place for the obligations of believers to God, but he conceives the satisfying of such obligations largely in organic terms. The good deeds of believers are "fruit" that arise spontaneously and freely. Luther points the way toward the modern view that "gift by definition should be free of reciprocity or return."[10]

The tension between the ideas of Barclay and those of Luther is clear here, but the same is not true with Calvin. Like Barclay, Calvin regards grace as strongly obligating (see 14.3 and 14.4) and emphasizes the need for believers to strive toward greater and greater sanctification (see 14.3). Barclay and Calvin are both interpreters for whom obeying the truth in response to the gift of Christ is of central significance. There is a major difference in how they discern the content of this obedience, with the law playing a central role for Calvin in a way that it does not for Barclay, who is focused on norms and patterns of communal life shaped by the incongruity of grace.[11] Nevertheless, they share a deep commitment to the circularity of grace.[12]

Barclay and Calvin also share other important commitments. They both regard the circularity of grace as consistent with the rejection of instrumental reciprocity. Far from acquiring the gift of Christ or any additional subsequent gift from God, obedience is part of the gift itself as God remakes believers. As Calvin puts it, "It is not the mere power of choosing aright, or some indefinable preparation, or assistance, but the right will itself, which is His workmanship" (*Comm. Eph.* 2:10, *CNTC* 11:146). That this work of renewing human agency is wholly an act of God makes redundant all notions of instrumentality and of merit. Yet at the same time, as Barclay points out, this act of God "generates and grounds an active, willed conformity to the Christ-life, in which believers become, like Christ, truly human as obedient agents."[13] Believers reciprocate the gift of Christ, but they do so with deeds that are both fully their own and fully those of God.

These features serve to clarify the ecumenical implications of Barclay's work, for his emphasis on the circularity of grace has understandably stimulated con-

---

10. Barclay, *Paul and the Gift*, 63.

11. Barclay develops this in relation to the contemporary world in *Paul and the Power of Grace*, 149–59.

12. In fact, the positions of Calvin and Barclay are also close together in other important respects. See Stephen J. Chester, "'Works Themselves Are a Part of Grace': John Calvin's Interpretation of Ephesians 2:8–10," in *The New Perspective on Grace: Paul and the Gospel after Paul and the Gift*, ed. Edward Adams et al. (Grand Rapids: Eerdmans, 2023).

13. Barclay, *Paul and the Gift*, 518–19. Barclay uses the same label for his own view of the relationship between divine agency and the human agency of believers as he does for that of Calvin. They are both examples of "energism." See *Paul and the Gift*, 442 and 129, respectively.

siderable interest from Roman Catholic scholars. Yet as the similarities between Barclay and Calvin illustrate, an emphasis on circularity does not necessarily lead Pauline scholarship back toward commitments typical of medieval interpretation. Circularity does not have to be explained in terms of created habits of grace and of meritorious deeds. Barclay insists that grace is not a "substance enhancing the natural powers of the human" and that "the future judgment of which Paul speaks does not ... determine salvation on the basis of human 'collaboration' with grace."[14] Barclay's commitment to the circularity of grace can be expressed in ways that resonate with the exegesis of the Reformers even if at important points it may involve a preference for positions held by some of them and not by others.

15.4. Conclusion: The Reformers and Barclay in Critical Dialogue

However, the relationship between Barclay's work and that of the Reformers need not stop at the level of general compatibility. Thinking about the two in relation to each other can help to clarify significant issues in Pauline interpretation. At some points, Barclay's focus on the circularity of grace may help us with issues left unresolved in the work of the Reformers. For example, we noted in the final section of the previous chapter that Calvin perhaps distinguishes more sharply than Paul's texts allow between justification and sanctification, while Luther avoids this but at the price of treating the good works of believers too exclusively as the good fruit spontaneously produced by good trees (see 14.5). Barclay does not do either of these things but employs the structure of gift and response to produce a more unified vision. The saving gift is thoroughly incongruous: it goes to the unworthy, unfitting, and unsuitable, and nothing that results from it by way of holiness could provide a basis for the gift. It is the source of everything believers are in Christ and therefore remains incongruous.

Yet the recipients will be changed by the gift, which "has a shape and a purpose, and will finally be completed (as gift) in the full transformation of fitting recipients. ... God is already at work in them in this life to press them towards that 'fit,' a work which is also theirs at the same time as it is God's (Phil 2:15–16)."[15] The works of believers matter greatly but do so in making their lives a fitting expression of

14. Barclay, *Paul and the Power of Grace*, 142.

15. John M. G. Barclay, "Believers and the 'Last Judgment' in Paul: Rethinking Grace and Recompense," in *Eschatologie = Eschatology: The Sixth Durham-Tübingen Research Symposium, Eschatology in Old Testament, Ancient Judaism and Early Christianity*, ed. Hans Joachim Eckstein, Christof Landmesser, and Hermann Lichtenberger, WUNT 2/272 (Tübingen: Mohr Siebeck, 2011), 207–8.

incongruous grace, not in moving beyond the incongruity of the gift. Barclay is striving toward a strong account of the obedience of believers that integrates their works into the single and complete gift of God in Christ, but he does so without thinking of those works solely in terms of organic spontaneity.

If Barclay can help with such unresolved issues in the Pauline interpretation of the Reformers, it is also the case that their exegetical legacy can complement his own work. Sometimes this is a matter of specific insights. As Jonathan Linebaugh points out, appreciation of the totally incongruous nature of the gift depends upon the law's revelation of the fallen human condition: "For the Reformers it is the law that identifies the site at which God's grace is given and at which it operates out of the opposite, justifying the ungodly and raising the dead."[16]

At other times, it is a matter of broad themes in Pauline theology. For although Barclay is clear that Christ is the gift received by believers, his focus on the theme of grace means that he does not say very much in detail about union with Christ or about justification.[17] Their importance for Paul is acknowledged, and they are discussed in Barclay's expositions of Romans and Galatians, but they are viewed from the perspective of their relationship to grace. In contrast, the Reformers give extensive consideration to these crucial themes, and, for this reason, their interpretation of Paul says more about the nature of the gift of Christ itself. Yet the Reformers' own commitment to the incongruity of grace means that what they say is largely compatible with Barclay's views and can also be heard as further explaining the distinctive nature of Paul's understanding of grace. Critical dialogue with their insights can help to strengthen thoughtful contemporary interpretations of Paul such as that offered by Barclay.

16. Jonathan A. Linebaugh, "Incongruous and Creative Grace: Reading *Paul and the Gift* with Martin Luther," *IJST* 22 (2020): 52.

17. On justification in Galatians and Romans, see Barclay, *Paul and the Gift*, 375–78, 475–76, 479–87. On participation in Christ, see 500–501.

CHAPTER SIXTEEN

Paul and the Reformers:
Resources for Contemporary Pauline Theology

The last chapter explored new developments within Pauline theology beyond the New Perspective on Paul (NPP). A largely antithetical relationship emerged with the "Paul within Judaism" movement's general claims, even if the specific claim that for Paul Jewish believers are obliged to remain observant does not itself alone result in any general incompatibility. In contrast, John Barclay's perspective on grace offers more scope for critical dialogue with the work of the Reformers. Resources drawn from their work can help us to relate Barclay's emphasis on the incongruity of Pauline grace to other important themes in the apostle's theology. This final chapter will explore and support this claim, showing how the appropriation of exegetical insights drawn from the Reformers can help us to interpret Paul's description of the reign of grace in the lives of believers (Rom 6–8), and also help us to interpret key Pauline texts like Rom 4, where Paul discusses the figure of Abraham, in a rounded and exegetically credible manner.

16.1. Reformation Principles for Pauline Interpretation Today

As I suggested at the end of chapter 14, of special benefit among the Reformers' exegetical insights is the way in which they integrate justification by faith and union with Christ (see 14.5). In particular, their insistence that the righteousness received by believers remains alien but does so as a principal dimension of union with Christ's person clarifies various aspects of what Paul means by being under grace (Rom 6:14, 15). This judgment represents a preference for the exegesis of Luther and Calvin over that of Melanchthon since, although, along with early Protestant interpreters in general, Melanchthon fully shares their commitment to alien righteousness, he does not make union with Christ central to justification. He instead explains the christological dimensions of justification with reference to the mediatorial role of Christ, who on account of his saving work can intercede with the Father on behalf of sinners (see 11.3). The result is that he largely fails to respond to Paul's language of being in Christ (see 12.6).

This judgment also represents something of a departure in relation to contemporary theology where extrinsic accounts of justification are unfashionable. Reformation accounts emphasize that the perfect righteousness granted to the believer in justification remains wholly and entirely that of Christ. It is received by faith through the preaching of the biblical word, with those who believe drawn out of themselves and into total reliance on the promises of God. People do not encounter God by looking inward, but instead they encounter God as the convicting power of the word turns them outward toward Christ.

The perceived problem with this emphasis on the external or alien nature of righteousness is that it separates justification from the transformation that Paul so clearly expects in the lives of believers. Reformation interpreters may hold that believers will experience ethical change, but if this change is something separate from the righteousness granted in justification, is that justification itself anything more than a legal fiction? And if justification is a legal fiction, will it not also become contractual, with faith filling the role of a human disposition that satisfies a divine requirement?

It is at this point that Luther's and Calvin's emphasis on union with Christ is especially vital. For the perceived dangers of an emphasis on alien righteousness become real only if union with Christ is neglected. Once union with Christ is made integral to justification, they are averted. There is no valid basis on which to accuse Luther of a legal fiction since, although he insists that righteousness remains alien to believers, he also insists that it is essential for believers to live an alien life (see 10.5). Similarly, such an accusation against Calvin is also unfounded since he insists that, alongside justification, sanctification is one of the simultaneous twin key aspects of union with Christ (see 13.2). Further, neither Luther nor Calvin can justly be accused of offering a contractual account of justification precisely because they emphasize this christological focus of faith. Far from holding that faith justifies because it is the right kind of religious disposition to fulfill the human side of a contract with God, both insist that faith justifies because it grasps hold of Christ and unites believers with him (see 14.5).

If union with Christ is treated as integral to justification in this way, then the Reformers' strong emphasis upon the extrinsic nature of justification does not imply the dangers that frequently make contemporary Pauline interpreters wary of it. Instead, it is left free to deliver considerable insights into the nature of the reign of grace, which Paul discusses in detail in Rom 6–8. This material is often treated as belonging to a later participatory phase in the letter's argument separate from the forensic account of justification offered in Rom 1–4.[1] But Paul in fact directly relates the reign of grace to justification.

The apostle says that grace exercises dominion "through righteousness" (*dia dikaiosynēs*, Rom 5:21), having previously said that Abraham's descendants inherit the promises of God made to the patriarch "through righteousness" (*dia dikaiosynēs*, 4:13). As Jewett points out, these are the only occurrences of this phrase in the New Testament.[2] By means of this phrase, Paul includes justification in the present reality of renewal in the lives of believers. Justification is indeed the way in which believers gain access to the grace in which they stand (Rom 5:1), but it does not then immediately go into retirement.

This point can also be illustrated with reference to Paul's argument about baptism in Rom 6. He says that those who have died with Christ in baptism will rise with him because in so dying they have been justified from sin (Rom 6:7). English translations usually read that those who have died with Christ have been "set free" from sin, and this obscures important connections between different phases of Paul's argument. The verb Paul uses is "justify" (*dikaioō*), and this statement about entering into newness of life in Christ is the prelude to the statement that those who have died with Christ in baptism "believe" (*pisteuō*) that they will also rise with him (Rom 6:8). Paul's previous use of the verb "believe" (*pisteuō*) came in Rom 4:24 where the reckoning of Abraham's faith as righteousness is said to be also for those who believe in "him who raised Jesus our Lord."

Shortly after this linking of justifying faith, resurrection, and baptism comes Paul's instruction to believers to "consider yourselves dead to sin and alive to God in Christ Jesus" (Rom 6:11). The verb "consider" or "reckon" (*logizomai*) also appears in the statement "Abraham believed God and it was reckoned to him as righteousness" (Gen 15:6; Rom 4:3, 22, 24). On the basis of Christ's once-and-for-all death to sin (Rom 6:10), those over whom grace reigns are to think about their own identity in Christ in a way that reflects their justification by God. As Karl Barth puts it, at Rom 6:11 "faith means . . . reckoning as God reckons."[3] Once again, justification is integral to the present reign of grace in the lives of believers.

---

1. Romans 5 is often treated as a bridge between the forensic and participatory parts of Paul's arguments. It should be remembered that this is different from Calvin's position that the earlier chapters concern justification and the later ones concern sanctification, since for Calvin forensic justification no less than sanctification is an aspect of union with Christ and hence a participatory concept (see 13.2).

2. Robert Jewett, *Romans*, Hermeneia (Minneapolis: Fortress, 2007), 389.

3. Karl Barth, *The Epistle to the Romans*, 6th ed., trans. Edwyn C. Hoskyns (Oxford: Oxford

Thus, if Luther and Calvin are correct that justification involves the receipt by believers of alien righteousness, then any account of the reign of grace must also include an extrinsic emphasis. Through justification, believers are united with Christ by faith so that their new lives are externally sourced, "wholly dependent on the life of Another, the One who is risen from the dead."[4] Further, that the righteousness received by believers is the alien righteousness of Christ, and does not become their own,[5] makes it clear that the nature of the grace that reigns in believer's lives conforms to Paul's distinctive emphasis upon its incongruity. Believers must respond to the gift of Christ in obedience, and they must be shaped into its fitting recipients, but their new lives are perpetually to reflect the incongruity of divine grace. The fit for which they are to strive is not one that enables them to leave the incongruity of grace behind. They are to grow in holiness (Rom 6:19), but this holiness is one that embodies incongruous grace. As it does so, believers bear witness to the divine love that led Christ to die for the ungodly (Rom 5:6).

If the reign of grace and the reality of justification are in fact interconnected in this way, what are the interpretative resources offered by Luther and Calvin's different ways of making both union with Christ and the alien nature of Christ's righteousness integral to justification? How do these resources allow Paul's distinctive emphasis on the incongruous nature of grace to be fully reflected in our accounts of what it means to live under grace? There are six aspects of their positions that should be particularly heeded by contemporary interpreters.

1. The extrinsic nature of justification explains why the union of believers with Christ does not simply deconstruct in the face of continued Christian sinfulness. It has often been observed that Paul knows that, living in the overlap of two ages, those to whom he writes continue to sin. Yet this does not lead him to doubt their ultimate acceptance by God. When Paul rebukes the behavior of some in the Corinthian church in bringing legal cases against one another (1 Cor 6:1–11), his objection is not based upon fear that they will lose their salvation but upon his confidence that as saints they will one day judge the world (1 Cor 6:2). Wrongdoers will certainly not inherit the kingdom of God (1 Cor 6:9), but the Corinthians no longer belong in this category (1 Cor 6:11). Because believers are united with Christ in justification, his death and resurrection are continuously present realities that deal with sin. The crucifixion of believers *with* Christ that is so central to union

---

University Press, 1933), 206. See also Samuli Siikavirta, *Baptism and Cognition in Romans 6–8,* WUNT 2/407 (Tübingen: Mohr Siebeck, 2015), 167–68.

4. John M. G. Barclay, "Under Grace: The Christ-Gift and the Construction of a Christian *Habitus,*" in *Apocalyptic Paul: Cosmos and Anthropos in Romans 5–8,* ed. Beverly R. Gaventa (Waco, TX: Baylor University Press, 2013), 65.

5. Note Paul's contrasts between the righteousness of God and human beings' own righteousness (Rom 10:3; Phil 3:9).

with Christ in justification for Paul does not stand alone. Alongside it belongs an equally strong emphasis on the fact that Christ's death is *for* them: "I have been crucified *with* Christ . . . who loved me and gave himself *for* me" (Gal 2:19–20).

2. That throughout their lives, justification continues to provide believers with alien righteousness is a crucial aspect of any appropriately apocalyptic account of Pauline theology. The invasive nature of the reign of grace is not rightly understood if justification is conceived exclusively as the crucial event that initiates the journey of the Christian life. Justification certainly is the genesis of the Christian life, and that life certainly is a journey away from sin, but the union with Christ involved in justification retains its dynamic character as event. Believers are continually set free, and the initial liberating event of justification is a continuously present reality. It does not simply yield or lead to something else. Justification not only was an apocalyptic event but continues to remain an apocalyptic event. Believers do not journey away from the apocalypse of Jesus Christ but are borne along by it. God's invasive grace in Christ is the flood upon which the ark of the Christian life floats. The transformation of believers and the continuing presence of the event of justification must therefore be conceptualized together. As Barclay writes of Galatians, "for Paul the decisive event is always now: Will Christ be formed in you (4:19)?"[6] Because Christ has been raised from the dead, his cross is a continuously disruptive, fracturing presence.

3. The external emphasis in Luther and Calvin's accounts of justification does not only bring assurance of forgiveness for the sins of believers. Rightly understood, it also counters any temptation to treat grace either as a possession or as an object of consumption. Assurance is possible only and precisely because the righteousness granted is not believers' own, and does not become their own, but remains that of Christ with whom believers are united. They are new creations continually resourced from the life of the risen Christ, and the miraculous appearance of such new creations requires the death of the self (Rom 6:6; Gal 2:19–20). This "is not some reformation of the self, or some newly discovered technique in self-mastery; it is an ectopic phenomenon, drawing on the 'life from the dead' that began with Jesus' resurrection."[7] Properly to grasp the permanently alien nature of new life in Christ involves rejection of any temptation to superiority in which "the religious person sees himself as an exception to sinful human possibilities."[8] It also rejects any claim to autonomy or for the capacity for the self repeatedly to remake identity according to personal preferences.

---

6. John M. G. Barclay, "Paul's Story: Theology as Testimony," in *Narrative Dynamics in Paul: A Critical Assessment*, ed. Bruce W. Longenecker (Louisville: Westminster John Knox, 2002), 146.

7. Barclay, "Under Grace," 65.

8. Eberhard Busch, *Karl Barth and the Pietists: The Young Karl Barth's Critique of Pietism and Its Response*, trans. Donald W. Bloesch (Downers Grove, IL: InterVarsity Press, 2004), 84.

4. Even as these dangers are avoided, the very insistence that believers are new creations requires a transformation in behavior without which faith is not authentic. As Luther puts it, "Paul's view is this: Faith is active in love, that is, that faith justifies which expresses itself in acts" (*LW* 54:74 [*Table Talk* no. 458]). Justification is by faith and not by deeds, but any notion of a passive, inactive faith is simply a contradiction in terms. Works of love either remain a constitutive part of justification (but not its basis, so Luther) or are distinguished from justification but are nevertheless intimately and inseparably connected to justification (so Calvin). Everyday practice therefore continues to be of profound significance. The continuous and intensive dependence of believers upon the crucified and risen Christ gives to such practice a sociological pattern that reflects the incongruity of grace: "it is true faith toward God, which loves and helps one's neighbor—regardless of whether the neighbor is a servant, a master, a king, a pope, a man, a woman; one who wears purple, one who wears rags, one who eats meat, or one who eats fish" (*LW* 27:31).

5. This has profound ecclesiological consequences. On the one hand, all of Paul's ideas are always directed toward the social practice of the church. The deep desire within contemporary scholarship to correct the excessive concern with self-understanding in existential accounts of Pauline theology like that of Bultmann is appropriate (see 2.5). We must be deeply engaged with what we can learn about the formation of early Christian communities and the patterns of their common life. This is because "what grace creates *ex nihilo* by raising humankind from the dead is not a mere empty space, an *absence*. . . . [A]n account of God's revelatory self-presence must necessarily be completed by an account of the church which is the first fruit of God's utterance . . . a community which engages in visible acts." For grace to be at all tangible, there must be the community of the church with its identifiable culture, tradition, and practices. Yet, on the other hand, if the church really is created by the grace of God expressed in a crucified and risen Messiah, then it will live "a common life centered on a confession which subverts." The church all too quickly degenerates into simply another human society if it forgets that its "being is characterized by externality: it is 'ectopic' because its 'place' is in the being and act of the communicative God of the gospel."[9] The calling of the people of God is to instantiate the incongruity of grace in social practice by attempting the (humanly speaking) impossible task of loving all who are unlovable.

6. This external character of the being of the church points to its dependence on God. The righteousness of the church is continuously constituted solely by the church's union with Christ in justification. Further, the church's very existence is not self-generated but depends on faith elicited by the proclaimed word of God.

9. John Webster, *Holy Scripture: A Dogmatic Sketch* (Cambridge: Cambridge University Press, 2003), 47, 57, 71.

The church is the church of the word (*not* Scripture the word of the church), and all the attempts of the church to practice righteousness in its common life result from receiving "the word of faith which we proclaim" (Rom 10:8). Theology and ethics must be held together in Pauline interpretation, but attempts to integrate the two can be successful only if they avoid neglect of Paul's emphasis on proclamation. For the apostle, the distinctive social practices of early Christian communities and a theology of the faith-eliciting word of God are not opposite concerns but correlates of each other. Paul has no difficulty in articulating a theology of the word (e.g., Rom 10:5–21; 1 Cor 1:18–25; Gal 3:1–5) in contexts in which he cares passionately about which practices his readers adopt.

These six aspects of what it means to live under grace constitute an important resource for contemporary Pauline interpretation since, if heeded, they make it possible to offer a rounded account of what Paul has to say about salvation. An extrinsic account of justification to which union with Christ is nevertheless essential leads to a simultaneous and equal emphasis in the economy of salvation on (1) the complete sufficiency of divine grace and its radical disregard of normal human estimations of worth, and (2) the transformation of believers and the significance of the church. Both are crucial. For if the extrinsic nature of justification is emphasized without union with Christ being made central, then legal fictions and a contractual soteriology become genuine dangers. Yet if an account of justification is offered in which union with Christ is central but there is little or no extrinsic emphasis, the likely result is just as serious: what Luther would disparagingly term theologies of glory that give too little attention to the necessity of continued dependence on the mercy of the cross.

Somewhat ironically given the often perceived overly extrinsic one-sidedness of Protestant soteriology, Luther and Calvin provide strong examples of interpreters who develop a well-balanced approach. Twenty-first-century interpreters may well accent the various aspects of what it means to live under grace somewhat differently from the Reformers in response to the demands of contemporary contexts. Yet if they want to respond effectively to the demands of these contexts, neither will today's Pauline interpreters ignore the Reformers' strong insistence that for Paul alien righteousness and union with Christ belong together in justification.

16.2. Romans 4 as an Exegetical Test Case

The ultimate test of the usefulness of the Reformers' insights for interpreting Paul today is exegetical. Can they help us to make sense of Paul's texts? Are there texts that can be more plausibly interpreted by drawing upon insights from both the Reformers and contemporary scholarship rather than by relying on contemporary scholarship alone? A particularly suitable text for this purpose is Rom 4 with its discussion of Abraham and his faith, a topic of intense debate both in the sixteenth century and today.

The structure of Rom 4 grants the argument of the chapter a double focus, with 4:1–8 and 4:19–25 emphasizing Abraham's faith and the basis on which it led to his justification, and 4:9–18 emphasizing the fulfillment of the divine promise that Abraham will be the father of a family composed of both Jews and gentiles (Gen 17:5; Rom 4:17). Recent interpreters have typically responded to this double focus by arguing that one of the two major components of Paul's argument is primary. The other component is then subordinated to their preferred focus. So marked is this tendency toward polarization, that Benjamin Schliesser organizes his discussion of the recent history of reception of Abraham in Rom 4 under the twin headings of "faith" and "fatherhood."[10]

Unsurprisingly the Reformers pay considerable attention to Abraham's faith and its implications for how believers are justified. For them Rom 4:1–8 is a crucial text that, by opposing faith and works, demonstrates that human obedience plays no instrumental role in justification. The example of Abraham excludes all theologies of merit, and the reference to God as the one who justifies the ungodly (Rom 4:5), along with the quotation from Ps 32 (Rom 4:7–8), demonstrates that justification is to be understood as concerning divine mercy and forgiveness for those unworthy of grace. Contemporary interpreters may reproduce these emphases if they are sympathetic to trajectories of Pauline interpretation that derive from the Reformers, but those who identify with the NPP often dispute this understanding of 4:1–8 or regard it as marginal to Paul's main purpose in the argument of the chapter.

For example, N. T. Wright argues that Paul's focus is instead on Abraham's fatherhood of a worldwide family composed of both Jews and gentiles (Rom 4:11–12).[11] It is Abraham's trust in the promise of such a family that is reckoned to him as righteousness (Rom 4:3). This fits with Wright's own conviction that the righteousness received by those who believe in Christ is covenant membership with faith as its badge (see 2.2). Those who are members of the covenant family do receive forgiveness of their sins, but it is inclusion in God's people that leads

---

10. Benjamin Schliesser, *Abraham's Faith in Romans 4: Paul's Concept of Faith in Light of the History of Reception of Genesis 15:6*, WUNT 2/224 (Tübingen: Mohr Siebeck, 2007), 222–36.

11. See N. T. Wright, "Paul and the Patriarch: The Role(s) of Abraham in Romans and Galatians," in *Pauline Perspectives: Essays on Paul, 1978–2013* (Minneapolis: Fortress, 2013), 554–92.

to forgiveness, not vice versa. The point of Paul's insistence that Abraham was not justified by works is not to deny that human obedience justifies but simply to highlight that God was not obligated to give the patriarch a worldwide family of descendants and did so as a gift.[12] Wright's definition of justification is his own, but he applies it to the interpretation of Rom 4 in a way that fits with the general emphasis of NPP interpreters on the breaking down of boundaries between Jews and gentiles entailed by the gospel Paul proclaims.

For his part, Michael Gorman emphasizes the significance of union with Christ in the argument of Rom 4. Gorman positions Rom 4 as part of an unfolding argument in which, from Rom 3:21 onward, Paul describes salvation in participatory terms: "In Christ, humans begin sharing in the righteousness of God and even begin the process of sharing in God's glory. This is because God's righteousness and glory are found in Christ."[13] Abraham is therefore to be understood as "an exemplum of Paul's unique participatory understanding of justification by faith as co-crucifixion and co-resurrection with Christ (4:16–17) . . . because Abraham himself was functionally dead (4:19a)—along with his wife's womb (4:19b)—his faith was that God could bring life out of *his* death, could transform *his* deadness into life" (Gorman, 23).

For Gorman, this stands in contrast to flat readings that emphasize that Abraham was justified by a passive, inactive trust that did not result in any fundamental change in his situation: "That he was *justified* by faith means not that he was fictitiously considered just or righteous but that he was granted the gracious gift of new life out of death, which was concretely fulfilled in the birth of a descendant" (Gorman, 23–24). In the argument of Romans, "Abraham's experience is prospectively analogous to what Paul says about all baptized believers in Rom 6: their justification by faith means a participatory experience of resurrection out of death" (Gorman, 24).

The interpretations of Wright and Gorman have much to offer in what they affirm. Wright is correct to emphasize Abraham's fatherhood of a family composed of both Jews and gentiles. Paul clearly does not only intend to say that since God justified Abraham by faith, gentiles must be justified in the same manner. Equally

12. Wright bases this assertion upon what he regards as an allusion by Paul to the promise given to Abraham at Gen 15:1, "your reward will be very great." In the Septuagint, the term used for "reward" (*misthos*) is the same as that used by Paul in Rom 4:4 (NRSV, "wages"). For further discussion of this and other detailed aspects of Wright's argument, see Stephen J. Chester, *Reading Paul with the Reformers: Reconciling Old and New Perspectives* (Grand Rapids: Eerdmans, 2017), 400–408.

13. Michael J. Gorman, "Romans: The First Christian Treatise on Theosis," *JTI* 5 (2011): 23. Page references are given in parentheses in the text.

emphatically, he emphasizes that, because gentiles are justified in this same way, they are children of Abraham along with Jewish believers (Rom 4:11–12, 17–18). Wright retrieves an important aspect of Paul's argument that has sometimes been neglected in Protestant exegesis.

Similarly, Gorman's emphasis on participation also responds to important aspects of Paul's argument. He connects the participatory nature of justification as an experience of resurrection out of death to the family that results from it: "This resurrection life is actualized, not merely in the birth of Isaac, but in the subsequent reality of many descendants" (Gorman, 24). Justification has a strongly ecclesial dimension that foreshadows the portrayal in Rom 12–15 of what it means for communities of believers to embody the gospel in social practice (Gorman, 32). On Gorman's account, God's calling into existence of a worldwide family of Abraham is not merely a circumstantial consequence of God's justifying activity in Christ. Instead, it is an expression of divine identity as one who has made Abraham the father of many nations and "who gives life to the dead and calls into existence the things that do not exist" (4:17). Gorman's perspective on the justification of Abraham complements and extends the strengths of Wright's interpretation in significant ways.

The deficiencies in Wright's and Gorman's interpretations relate not to what they affirm but instead to what they neglect or deny. The importance of Abraham's fatherhood of a multinational family and the importance of faith as participation are not asserted alongside an emphasis on Paul's opposing of faith and works (Rom 4:2–5). Instead, they are asserted in place of it in ways that ignore or deny things that Paul clearly says. Gorman's contrasting of his participatory account of Abraham's faith with what he sees as an undue emphasis on passive trust neglects the fact that Abraham's trusting reception of the promise of Gen 15:6 bookends the chapter (Rom 4:3–5, 20–22). Even if trust is not the only dimension of Abraham's faith that is important to Paul, he makes its significance very clear. It and the participatory nature of faith therefore ought not to be set against each other.[14]

Wright's desire to interpret Rom 4 exclusively with reference to Abraham's fatherhood of all who believe strongly impacts his interpretation of 4:1–8. He wishes to eliminate explanations of Abraham's faith and how it justifies that stem from Reformation exegesis. What results is several exegetically implausible denials, one of which is that Paul has no intention to dispute that justification is received in

---

14. This criticism does not apply to Gorman's recent *Romans: A Pastoral and Theological Commentary* (Grand Rapids: Eerdmans, 2022), where he offers a more balanced and even more compelling treatment of Rom 4 that includes significant emphasis on the character of faith as trust alongside an appropriate highlighting of faith's participatory nature.

response to human obedience to torah. This ignores the considerable evidence in Second Temple literature of other interpretations of Gen 15:6 that insist on the significance of Abraham's obedience. They "are concerned to present Abraham as an exemplary figure or role model for human conduct in relation to God.... Apart from Paul, Jewish interpreters regard the promise motif as secondary to a story whose primary aim is to celebrate Abraham's outstanding piety and virtue."[15] Even if Paul is not opposing Jewish commitment to salvation by works, but instead simply insisting that grace is incongruous and goes to the unworthy, a denial that God's promises were given to Abraham because of his virtue is necessary to Paul's argument.

Wright also denies that Paul numbers Abraham among the ungodly and argues that Paul's reference to God's justification of the ungodly (Rom 4:5) refers exclusively to Abraham's gentile descendants by faith. This denial of Abraham's ungodliness ignores the witness of Josh 24:2 that the patriarch and his family "lived beyond the Euphrates and served other gods," that is, they had been idolaters just as Paul's gentile converts were idolaters. Further, Paul's insistence that Jew and gentile alike are "under sin" (Rom 3:9), and his parallel statements that Christ died for the ungodly "while we were still weak" (Rom 5:6) and that Christ died for us "while we were still sinners" (Rom 5:9), clarifies that "the ungodly" is not an exclusively gentile category. Abraham's sinful humanity itself places him among the ungodly.

Similarly, Wright argues that Paul's quotation of Ps 32:1–2 does not speak of David himself as a sinner in need of forgiveness but rather invokes the king "as one who gives testimony to the blessing of forgiveness on anyone who has no 'works,' no outward sign of belonging to God's people."[16] Yet Paul specifically identifies the psalmist as David, Israel's greatest king, and therefore as one who is within the covenant and does not lack outward signs of belonging to it.[17] Far from speaking of gentile sin and its forgiveness, Ps 32 focuses on the author's personal experience of sin and divine forgiveness (cf. Ps 32:5). It is difficult to understand why Paul would ever have quoted this text had he wished to restrict the category of the "ungodly" to Abraham's gentile descendants.

All these deficiencies stem from a one-sided account of Rom 4. To do justice to Paul's argument, we must "integrate Paul's dual portrayal of Abraham, as both

---

15. Francis Watson, *Paul and the Hermeneutics of Faith* (London: T&T Clark, 2004), 268. See, for example, Philo, *Who Is the Heir?* 91 (Colson and Whitaker, LCL); Philo, *On the Life of Abraham* 276 (Colson, LCL); and Josephus, *Jewish Antiquities* 1.183 (Thackeray, LCL).

16. Wright, "Paul and the Patriarch," 588.

17. See Simon J. Gathercole, *Where Is Boasting? Early Jewish Soteriology and Paul's Response in Romans 1–5* (Grand Rapids: Eerdmans, 2002), 247: "David although circumcised, sabbatarian, and kosher, is described as without works because of his disobedience."

believer in God and *father* of a multinational family."[18] Given their emphasis on Abraham's justification exclusively by his trust in God's promises and not by his own works, the Reformers might be expected also to fail to integrate the dual aspects of Paul's arguments and to be equally one-sided but in the opposite direction. Yet, in fact, a striking example of an interpreter who achieves such integration is provided by Calvin, who pays attention both to Abraham's faith and how it justifies and to Abraham's fatherhood of the family of faith.

Unsurprisingly, Calvin places considerable emphasis on the need to be justified by faith and not by works after the pattern of Abraham. The patriarch's justification was a consequence of divine grace and in no way a result of his meritorious deeds: "Paul is assuming that the righteousness of faith is the place of help and refuge for the sinner who is destitute of works. If there were any righteousness by the law or by works, it would reside in men themselves. But men get the faith which they lack from elsewhere. It is for this reason rightly termed the imputed righteousness of faith" (*Comm. Rom.* 4:3, *CNTC* 8:83). This righteousness is itself "nothing other than the remission of sins" (*Comm. Rom.* 4:6, *CNTC* 8:86). Calvin regards Abraham as typifying the need of sinners for an alien righteousness that comes entirely from outside themselves: "faith adorns us with the righteousness of another, which it begs from God" (*Comm. Rom.* 4:5, *CNTC* 8:85). Clearly Calvin would not share Wright's definition of justification as covenant membership.

However, this does not mean that the theme of the covenant family is in the slightest neglected in Calvin's treatment of Rom 4. Calvin not only gives attention to how Abraham was justified but also to Abraham's role as the father of the family of faith. He argues that Paul does not quote Gen 15:6 because it demonstrates that Abraham believed only the details of the individual promise of a son. Instead, Abraham embraced this particular promise as indicative of God's broader desire to be a true father to him. God gives, and Abraham receives, embracing the favor offered to him, a favor that assured Abraham of God's "adoption and His fatherly favour, in which is included eternal salvation by Christ" (*Comm. Rom.* 4:3, *CNTC* 8:84). The promise of the gift of Isaac was grounded upon God's adoption of Abraham (see 14.1). The promise of a family for Abraham comes in the context of Abraham's own inclusion in God's family.

As Calvin hears Paul, Abraham trusts in God's fatherly kindness and so becomes a child of God, while those who share the faith of Abraham become children of Abraham, which means that they, too, are children of God. The result is that although justification itself concerns the forgiveness of sins, this by no means displaces or excludes family membership as a crucial component of soteriology:

---

18. John M. G. Barclay, *Paul and the Gift* (Grand Rapids: Eerdmans, 2015), 481.

"To be of faith, therefore, is to place one's righteousness and hope of salvation in the mercy of God. That such are the children of Abraham he concludes from the preceding statement. For if Abraham was justified by faith, those who wish to be his children must likewise stand firmly in faith. He has omitted one fact, which may easily be supplied, that there is no place in the Church for any man who is not a son of Abraham."[19]

Calvin thus brings together Abraham's role as an exemplar of justification by faith with his role as father of a multinational family. Although he does not offer a single neat definition, it appears that if asked to define the nature of justification by faith, Calvin's answer would be, in positive terms, the forgiveness of sins and receipt of the alien righteousness of Christ, and, in negative terms, refusal to rely on righteousness by works. Yet it also seems that he would immediately want to add that the *result* of justification is to make those who believe members of Abraham's family and hence children of God. For Calvin, faith justifies from sin because it grasps hold of Christ and receives his righteousness, and, as it does so, the church, the family of Abraham in the world, is created.

As part of his dual focus on Abraham's faith and his fatherhood of all who believe, Calvin is even able to include in his exegesis the theme of participation in resurrection. When Paul defines the God who is able to make the aged Abraham the father of many nations as the "one who gives life to the dead and calls into existence the things that do not exist" (Rom 4:17), Calvin follows the apostle's connections between Abraham's faith in the promise of life from his functionally dead body and the resurrecting power of God: "He was promised a seed as though he were in virility and full vigour. He was, however, past procreation, and therefore it was necessary for him to raise his thoughts to the power of God which gives life to the dead. There is, therefore, no absurdity if the Gentiles, who are otherwise barren and dead, are brought into the fellowship."[20]

Calvin returns to this theme when commenting on Gen 12:1, where he interprets the circumstances of Abraham's calling by God in light of the reference in Josh 24:2 to the patriarch worshiping other gods: "He is an example of the

19. *Comm. Gal.* 3:7, *CNTC* 11:52. Calvin here cross-references Rom 4:4–5, and in fact, he develops the theme of Abraham as father of those who believe even further in his commentaries and sermons on Galatians and Genesis than he does in his exegesis of Rom 4 itself. See Stephen J. Chester, "Faith and Family: Calvin, the Figure of Abraham, and the New Perspective on Paul," in *Reformatorische Paulusauslegungen*, ed. Stefan Krauter and Manuel Nägele (Tübingen: Mohr Siebeck, 2023), 479–502.

20. *Comm. Rom.* 4:17, *CNTC* 8:95. Calvin also notes Paul's use of a similar circumlocution at Rom 4:24 where God is described as "him who raised Jesus our Lord from the dead." See *Comm. Rom.* 4:24, *CNTC* 8:101–2.

vocation of us all; for in him we perceive, that, by the mere mercy of God, those things which are not are raised from nothing, in order that they may begin to be something" (*Comm. Gen.* 12:1, *CTS* 1:343). For Calvin, the rescue of Abraham from idolatry, the gifting to him of a son when in old age, and the justification of gentile believers all reflect the creative and resurrecting power of God.

Calvin thus seems to grasp the important point made by Gorman that Abraham's experience of justification anticipates the participatory experience of resurrection out of death granted to believers in baptism (Rom 6:3–6). Calvin does not share Gorman's conviction that when Paul talks of dying and rising in Christ in baptism, he is discussing justification, but the fact that for Calvin sanctification no less than justification is an aspect of union with Christ means that he has no difficulty in discussing the later text in a parallel way: "our old man is destroyed by the death of Christ, so that His resurrection may restore our righteousness, and make us new creatures" (*Comm. Rom.* 6:4, *CNTC* 8:122).

16.3. Conclusion: Toward Hearing All of Paul

Calvin's interpretation of Paul's discussion of the faith of Abraham exhibits the same strengths as those found in the work of important recent interpreters like Wright and Gorman. He emphasizes Abraham's fatherhood of the family of faith and the participatory aspects of Abraham's trust in the resurrecting power of God. Yet Calvin does not achieve this by eliminating significant elements of the theme of Abraham as believer. He can integrate the different aspects of Paul's argument and does not need to neglect or deny in an exegetically unsustainable way significant parts of what the apostle wants to say.

It is this capacity to integrate themes that makes Calvin's treatment of the figure of Abraham of continuing relevance. It may not be possible or desirable to perform this integration today in exactly the same manner as Calvin. His handling of the theme of works-righteousness certainly provides an example of a way in which his approach requires amendment.[21] Yet what paying attention to Calvin's exegesis can do is to help contemporary interpreters to avoid selective deafness and to hear all the different dimensions of Paul's argument concerning Abraham.

---

21. Another may be Calvin's use of Gen 15:1, which he takes to mean, "I am thy shield and thy exceeding great reward" (KJV), and therefore as indicating that Abraham is to be united with God and become a child of God. The overwhelming majority of recent commentators and Bible translations take the verse instead to mean, "I am your shield; your reward shall be very great" (NRSV). See Chester, "Faith and Family," 486–87, 496.

Calvin's treatment of Rom 4 provides a compelling example of the exegetical application of his insistence on the importance of union with Christ combined with his emphatic conviction that justification is extrinsic, with believers receiving Christ's alien righteousness. His sensitivity to Paul's participatory themes allows Calvin to recognize the significance both of Abraham's fatherhood of the family of faith and of his trust in the resurrecting power of God, while his extrinsic understanding of justification allows Calvin to hear with proper force Paul's quite obvious emphasis on forgiveness (Rom 4:7–8). As with Luther, Calvin does not perceive union with Christ and the extrinsic nature of justification as themes that stand in tension or need of reconciliation since it is when united with Christ by faith that believers receive his righteousness. Theological insights that belong together for Paul are not pulled apart in the manner typical of more recent interpretation. When themselves rightly understood, the Reformers offer exegetical insights of continuing relevance for our efforts to interpret Paul's theology for today.

Bibliography

Allen, Michael, and Jonathan A. Linebaugh, eds. *Reformation Readings of Paul: Explorations in History and Exegesis*. Downers Grove, IL: InterVarsity Press, 2015.

Anonymous. "Cordatus' Controversy with Melanchthon." *ThQ* 11 (1907): 193–207.

Aquinas, Thomas. *Commentary on Saint Paul's Epistle to the Galatians*. Translated by Fabian R. Larcher. Albany, NY: Magi, 1966.

Augustine. *Augustine's Commentary on Galatians: Introduction, Text, Translation, and Notes*. Translated by Eric A. Plumer. Oxford: Oxford University Press, 2003.

———. *The City of God against the Pagans*. Translated by R. W. Dyson. Cambridge: Cambridge University Press, 1998.

———. *Expositions of the Psalms 99–120*. Translated by Maria Boulding. The Works of St. Augustine III/19. New York: New City, 2003.

———. *Homilies on the Gospel of John 1–40*. Translated by Edmund Hill. The Works of St. Augustine III/12. New York: New City, 2009.

———. *Letters 156–210*. Translated by Roland J. Teske. The Works of St. Augustine II/3. New York: New City, 2004.

———. *Sermons 148–183*. Translated by Edmund Hill. The Works of St. Augustine III/5. New York: New City, 1992.

———. "The Spirit and the Letter." In *Answer to the Pelagians*. Translated by Roland J. Teske. The Works of St. Augustine I/23. New York: New City, 1997.

Aulén, Gustav. *Christus Victor: An Historical Study of the Three Main Types of the Idea of the Atonement*. London: SPCK, 1931.

Ayres, Lewis. "Augustine." Pages 345–60 in *The Blackwell Companion to Paul*. Edited by Stephen Westerholm. Oxford: Wiley-Blackwell, 2011.

Babcock, William S. "Augustine on Sin and Moral Agency." Pages 87–113 in *The Ethics of St. Augustine*. Edited by William S. Babcock. Atlanta: Scholars Press, 1991.

Bainton, Roland. *Here I Stand: A Life of Martin Luther*. New York: Abingdon-Cokesbury, 1950.

Barclay, John M. G. "Believers and the 'Last Judgment' in Paul: Rethinking Grace and Recompense." Pages 195–208 in *Eschatologie = Eschatology: The Sixth Durham-Tübingen Research Symposium, Eschatology in Old Testament, Ancient Judaism and Early Christianity*. Edited by Hans Joachim Eckstein, Christof Landmesser, and Hermann Lichtenberger. WUNT 2/272. Tübingen: Mohr Siebeck, 2011.

———. "Humanity under Faith." Pages 79–100 in *Beyond Bultmann: Reckoning a New Testament Theology*. Edited by Bruce W. Longenecker and Mikeal C. Parsons. Waco, TX: Baylor University Press, 2014.

———. *Judaism in the Mediterranean Diaspora*. Edinburgh: T&T Clark, 1996.

———. *Obeying the Truth: Paul's Ethics in Galatians*. Edinburgh: T&T Clark, 1988.

———. *Paul and the Gift*. Grand Rapids: Eerdmans, 2015.

———. *Paul and the Power of Grace*. Grand Rapids: Eerdmans, 2020.

———. "Paul's Story: Theology as Testimony." Pages 133–56 in *Narrative Dynamics in Paul: A Critical Assessment*. Edited by Bruce W. Longenecker. Louisville: Westminster John Knox, 2002.

———. "Pure Grace? Paul's Distinctive Jewish Theology of Gift." *ST* 68 (2014): 4–20.

———. Review of *Paul and the Faithfulness of God*, by N. T. Wright. *SJT* 68 (2015): 235–43.

———. "Under Grace: The Christ-Gift and the Construction of a Christian *Habitus*." Pages 59–76 in *Apocalyptic Paul: Cosmos and Anthropos in Romans 5–8*. Edited by Beverly R. Gaventa: Waco, TX: Baylor University Press, 2013.

Barth, Karl. *The Epistle to the Romans*. 6th ed. Translated by Edwyn C. Hoskyns. Oxford: Oxford University Press, 1933.

Batka, L'ubomír. "Luther's Teaching on Sin and Evil." Pages 233–53 in *The Oxford Handbook of Martin Luther's Theology*. Edited by Robert Kolb, Irene Dingel, and L'ubomír Batka. Oxford: Oxford University Press, 2014.

Bayer, Oswald. *Martin Luther's Theology: A Contemporary Interpretation*. Grand Rapids: Eerdmans, 2008.

Bernardo, Aldo. *Petrarch, Scipio, and the "Africa": The Birth of Humanism's Dream*. Baltimore: Johns Hopkins University Press, 1962.

Billings, J. Todd. *Calvin, Participation, and the Gift: The Activity of Believers in Union with Christ*. Oxford: Oxford University Press, 2007.

———. "Union with Christ and the Double Grace: Calvin's Theology and Its Early Reception." Pages 49–71 in *Calvin's Theology and Its Reception*. Edited by J. Todd Billings and I. John Hesselink. Louisville: Westminster John Knox, 2012.

Billings, J. Todd, and I. John Hesselink, eds. *Calvin's Theology and Its Reception: Disputes, Developments, and New Possibilities*. Louisville: Westminster John Knox, 2012.

Boer, Martinus C. de. *The Defeat of Death: Apocalyptic Eschatology in 1 Corinthians 15 and Romans 5*. Sheffield: JSOT Press, 1988.

Bornkamm, Karin. *Luthers Auslegungen des Galaterbriefs von 1519 bis 1531: Ein Vergleich.* Berlin: de Gruyter, 1963.

Braaten, Carl E., and Robert W. Jenson, eds. *Union with Christ: The New Finnish Interpretation of Luther.* Grand Rapids: Eerdmans, 1998.

Briskina, Anna. "An Orthodox View of Finnish Luther Research." *LQ* 22 (2008): 16–39.

Bullinger, Heinrich. *Bullinger's Decades: The Fourth Decade.* Edited by Thomas Harding. Parker Society 9. Cambridge: Cambridge University Press, 1851.

———. *Bullinger's Decades: The Third Decade.* Edited by Thomas Harding. Parker Society 8. Cambridge: Cambridge University Press, 1851.

Bultmann, Rudolf, *Theology of the New Testament.* 2 vols. London: SCM, 1952.

Busch, Eberhard. *Karl Barth and the Pietists: The Young Karl Barth's Critique of Pietism and Its Response.* Translated by Donald W. Bloesch. Downers Grove, IL: InterVarsity Press, 2004.

Butin, Philip W. *Revelation, Redemption, and Response: Calvin's Trinitarian Understanding of the Divine-Human Relationship.* Oxford: Oxford University Press, 1995.

Calvin, John. *Institutes of the Christian Religion: 1541 French Edition.* Translated by Elsie A. McKee. Grand Rapids: Eerdmans, 2009.

———. *On the Bondage and the Liberation of the Will: A Defense of the Orthodox Doctrine of Human Choice against Pighius.* Edited by Anthony N. S. Lane. Translated by G. I. Davies. Grand Rapids: Baker, 1996.

———. *Sermons on Genesis: Chapters 11–20.* Translated by Rob Roy McGregor. Edinburgh: Banner of Truth, 2012.

———. *Sermons on the Epistle to the Galatians.* Translated by Kathy Childress. Edinburgh: Banner of Truth, 1997.

———. *Sermons on the Epistle to the Ephesians.* Edinburgh: Banner of Truth, 1973.

Campbell, Constantine R. *Paul and Union with Christ: An Exegetical and Theological Study.* Grand Rapids: Zondervan, 2012.

Campbell, Douglas A. *The Deliverance of God: An Apocalyptic Rereading of Justification in Paul.* Grand Rapids: Eerdmans, 2009.

Canlis, Julie. *Calvin's Ladder: A Spiritual Theology of Ascent and Ascension.* Grand Rapids: Eerdmans, 2010.

Chemnitz, Martin. *Examination of the Council of Trent.* Vol. 1. Translated by Fred Kramer. Saint Louis: Concordia, 1971.

Chester, Stephen J. *Conversion at Corinth: Perspectives on Conversion in Paul's Theology and the Corinthian Church.* London: T&T Clark, 2003.

———. "Faith and Family: Calvin, the Figure of Abraham, and the New Perspective on Paul." Pages 479–502 in *Reformatorische Paulusauslegungen.* Edited by Stefan Krauter and Manuel Nägele. Tübingen: Mohr Siebeck, 2023.

———. "Paul and the Introspective Conscience of Martin Luther." *BibInt* 14 (2006): 508–36.

———. *Reading Paul with the Reformers: Reconciling Old and New Perspectives.* Grand Rapids: Eerdmans, 2017.

———. "Romans 7 and Conversion in the Protestant Tradition." *ExAud* 25 (2009): 135–71.

———. "'Works Themselves Are a Part of Grace': John Calvin's Interpretation of Ephesians 2:8–10." Pages 236–50 in *The New Perspective on Grace: Paul and the Gospel after Paul and the Gift.* Edited by Edward Adams, Dorothea H. Bertschmann, Stephen J. Chester, and Todd D. Still. Grand Rapids: Eerdmans, 2023.

Christ-von Wedel, Christine. *Erasmus of Rotterdam: Advocate of a New Christianity.* Toronto: University of Toronto Press, 2013.

Cochrane, Arthur C., ed. *Reformed Confessions of the Sixteenth Century.* Louisville: Westminster John Knox, 2003.

Corley, Bruce. "Interpreting Paul's Conversion—Then and Now." Pages 1–17 in *The Road from Damascus: The Impact of Paul's Conversion on His Life, Thought, and Ministry.* Edited by Richard N. Longenecker. Grand Rapids: Eerdmans, 1997.

Davies, Jamie. *The Apocalyptic Paul.* Cascade Library of Pauline Studies. Eugene, OR: Cascade, 2022.

Dunn, James D. G. "The New Perspective on Paul." Pages 99–120 in *The New Perspective on Paul.* Rev. ed. Grand Rapids: Eerdmans, 2008.

———. "New Perspective View." Pages 176–218 in *Justification: Five Views.* Edited by James K. Beilby and Paul R. Eddy. Downers Grove, IL: InterVarsity Press, 2011.

———. "The New Perspective: Whence, What and Whither?" Pages 1–97 in *The New Perspective on Paul.* Rev. ed. Grand Rapids: Eerdmans, 2005.

———. *The Theology of Paul the Apostle.* Edinburgh: T&T Clark, 1998.

Ebeling, Gerhard. "On the Doctrine of the *Triplex Usus Legis* in the Theology of the Reformation." Pages 62–78 in *Word and Faith.* Translated by James W. Leitch. Philadelphia: Fortress, 1963.

Emmert, Kevin P. *John Calvin and the Righteousness of Works.* Göttingen: Vandenhoeck & Ruprecht, 2021.

Evans, Gillian R. *The Roots of the Reformation: Tradition, Emergence, and Rupture.* Downers Grove, IL: InterVarsity Press, 2012.

Evans, Robert. *Reception History, Tradition and Biblical Interpretation: Gadamer and Jauss in Current Practice.* London: T&T Clark, 2014.

Farthing, John L. *Thomas Aquinas and Gabriel Biel.* Durham, NC: Duke University Press, 1988.

Flogaus, Reinhard. "Justification or Deification: Luther's Soteriology in Ecumenical Perspective." Pages 185–215 in *Theological Anthropology, 500 Years after Martin*

Luther: Orthodox and Lutheran Perspectives. Edited by Christophe Chalamet, Konstantinos Delikostantis, Job Getcha, and Elisabeth Parmentier. Leiden: Brill, 2021.

Fredriksen Landes, Paula. *Augustine on Romans: Propositions from the Epistle to the Romans, Unfinished Commentary on the Epistle to the Romans.* Chico, CA: Scholars Press, 1982.

Garcia, Mark A. *Life in Christ: Union with Christ and Twofold Grace in Calvin's Theology.* Eugene, OR: Wipf & Stock, 2008.

Gathercole, Simon J. *Where Is Boasting? Early Jewish Soteriology and Paul's Response in Romans 1–5.* Grand Rapids: Eerdmans, 2002.

The Geneva Bible: A Facsimile of the 1560 Edition. Peabody, MA: Hendrickson, 2007.

George, Timothy. "Modernizing Luther, Domesticating Paul: Another Perspective." Pages 437–63 in *Justification and Variegated Nomism II.* Edited by Donald A. Carson, Peter T. O'Brien, and Mark T. Seifrid. Grand Rapids: Baker, 2004.

Gerrish, Brian. *Grace and Gratitude: The Eucharistic Theology of John Calvin.* Minneapolis: Fortress, 1993.

Gordon, Bruce. *Calvin.* New Haven: Yale University Press, 2009.

Gorman, Michael J. *Participating in Christ: Explorations in Paul's Theology and Spirituality.* Grand Rapids: Baker, 2019.

———. *Romans: A Pastoral and Theological Commentary.* Grand Rapids: Eerdmans, 2022.

———. "Romans: The First Christian Treatise on Theosis." *JTI* 5 (2011): 13–34.

Grabowski, Stanislaus J. *The Church: An Introduction to the Theology of St. Augustine.* Saint Louis: Herder, 1957.

Greschat, Martin. *Melanchthon neben Luther: Studien zur Gestalt der Rechfertigungslehre zwischen 1528 und 1537.* Wittenberg: Luther-Verlag, 1965.

Haas, Günther H. "Ethics and Church Discipline." Pages 332–44 in *The Calvin Handbook.* Edited by Herman J. Selderhuis. Grand Rapids: Eerdmans, 2009.

Hamm, Berndt. *The Early Luther: Stages in a Reformation Reorientation.* Grand Rapids: Eerdmans, 2014.

———. "How Innovative Was the Reformation?" Pages 254–72 in *The Reformation of Faith in the Context of Late Medieval Theology and Piety: Essays by Berndt Hamm.* Edited by Robert J. Bast. Leiden: Brill, 2004.

———. "Impending Doom and Imminent Grace: Luther's Early Years in the Cloister as the Beginning of His Reformation Reorientation." Pages 26–58 in *The Early Luther: Stages in a Reformation Reorientation.* Grand Rapids: Eerdmans, 2014.

———. "Justification by Faith Alone: A Profile of the Reformation Doctrine of Justification." Pages 233–57 in *The Early Luther: Stages in a Reformation Reorientation.* Grand Rapids: Eerdmans, 2014.

———. "The Place of the Reformation in the Second Christian Millennium." Pages 273–300 in *The Reformation of Faith in the Context of Late Medieval Theology and Piety: Essays by Berndt Hamm*. Edited by Robert J. Bast. Leiden: Brill, 2004.

———. "What Was the Reformation Doctrine of Justification?" Pages 179–216 in *The Reformation of Faith in the Context of Late Medieval Theology and Piety: Essays by Berndt Hamm*. Edited by Robert J. Bast. Leiden: Brill, 2004.

Hampson, Daphne. *Christian Contradictions: The Structures of Lutheran and Catholic Thought*. Cambridge: Cambridge University Press, 2001.

Hays, Richard B. *The Faith of Jesus Christ: The Narrative Substructure of Galatians 3:1–4:11*. 2nd ed. Grand Rapids: Eerdmans, 2002.

Helm, Paul. *Calvin at the Centre*. Oxford: Oxford University Press, 2010.

Helmer, Christine, and Bo Kristian Holm, eds. *Lutherrenaissance: Past and Present*. Göttingen: Vandenhoeck & Ruprecht, 2015.

Hendrix, Scott H. "The Work of Heiko A. Oberman (1930–2001)." *RSR* 28 (2002): 123–30.

Hesselink, I. John. *Calvin's Concept of the Law*. Allison Park, PA: Pickwick, 1992.

———. "The Revelation of God in Creation and Scripture." Pages 3–24 in *Calvin's Theology and Its Reception*. Edited by J. Todd Billings and I. John Hesselink. Louisville: Westminster John Knox, 2012.

Hildebrand, Pierrick. "Calvin and the Covenant: The Reception of Zurich Theology." Pages 57–73 in *The Oxford Handbook of Calvin and Calvinism*. Edited by Bruce Gordon and Carl Trueman. Oxford: Oxford University Press, 2021.

Hindmarsh, Bruce C. *The Evangelical Conversion Narrative: Spiritual Autobiography in Early Modern England*. Oxford: Oxford University Press, 2005.

Holder, R. Ward, ed. *A Companion to Paul in the Reformation*. Leiden: Brill, 2009.

———. "Introduction—Paul in the Sixteenth Century: Invitation and a Challenge." Pages 1–12 in *A Companion to Paul in the Reformation*. Edited by R. Ward Holder. Leiden: Brill, 2009.

Horton, Michael S. "Calvin's Theology of Union with Christ and the Double Grace: Modern Reception and Contemporary Possibilities." Pages 72–96 in *Calvin's Theology and Its Reception: Disputes, Developments, and New Possibilities*. Edited by J. Todd Billings and I. John Hesselink. Louisville: Westminster John Knox, 2012.

Huggins, Jonathan. *Living Justification: A Historical-Theological Study of the Reformed Doctrine of Justification in the Writings of John Calvin, Jonathan Edwards, and N. T. Wright*. Eugene, OR: Wipf & Stock, 2013.

Jenkins, Allan K., and Patrick Preston. *Biblical Scholarship and the Church: A Sixteenth-Century Crisis of Authority*. Aldershot: Ashgate, 2007.

Jewett, Robert. *Romans*. Hermeneia. Minneapolis: Fortress, 2007.

Jüngel, Eberhard. *Justification: The Heart of the Christian Faith*. Edinburgh: T&T Clark, 2001.

Juntunen, Sammeli. "Luther and Metaphysics: What Is the Structure of Being according to Luther?" Pages 129–60 in *Union with Christ: The New Finnish Interpretation of Luther*. Edited by Carl E. Braaten and Robert W. Jenson. Grand Rapids: Eerdmans, 1998.

Käsemann, Ernst. *Commentary on Romans*. Grand Rapids: Eerdmans, 1980.

———. "On the Subject of Primitive Christian Apocalyptic." Pages 108–37 in *New Testament Questions of Today*. London: SCM, 1969.

———. *Perspectives on Paul*. Philadelphia: Fortress, 1971.

Kim, Seyoon. *The Origin of Paul's Gospel*. 2nd ed. WUNT 2/4. Tübingen: Mohr Siebeck, 1984.

Kim, Sun-young. *Luther on Faith and Love: Christ and the Law in the 1535 Galatians Commentary*. Minneapolis: Fortress, 2014.

Kolb, Robert. *Bound Choice, Election, and Wittenberg Theological Method*. Grand Rapids: Eerdmans, 2005.

———. *Martin Luther: Confessor of the Faith*. Oxford: Oxford University Press, 2009.

Kolb, Robert, and Timothy J. Wengert, eds. *The Book of Concord: The Confessions of the Evangelical Lutheran Church*. Minneapolis: Fortress, 2000.

Lane, Anthony N. S. *Justification by Faith in Catholic-Protestant Dialogue: An Evangelical Assessment*. London: T&T Clark, 2002.

Lauster, Jörg. "Luther—Apostle of Freedom? Liberal Protestant Interpretations of Luther." Pages 127–43 in *Lutherrenaissance: Past and Present*. Edited by Christine Helmer and Bo Kristian Holm. Göttingen: Vandenhoeck & Ruprecht, 2015.

Leppin, Volker. "Luther's Transformation of Medieval Thought: Continuity and Discontinuity." Pages 115–24 in *The Oxford Handbook of Martin Luther's Theology*. Edited by Robert Kolb, Irene Dingel, and L'ubomír Bakta. Oxford: Oxford University Press, 2014.

———. "Martin Luther, Reconsidered for 2017." *LQ* 22 (2008): 373–87.

Levering, Matthew. *Paul in the Summa Theologiae*. Washington, DC: Catholic University of America Press, 2014.

Lienhard, Marc. *Luther: Witness to Jesus Christ; Stages and Themes of the Reformer's Christology*. Minneapolis: Augsburg, 1982.

Lillback, Peter. *The Binding of God: Calvin's Role in the Development of Covenant Theology*. Grand Rapids: Baker, 2001.

Linebaugh, Jonathan A. "The Christocentrism of Faith in Christ: Martin Luther's Reading of Galatians 2:16, 19–20." Pages 199–210 in *The Word of the Cross: Reading Paul*. Grand Rapids: Eerdmans, 2022.

———. "Incongruous and Creative Grace: Reading *Paul and the Gift* with Martin Luther." *IJST* 22 (2020): 47–59.

Lohse, Bernhard. *Martin Luther's Theology: Its Historical and Systematic Development.* Edinburgh: T&T Clark, 1999.

Longenecker, Bruce W., and Mikeal C. Parsons, eds. *Beyond Bultmann: Reckoning a New Testament Theology.* Waco, TX: Baylor University Press, 2014.

Lugioyo, Brian. *Martin Bucer's Doctrine of Justification: Reformation Theology and Early Modern Irenicism.* Oxford: Oxford University Press, 2011.

Luther, Martin. *Advent and Christmas Season.* Vol. 1 of *Luther's Epistle Sermons.* Translated by John Nicholas Lenker. Minneapolis: Luther, 1908.

———. *Gospels: Advent, Christmas, and Epiphany Seasons.* Vol. 1 of *Luther's Church Postil.* Translated by John Nicholas Lenker. Minneapolis: Lutherans in All Lands, 1905.

Luy, David. "Sixteenth-Century Reception of Aquinas by Luther and Lutheran Reformers." Pages 104–20 in *The Oxford Handbook of the Reception of Aquinas.* Edited by Matthew Levering and Marcus Plested. Oxford: Oxford University Press, 2021.

Macaskill, Grant. *Union with Christ in the New Testament.* Oxford: Oxford University Press, 2013.

Mannermaa, Tuomo. *Christ Present in Faith: Luther's View of Justification.* Minneapolis: Fortress, 2005.

Marshall, Bruce. "*Beatus Vir*: Aquinas, Romans 4, and the role of 'Reckoning' in Justification." Pages 216–37 in *Reading Romans with St. Thomas Aquinas.* Edited by Matthew Levering and Michael Dauphinais. Washington, DC: Catholic University of America Press, 2012.

Martyn, J. Louis. "Apocalyptic Antinomies." Pages 111–24 in *Theological Issues in the Letters of Paul.* Edinburgh: T&T Clark, 1997.

———. *Galatians.* AB 33A. New York: Doubleday, 1997.

———. *Theological Issues in the Letters of Paul.* Edinburgh: T&T Clark, 1997.

McCormack, Bruce L. "What's at Stake in Current Debates over Justification? The Crisis of Protestantism in the West." Pages 81–117 in *Justification: What's at Stake in the Current Debates?* Edited by Mark Husbands and Daniel J. Treier. Downers Grove, IL: InterVarsity Press, 2004.

McCulloch, Diarmaid. "Calvin: Fifth Latin Doctor of the Church?" Pages 33–45 in *Calvin and His Influence 1509–2009.* Edited by Irena Backus and Philip Benedict. Oxford: Oxford University Press, 2011.

McGrath, Alister E. *Iustitia Dei: A History of the Christian Doctrine of Justification.* 3rd ed. Cambridge: Cambridge University Press, 2005.

———. *Luther's Theology of the Cross: Martin Luther's Theological Breakthrough.* 2nd ed. Oxford: Wiley-Blackwell, 2010.

Melanchthon, Philip. *Commentary on Romans*. Translated by Fred Kramer. Saint Louis: Concordia, 1992.

———. *Loci Communes 1543*. Translated by J. A. O. Preus. Saint Louis: Concordia, 1992.

———. "Loci Communes Theologici." Pages 3–152 in *Melanchthon and Bucer*. Edited by Wilhelm Pauck. Philadelphia: Westminster, 1969.

———. *Melanchthon on Christian Doctrine*. Translated by Clyde L. Manschreck. New York: Oxford University Press, 1965.

———. *Paul's Letter to the Colossians*. Translated by D. C. Parker. Sheffield: Almond, 1989.

Milbank, John. "Alternative Protestantisms." Pages 25–41 in *Radical Orthodoxy and the Reformed Tradition: Creation, Covenant, and Participation*. Edited by James K. Smith and James H. Olthuis. Grand Rapids: Baker, 2005.

Moore, George F. *Judaism in the First Centuries of the Christian Era: The Age of the Tannaim*. 3 vols. Cambridge: Harvard University Press, 1927–1930.

Müller, Gerhard. "Luther's Transformation of Medieval Thought: Discontinuity and Continuity." Pages 105–14 in *The Oxford Handbook of Martin Luther's Theology*. Edited by Robert Kolb, Irene Dingel, and L'ubomír Bakta. Oxford: Oxford University Press, 2014.

Oberman, Heiko A. "Headwaters of the Reformation." Pages 39–83 in *The Dawn of the Reformation: Essays in Late Medieval and Early Reformation Thought*. Edinburgh: T&T Clark, 1986.

———. "*Iustitia Christi* and *Iustitia Dei*: Luther and the Scholastic Doctrines of Justification." Pages 104–25 in *The Dawn of the Reformation: Essays in Late Medieval and Early Reformation Thought*. Edinburgh: T&T Clark, 1986.

———. *Luther: Man between God and the Devil*. New York: Image, 1992.

Ozment, Steven. *The Age of Reform 1250–1550: An Intellectual and Religious History of Late Medieval and Reformation Europe*. New Haven: Yale University Press, 1980.

Paulson, Steven. "Luther's Doctrine of God." Pages 187–200 in *The Oxford Handbook of Martin Luther's Theology*. Edited by Robert Kolb, Irene Dingel, and L'ubomír Batka. Oxford: Oxford University Press, 2014.

Perkins, William. *A Commentary on Galatians*. Edited by Gerald T. Sheppard. New York: Pilgrim, 1989.

Peura, Simo. "Christ as Favor and Gift: The Challenge of Luther's Understanding of Justification." Pages 42–69 in *Union with Christ: The New Finnish Interpretation of Luther*. Edited by Carl E. Braaten and Robert W. Jenson. Grand Rapids: Eerdmans, 1998.

Piper, John. *The Future of Justification: A Response to N. T. Wright*. Wheaton, IL: Crossway, 2007.

Pitkin, Barbara. *What Pure Eyes Could See: Calvin's Doctrine of Faith in Its Exegetical Context.* Oxford: Oxford University Press, 1999.

Prothro, James B. "An Unhelpful Label: Reading the 'Lutheran' Reading of Paul." *JSNT* 39 (2016): 119–40.

The Rhemes New Testament. Rhemes: John Fogny, 1582.

Riches, John K. *Galatians through the Centuries.* Oxford: Blackwell, 2008.

———. "Reception History as a Challenge to Biblical Theology." *JTI* 7 (2013): 171–85.

Roper, Lyndal. *Martin Luther: Renegade and Prophet.* New York: Random House, 2017.

Rosemann, Phillip W. *Peter Lombard.* Oxford: Oxford University Press, 2004.

Rudolph, David J. *A Jew to the Jews: Jewish Contours of Pauline Flexibility in 1 Cor 9:19–23.* WUNT 2/304. Tübingen: Mohr Siebeck, 2011.

———. "Paul and the Food Laws: A Reassessment of Romans 14:14, 20." Pages 151–82 in *Paul the Jew: Rereading the Apostle as a Figure of Second Temple Judaism.* Edited by Gabrielle Boccaccini and Carlos A. Segovia. Minneapolis: Fortress, 2016.

Rummel, Erika. *Erasmus.* London: Continuum, 2004.

———. *The Humanist-Scholastic Debate in the Renaissance and Reformation.* Cambridge: Harvard University Press, 1995.

Ruokanen, Miikka. *Trinitarian Grace in Martin Luther's* The Bondage of the Will. Oxford: Oxford University Press, 2021.

Saak, Eric L. *High Way to Heaven: The Augustinian Platform between Reform and Reformation 1292–1524.* Leiden: Brill, 2002.

Saarinen, Risto. *Luther and the Gift.* Tübingen: Mohr Siebeck, 2017.

Sanders, E. P. *Judaism: Practice and Belief 63 BCE–66 CE.* London: SCM; Philadelphia: Trinity International, 1992.

———. *Paul.* Oxford: Oxford University Press, 1991.

———. *Paul and Palestinian Judaism.* London: SCM, 1977.

———. *Paul, the Law, and the Jewish People.* Philadelphia: Fortress, 1983.

Schäfer, Rolf. "Melanchthon's Interpretation of Romans 5.15: His Departure from the Augustinian Concept of Grace Compared to Luther's." Pages 79–104 in *Philip Melanchthon (1497–1560) and the Commentary.* Edited by Timothy J. Wengert and M. Patrick Graham. Sheffield: Sheffield Academic, 1997.

Scheible, Heinz. "Luther and Melanchthon." *LQ* 4 (1990): 317–39.

Schliesser, Benjamin. *Abraham's Faith in Romans 4: Paul's Concept of Faith in Light of the History of Reception of Genesis 15:6.* WUNT 2/224. Tübingen: Mohr Siebeck, 2007.

Schroeder, Henry J., trans. *Canons and Decrees of the Council of Trent: Original Text with English Translation.* Saint Louis: Herder, 1941.

Schweitzer, Albert. *The Mysticism of Paul the Apostle.* London: Black, 1931.

———. *Paul and His Interpreters.* London: Black, 1912.

Seeberg, Reinhold. *Textbook of the History of Doctrines*. Translated by Charles E. Hay. Philadelphia: Lutheran Publication Society, 1905.

Seifrid, Mark. "The Text of Romans and the Theology of Melanchthon: The Preceptor of the Germans and the Apostle to the Gentiles." Pages 97–120 in *Reformation Readings of Paul: Explorations in History and Exegesis*. Edited by Michael Allen and Jonathan A. Linebaugh. Downers Grove, IL: InterVarsity Press, 2015.

Sheppard, Gerald T. "Between Reformation and Modern Commentary: The Perception of the Scope of Biblical Books." Pages xlviii–lxxvii in William Perkins, *A Commentary on Galatians*. Edited by Gerald T. Sheppard. New York: Pilgrim, 1989.

Sider, Robert D. "Historical Imagination and the Representation of Paul in Erasmus' Paraphrases on the Pauline Epistles." Pages 85–109 in *Holy Scripture Speaks: The Production and Reception of Erasmus' Paraphrases on the New Testament*. Edited by Hilmar M. Pabel and Mark Vessey. Toronto: University of Toronto Press, 2002.

Siggins, Ian D. K. *Martin Luther's Doctrine of Christ*. New Haven: Yale University Press, 1970.

Siikavirta, Samuli. *Baptism and Cognition in Romans 6–8*. WUNT 2/407. Tübingen: Mohr Siebeck, 2015.

Steinmetz, David C. "Abraham and the Reformation." Pages 32–46 in *Luther in Context*. 2nd ed. Grand Rapids: Baker, 2002.

———. "Luther against Luther." Pages 1–11 in *Luther in Context*. 2nd ed. Grand Rapids: Baker, 2002.

———. "Luther among the Anti-Thomists." Pages 47–58 in *Luther in Context*. 2nd ed. Grand Rapids: Baker, 2002.

———. *Luther and Staupitz: An Essay in the Intellectual Origins of the European Reformation*. Durham, NC: Duke University Press, 1980.

Stendahl, Krister. *Paul among Jews and Gentiles*. Philadelphia: Fortress, 1976.

Stowers, Stanley. *A Rereading of Romans: Justice, Jews, and Gentiles*. New Haven: Yale University Press, 1994.

Stupperich, Robert. "Die Rechfertigungslehre bei Luther und Melanchthon 1530–1536." Pages 73–88 in *Luther and Melanchthon in the History and Theology of the Reformation*. Edited by Vilmos Vajta. Philadelphia: Muhlenberg, 1961.

Tait, Edwin. "The Law and Its Works in Martin Bucer's 1536 Romans Commentary." Pages 57–59 in *Reformation Readings of Romans*. Edited by Kathy Ehrensperger and R. Ward Holder. New York: T&T Clark, 2008.

TeSelle, Eugene. "Exploring the Inner Conflict: Augustine's Sermons on Romans 7 and 8." Pages 111–28 in *Engaging Augustine on Romans: Self, Context, and Theology in Interpretation*. Edited by Daniel Patte and Eugene TeSelle. Harrisburg, PA: Trinity International, 2002.

Thate, Michael J., Kevin J. Vanhoozer, and Constantine R. Campbell, eds. *In Christ in Paul: Explorations in Paul's Theology of Union and Participation*. WUNT 2/384. Tübingen: Mohr Siebeck, 2014.

Thiselton, Anthony C. "Reception Theory, H. R. Jauss and the Formative Power of Scripture." *SJT* 65 (2012): 289–308.

Tomlin, Graham. "Luther and the Deliverance of God." Pages 23–33 in *Beyond Old and New Perspectives on Paul: Reflections on the Work of Douglas Campbell*. Edited by Chris Tilling. Eugene, OR: Wipf & Stock, 2014.

Tucker, J. Brian. *Reading Romans after Supersessionism: The Continuation of Jewish Covenantal Identity*. Eugene, OR: Wipf & Stock, 2018.

Tylanda, Joseph. "Christ the Mediator: Calvin versus Stancaro." Pages 161–72 in vol. 5 of *Articles on Calvin and Calvinism*. Edited by Richard C. Gamble. 14 vols. New York: Garland, 1992.

Vainio, Olli-Pekka. *Justification and Participation in Christ: The Development of the Lutheran Doctrine of Justification from Luther to the Formula of Concord (1580)*. Leiden: Brill, 2008.

Vainio, Olli-Pekka, ed. *Engaging Luther: A (New) Theological Perspective*. Eugene, OR: Wipf & Stock, 2010.

Van Engen, John. "Faith as a Concept of Order in Medieval Christendom." Pages 19–67 in *Belief in History: Innovative Approaches to European and American Religion*. Edited by Thomas Kselman. Notre Dame: University of Notre Dame Press, 1991.

Vermigli, Peter Martyr. *Most Learned and Fruitful Commentaries upon the Epistle of S. Paul to the Romanes*. Translated by Sir Henry Billingsley. London: John Daye, 1568.

———. *Predestination and Justification: Two Theological Loci*. Translated and edited by Frank A. James III. Peter Martyr Library 8. Kirksville, MO: Sixteenth-Century Essays and Studies, 2003.

Vorster, Nico. *The Brightest Mirror of God's Works: John Calvin's Theological Anthropology*. PrTMS 236. Eugene, OR: Pickwick, 2019.

Wasserman, Emma. *The Death of the Soul in Romans 7: Sin, Death, and the Law in Light of Hellenistic Moral Psychology*. WUNT 2/256. Tübingen: Mohr Siebeck, 2008.

Watson, Francis. "New Directions in Pauline Theology." *EC* 1 (2010): 11–14.

———. *Paul and the Hermeneutics of Faith*. London: T&T Clark, 2004.

———. *Paul, Judaism, and the Gentiles: Beyond the New Perspective*. 2nd ed. Grand Rapids: Eerdmans, 2007.

Wawrykow, Joseph P. *God's Grace and Human Action: 'Merit' in the Theology of Thomas Aquinas*. Notre Dame: University of Notre Dame Press, 1995.

Webster, John. *Holy Scripture: A Dogmatic Sketch*. Cambridge: Cambridge University Press, 2003.

Weigle, Luther A., ed. *The New Testament Octapla: Eight English Versions of the New Testament in the Tyndale-King James Tradition*. New York: Nelson, 1962.

Wendel, François. *Calvin: Origins and Development of His Religious Thought*. Grand Rapids: Baker, 1997.

Wengert, Timothy J. *Defending Faith: Lutheran Responses to Andreas Osiander's Doctrine of Justification, 1551–1559*. Tübingen: Mohr Siebeck, 2012.

———. *Human Freedom, Christian Righteousness: Philip Melanchthon's Exegetical Dispute with Erasmus of Rotterdam*. Oxford: Oxford University Press, 1998.

———. *Law and Gospel: Philip Melanchthon's Debate with John Agricola of Eisleben over Poenitentia*. Grand Rapids: Baker, 1997.

———. "Melanchthon and Luther/Luther and Melanchthon." Pages 55–88 in *Philip Melanchthon, Speaker of the Reformation: Wittenberg's Other Reformer*. Burlington, VT: Ashgate Variorum, 2010.

———. "Philip Melanchthon and Augustine of Hippo." Pages 235–67 in *Philip Melanchthon, Speaker of the Reformation: Wittenberg's Other Reformer*. Burlington, VT: Ashgate Variorum, 2010.

———. "Philip Melanchthon's 1522 Annotations on Romans and the Lutheran Origins of Rhetorical Criticism." Pages 118–40 in *Biblical Interpretation in the Era of the Reformation*. Edited by Richard A. Muller and John Lee Thompson. Grand Rapids: Eerdmans, 1996.

———. "The Rhetorical Paul: Philip Melanchthon's Interpretation of the Pauline Epistles." Pages 129–64 in *A Companion to Paul in the Reformation*. Edited by R. Ward Holder. Leiden: Brill, 2009.

Westerholm, Stephen. "The First Readers of Romans and the 'Paul within Judaism' School." Pages 43–75 in *Romans: Text, Readers, and the History of Interpretation*. Grand Rapids: Eerdmans, 2022.

———. *Israel's Law and the Church's Faith: Paul and His Recent Interpreters*. Grand Rapids: Eerdmans, 1988.

———. *Justification Reconsidered*. Grand Rapids: Eerdmans, 2013.

———. *Perspectives Old and New on Paul: The "Lutheran" Paul and His Critics*. Grand Rapids: Eerdmans, 2004.

Wrede, William. *Paul*. London: Green, 1907.

Wright, David F. "Justification in Augustine." Pages 55–72 in *Justification in Perspective: Historical Developments and Contemporary Challenges*. Edited by Bruce L. McCormack. Grand Rapids: Baker, 2006.

Wright, N. T. *Justification*. Downers Grove, IL: InterVarsity Press, 2009.

———. *Paul and His Recent Interpreters*. Minneapolis: Fortress, 2015.

———. *Paul and the Faithfulness of God*. 2 vols. Minneapolis: Fortress, 2013.

———. "Paul and the Patriarch: The Role(s) of Abraham in Romans and Galatians."

Pages 554–92 in *Pauline Perspectives: Essays on Paul, 1978–2013*. Minneapolis: Fortress, 2013.

———. "The Paul of History and the Apostle of Faith." *TynBul* 29 (1978): 61–88.

Yinger, Kent L. *The New Perspective on Paul*. Eugene, OR: Wipf & Stock, 2011.

Yule, George. "Luther's Understanding of Justification by Grace Alone in Terms of Catholic Christology." Pages 87–112 in *Luther: Theologian for Catholics and Protestants*. Edited by George Yule. Edinburgh: T&T Clark, 1985.

Zachmann, Randall C. *The Assurance of Faith: Conscience in the Theology of Martin Luther and John Calvin*. Louisville: Westminster John Knox, 2005.

Zemon Davis, Natalie. *The Gift in Sixteenth-Century France*. Madison: University of Wisconsin Press, 2000.

Index of Authors

Index of Scripture and Other Ancient Texts

Index of Medieval and Reformation Texts